HARRY BOLAND

JIM MAHER

MERCIER PRESS

IRISH AMERICAN BOOK COMPANY (IABC)
Boulder, Colorado

MERCIER PRESS
PO Box 5, 5 French Church Street, Cork
16 Hume Street, Dublin 2

Trade enquiries to CMD DISTRIBUTION,
55a Spruce Avenue, Stillorgan Industrial Park, Blackrock, Dublin

Published in the US and Canada by the
IRISH AMERICAN BOOK COMPANY
6309 Monarch Park Place, Niwot, Colorado, 80503
Tel: (303) 652 2710, (800) 452-7115
Fax: (303) 652 2689, (800) 401-9705

© Jim Maher 1998

ISBN 1 85635 236 6
10 9 8 7 6 5 4 3 2 1

DEDICATED TO
MARY AND MY FATHER AND MOTHER

Printed in Ireland by Colour Books Ltd.

CONTENTS

ACKNOWLEDGEMENTS

Only the assistance of many people has made it possible for me to complete this project. My wife, Mary, helped me in researching the book, in organising my research material and in proof-reading. Mrs Patricia O'Reilly, Dublin, acted for me in securing a publisher and I am indebted to her. Arthur Flynn (Irish Pen) gave me guidance all along the way.

The Boland family was courteous and co-operative. Harry Boland's eldest nephew, Kevin, assisted me with reminiscences and information and we travelled many places, visiting all the haunts that Harry frequented during his short life. Harry's other nephew, Annraoi, provided me with recollections, photographs, letters and papers that were invaluable to me in this work. Harry's niece, Eileen Barrington, answered, at all times, any queries of mine by phone or personal contact. Fionnuala Crowley, Cork, another of Harry's nieces, opened her door to me and put all her documents, letters and photographs at my disposal.

During my long years' research into the Civil War I spent much time in the Franciscan Library, Killiney. Father Ignatius, the Curator of the Library, and Ciara looked after me and I value their friendship. Breandán MacGiolla Choille who catalogued the De Valera Papers gave me personal insights into Civil War matters.

I greatly appreciate the assistance and courtesy of the following: Séamus Helferty, Kerry Holland and all others in the UCD Archives: the keeper of Trinity College manuscripts; Commandant Peter Young and Commandant Victor Lang and their assistants in the Military Archives, Cathal Brugha Barracks; my acquaintances in the National Archives, Bishop Street; the staff of the National Library of Ireland; Maura Kennedy and her co-workers at the Gilbert Library, Dublin; the personnel of the Public Record Office at Kew who made me so welcome.

In the USA I thank all those I met in the various universities, archives and libraries, and the staff of the National Archives, Washington.

I wish to thank all my good friends in the Irish public libraries that I visited. I thank Jim Fogarty and his staff in Kilkenny County Library for procuring for me many texts which were out of print through the Library Loan scheme.

I am grateful to all those who gave me private family papers. I thank Kieran White, Kilkenny for re-producing my photographs of Harry Boland and particularly the one which graces the cover. My sincere thanks to Tom Nolan for his work on the index and John Mulloney for proof-reading. Thanks to Mary Feehan and the staff of Mercier Press who have supported this project from the beginning.

I regret if I inadvertently omitted to mention any particular name.

JIM MAHER

BORN INTO PATRIOTISM

Irish freedom meant everything to Harry Boland. This yearning had been handed down to him from past generations on both sides of his family.[1] Harry's father, Jim, met Catherine Woods in Manchester while he was working at the laying of the Manchester Tramways. Catherine was born in Manchester in 1861 of Co. Louth lineage. Her father Philip Woods came from the Carlingford area. Her great-grandfather, James Woods, a blacksmith from Cooley, was whipped through the streets of Carlingford, tied to the back of a cart, for making pikes for the rebels in the 1798 Rising.[2]

Jim could trace his roots to the townland of Cams in the parish of Fuerty, Co. Roscommon but he was born in Manchester in 1857. His father, Patrick, was very active in the IRB in that city.[3]

Jim Boland came to Dublin for the first time in 1880 as a foreman with the Liverpool firm, Worthingtons, which had secured the contract for paving Dublin's streets. Shortly afterwards the city council decided to do the work by direct labour and Jim was given the job as overseer with a weekly wage of £2. While in Dublin Jim became a member of the Supreme Council of the IRB, he was the Centre for the province of Leinster and at one time chairman of the Dublin Directory IRB.[4] On 21 October, 1882 he married his Manchester girlfriend, Catherine Woods, in St Kevin's Church, Harrington Street.

In the Dublin Directory of the IRB Jim was very friendly with Denis Seery. Denis was a first cousin of Thomas Tynan, a strong Land Leaguer and also a member of the IRB organisation in Leinster. Denis often visited the Tynan home, Peafield House, Mountrath and introduced Jim Boland to the Tynan family. In September 1882 an attempt was made to evict the Tynans as they were unable to pay the increased rack rent of £4 an acre which the land agent demanded on behalf of the landlord. The Tynan family's twelve-roomed imposing two storey house stood on 175 acres of good Queen's County land. Almost 400 people from the local community assembled to prevent the bailiffs from seizing the cattle and horses on the farm or to occupy the dwelling house. The bailiffs and police withdrew but were expected to return. Jim and Denis decided to try to frighten them and Jim made a bomb in Dublin and gave it to Denis who planted it near the land agent's house in Cool, not far from Maryborough. The bomb went off at 2am on Christmas morning, 1882. It did considerable damage to property but no one was injured. However the landlord became worried and came to an arrangement with Thomas Tynan and the rack rent was reduced from £4 per acre to £1 per acre. Heavy police surveillance on Jim forced him to leave Ireland for America with his young bride. The Tynans of Peafield House always remembered the help Jim gave them.[5]

Jim organised Fenian activities in many parts of the USA for two and a half years. A younger brother (John P.) was already a Fenian organiser in the USA and had been sent out by the IRB to keep in touch with the Clan-na-Gael movement in New York.[6]

Jim and Catherine's first child, Nellie, was born in America in 1884. They left America in 1885, having spent two years and four months there, and went to Manchester, not Dublin. Their first son, Gerry, was born in May, 1885 in Manchester. When Gerry was still only six months old Jim and his family came back to Dublin where he resumed his daytime job in the Paving Department of Dublin Corporation.[7] When the family returned they went to live in 6 Dalymount Terrace, Phibsborough. Jim became a member of the Nationalist Club in Rutland Square and he enthusiastically supported Charles Stewart Parnell. The police kept him under surveillance and a detective could be seen constantly outside the Boland home because Jim was still in the IRB.[8] Their second son, Harry was born on 27 April 1887, Kathleen was born in 1890 and Edmund, the youngest was born in 1893.[9]

In the years after Jim returned to Dublin he was very active in Dublin GAA circles. He was chairman of Dublin County Board of the GAA in 1892 and the following year he represented Co. Dublin on the Central Council of the infant organisation.[10] Jim played with his young sons in the open green spaces near his own home and he gave Harry his first lessons in wielding the camán. The family lived near Dalymount Park, headquarters of the Bohemians Soccer Club, and the playing pitch was grazed by sheep. Harry and Gerry spent many afternoons riding the sheep around the playing field and falling off their backs just for the thrill of being thrown off.[11]

After the death of Parnell Jim opposed Tim Healy and his supporters for control of the Irish Party. The Healyites took over possession of the Dublin premises of the Parnellite newspaper, *United Irishman*. A group of Parnellites decided to regain control of the newspaper offices and Jim recruited a small number of IRB men to invade the premises. The two opposing sides, Parnellites and Healyites, became involved in a fracas and Jim received a heavy blow to the top of his head with the leg of a chair. At first it did not seem to be a serious injury, but a cyst developed inside his skull and exerted pressure on his brain. As time went on his health gradually deteriorated causing him severe headaches and then some loss of memory.[12] He had to go on extended sick leave from his Dublin corporation job and went to the Mater Hospital where he underwent unsuccessful brain surgery. As Catherine saw Jim sinking rapidly she sent for a priest from Phibsborough church to give her husband the last rites of the Catholic Church. The priest approached Jim in a stony fashion and said, 'I believe Mr Boland, you are a great Fenian'.

Even though very ill, Jim sensed the cool greeting. 'Not a great Fenian,' he answered, 'but a Fenian all the time.'

'Of course in that case, I can't give you absolution,' admonished the priest.

Jim looked at him unmoved and said, 'I won't die with a lie on my mouth, so I must go to God as I am.'[13]

Catherine sent for Fr Headley, a sympathetic Dominican priest who gave Jim the last anointing. He died in the Mater Hospital on the 11 March, 1895 having spent five months as a patient there.[14] Harry was eight years old when he lost a father he loved and admired very much.

Jim Boland had been out of work for a considerable time before his death. The family was left without a breadwinner but his nationalist friends rallied around the widow and family. The Tynans of Peafield House, did not forget the help Jim gave when they were in danger of eviction and Thomas took a prominent position on the fundraising committee. Others on the committee included Fred Allen then manager of the *Irish Independent*, William Field, MP, and Pat O'Brien. The final report of the Boland Family Fund stated: 'A meeting of the committee and subscribers of the Boland Family fund was held last night in the National Club. A balance sheet was submitted which showed that the total income reached the handsome sum of £293. After deducting the purchase of a first class going business in the tobacconist trade at 28 Wexford Street it leaves a handsome balance in the bank to the credit of Mrs Boland and the family.' With this money and Catherine set up in business the family went to live in Wexford Street.[15] This building consisted of a shop and a house with four rooms. Catherine was in her mid-thirties when she took over the new business.

Further help came from the Dublin County Board GAA who held a special tournament at Clonturk Park on 9 June, 1895 in which football and hurling teams from places as far apart as Thurles and Cavan took part. The Boland family received a good sum of money from the tournament.[16]

The Boland Fund kept the family going for up to five years after the death of their father. Nellie, the eldest, stayed at home helping with the family business but she was not a healthy child. Gerry and Harry were at the point where their second-level schooling had to be considered. Only a minority of families could afford to give their children second-level education then. The shop was not turning over enough of a profit for Catherine to give them further education because she was not a good business woman and she had a big soft-heart. Her son, Gerry, said that 'she could not refuse the poor, whether they had money or not'.[17]

Pat O'Brien, MP and former IRB friend of Jim's, arranged for the Irish Christian Brothers to admit Gerry to the new O'Brien Institute in Marino, Dublin, which was a semi-orphanage for children with only one parent alive. Harry went to school in Synge Street CBS but he had a personality clash with one Christian Brother and he refused to return to school.[18] Catherine had many problems at the time and was becoming increasingly worried about the health of her daughter, Nellie, who had contacted TB and was getting weaker. Denis Seery asked Thomas Tynan and his wife, Anna, to help out with Harry's schooling. They decided to bring Harry to their home and to look after his second-level education. In nearby Castletown, the De La Salle Brothers had a novitiate boarding college reserved for novices of the order. Thomas got in touch with the De La Salle Brothers and asked them to make an exception and take Harry in as a boarder. They agreed to admit Harry for a very nominal sum of money and he spent three years in the novitiate. During his school holidays after each term, he went to Peafield House. The environment in Peafield House was very nationalistic.[19]

There were great facilities for study in Castletown and a great spirit of learning. Harry excelled in the sporting arena in the college. Hurling was the dominant game in the junior school and every student was expected to try his skills at hurling. He brought the hurling skills with him that he had learned from his father. Every student had to learn to swim in the River Nore which flowed through the college lands.[20]

While Harry spent his holidays in Peafield House he was reared as a young country farmer. He did the same work on the farm as any of the three Tynan brothers, John, Michael and Thomas Jnr. Thomas was the same age as Harry and they played together every day. Thomas always said that Harry would never back off anything. 'It was not his nature even to back away from a bigger lad if a row started. Even as a schoolboy he was a bit of a "divil".'[21] The eldest Tynan brother, John who was then 25 years of age, was 11 years older than Harry. He kept a watchful 'big brother' eye on him and they became inseparable friends.[22] Harry's stay in Peafield House gave him an understanding of life in rural Ireland and he brought many of his Castletown and Peafield House educational, sporting and farming experiences with him right through his life.

In the GAA

The Boland family suffered another bereavement when, Nellie, the eldest child, who was suffering from the dreaded disease TB, died.[1] For the second time Harry felt the deep pangs of loss. Pat O'Brien, MP, looked after the Boland family until 1900 when they were able to provide for themselves. That year Gerry left school at 15 years of age and became an apprentice fitter on the Midland and Great Western Railway at Broadstone Station, but 'poverty sent Harry to live in Manchester'.[2] He stayed with an aunt on the Boland side in the Oxford Road area of Manchester and he also had many cousins from both sides of his family there.[3] He soon returned to Dublin but not before he had become a fan of the Manchester United soccer team.[4] Both he and his brother Gerry joined the IRB on the same day in 1904.[5]

After a period in the tailoring department of Todd, Burns and Co. Ltd., General Outfitters in Mary Street, Dublin, Harry was an excellent, fully qualified, tailor and a superb cutter of gents' and ladies' attire. He became a permanent member of the tailoring staff of Todd, Burns, one of the biggest stores in Dublin at this time.[6] He joined the Keating Branch of the Gaelic League and studied Irish.[7] Always an athlete at heart he was not long back in Ireland before he began to take an interest in the GAA and it was chiefly through the GAA and his exploits with the Dublin hurling team that he first became widely known. An unusual factor about Harry's GAA career was that he was involved from the beginning both in the administration of GAA affairs in Dublin and the game of hurling itself – his enthusiasm was inherited from his father's association with the national games. When Harry first came on the GAA scene many of those who were on league committees with him could remember Jim, his father, as a former county chairman.

Harry was interested in the running of Saturday and Sunday Hurling Leagues in Dublin because he hurled in the competitions himself. He is recorded as being present at a Sunday Hurling League meeting in 68 Sackville Street, Dublin on 5 April, 1906 and at a meeting of the Saturday Hurling League three weeks later.[8] He and his brothers, Gerry and Ned, first joined the O'Donovan Rossa football team and Rathmines Hurling Club. This hurling

14

club had an athletic section also as was common in GAA clubs then and it also had a gymnastic group. On Sunday, 16 December, 1906, Rathmines won first place in the Middle League when they beat Ua Tuathails. Harry lined out as full back on the Rathmines team and he distinguished himself by his long clearances under pressure from the Rathmines goal-mouth. This was his first major win in a hurling match.[9] In December, 1907, he became a member of the Dublin County Board GAA at the unusual early age of 20.

It was at this time that the Boland family closed their tobacconist shop at 28 Wexford Street and went to live at 26 Lennox Street Dublin. Gerry, Harry and Ned were bringing home an increasing amount of money from their daytime jobs and Kathleen was working as an assistant in a jeweller's shop in Grafton Street.[10]

Between 1908 and 1910 young men of a new generation were being secretly recruited into the IRB – many of them having come to the fore in the GAA. Amongst the most prominent were Austin Stack in Kerry, J. J. Walsh in Cork, and Harry in Dublin.[11] Harry brought an enquiring mind to GAA affairs from the start and he was not satisfied with the ways many things were being done. At the annual convention of the Sunday Hurling League at Rutland Square on 21 February, 1909, he seconded a motion proposed by D. Burke of the Davis club to give more games to each club in the Dublin area. The motion was passed and put into operation. He supported a suggestion to encourage schoolboys and minors to interest themselves in hurling – they were entitled to attend GAA games at one-third the cost of ordinary admission. He recommended that invitations be extended to such institutions as Artane and Carriglea to view Gaelic games free of charge.[12]

In early January, 1909, a junior championship tie was played between Rathmines and Ard Craobh. Lining out for Rathmines were Harry and his brother Gerry. Rathmines eventually won by a margin of two goals and Harry earned a place on the junior Dublin county team.[13] Dublin reached the Leinster final and played against King's County at Maryborough. There was a sudden end to this final because during the first fifteen minutes of the second half a King's County player committed a foul and the referee ordered him off the field. He refused to go and the referee promptly awarded the match to Dublin who were leading by four points at the time. Harry won his first inter-county medal – a Leinster Junior Hurling Championship one.[14]

The final of the 1908 all-Ireland Senior Championship final between Dublin and Tipperary had been delayed due to inter-county disputes at administration level but was finally fixed for Jones' Road on Sunday, 25 April, 1909. The Kickhams were Dublin County champions with the right to select the Dublin team but they decided to hold a trial match between a Kickhams Selection and the Rest of Dublin. Harry played very well and after a second trial he was picked for the Dublin senior team to contest the All-Ireland final against Tipperary. A crowd of 6,000 people gathered in Jones' Road for the final. This playing field (now Croke Park) had been levelled and rolled before the game and both teams gave a first-class exhibition of hurling. Harry combined with W. Leonard, the star Dublin forward, to score one point in the first half and to make another. In the second half another bout of play between Boland and Leonard ended in a goal. Tipperary led through most of the game but they found it difficult to draw away from their opponents. A point scored by Harry and another by Leonard evened the score just before the final whistle.[15] The replay took place at the Agricultural Society's ground in Athy on 27 June, 1909. The Dublin selectors made many changes to the team and Harry was not on the Dublin team for the replay. Tipperary won easily.[16]

The IRB were at work quietly and unobtrusively in the GAA around this time. Harry, though only twenty-two years old, never missed an opportunity to further IRB principles of Irish freedom. P. T. Daly, Hon. Secretary John O'Leary Memorial Committee, wrote to the 1909 May meeting of the Dublin County Board saying that the inscription on the monument to John O'Leary would be unveiled on the third Sunday of that month. A public procession starting from Rutland Square to Glasnevin was planned and the Memorial Committee would be obliged if all fixtures arranged by the Dublin County Board be postponed. Harry proposed that the County Dublin Committee accede to the request: 'Mr John O'Leary, was a patron of this association,' he said, 'and he made many sacrifices for Irish freedom during the course of his life. I propose that this date be made a closed day in our capital city for all Gaelic games'.[17] The fact that this proposition was made by a Dublin inter-county hurler made it easier for the delegates to accept the request.

When Harry went to London in 1909 on GAA business he met Michael Collins for the first time. Collins was involved in the

GAA in London and was treasurer of the Geraldines club. Boland suggested to Collins that he join the IRB[18] and Harry then brought him to Sam Maguire who initiated Collins into the organisation.[19]

During 1910 Harry continued hurling with the Rathmines Hurling Club but did not play on any Dublin county teams. He was, however, a regular attender at the meetings of the Dublin County Board and in August he helped to organise an athletics meeting for the Dublin GAA clubs. In his capacity as a GAA administrator in the Dublin area, Harry was becoming well-known. On 22 October 1911 the annual convention of the Dublin County Board was held at 41 Rutland Square. Delegates from forty-seven clubs in Dublin were present. Three candidates were nominated for the position of chairman – Harry received 45 votes, J. Quigley 15 and D. McCormack 10. Harry was elected and M. F. Crowe was unanimously re-elected as secretary and treasurer.[20] Considering he was now only twenty-four years of age, he was unusually young for this exacting role. But he brought the fresh ideas of young men into action in an association that was largely ruled by older men. Harry played with Dublin against Kilkenny in the Leinster Senior Hurling final at Maryborough in 1911. Kilkenny won easily.

Harry lined out with the Dublin team in the Croke Hurling final against Tipperary in Thurles on 21 April 1912 and Tipperary won by two goals. The revenue from the game went towards paying for the erection of the Croke Monument in Thurles and the payment of the first instalment of £1,500, out of a total purchase price of £3,500, for the Jones' Road grounds in Dublin. These grounds were soon to be known as Croke Park where 'no other games but those of the Gael were to be played'.[21]

Not satisfied with his playing and administrative roles in the GAA, Harry took to refereeing both hurling and football matches in 1912 and refereed the substituted and postponed 1911 All-Ireland hurling final between Kilkenny and Tipperary played in Fraher's field in Dungarvan. The game, played before a huge crowd, turned out to be a thriller with Kilkenny beating Tipperary by two points. Harry was complimented for keeping the game going at a fast pace. [Dan Fraher of Dungarvan, a trustee of the GAA, continued his late father's practice of giving this field, free of charge, to the GAA for inter-county matches. Dan's son, Maurice, was a promising athlete, excelling as a long-jumper.]

Harry blossomed as a GAA administrator when he represented Dublin at the 1913 Congress which was held in the council chamber of the City Hall in Dublin. Delegates attended from all over Ireland and from Lancashire and Scotland. Harry will be remembered as an administrator of great foresight for being associated with three motions at that congress. The first proposal came from Dublin County Board and it stated that 'where a man is fouled but succeeds in playing the ball, the referee shall allow the game to proceed'. Harry was behind this motion because he felt football and hurling games should not be slowed down by an official blowing his whistle too often for minor infringements. Another proposal, seconded by Harry, came from the Cork County Board and was moved by P. D. Mehigan (Carbery), the well-known writer of Gaelic games. 'That a distinctive county colour be compulsory for inter-county, inter-provincial and All-Ireland contests, such colours to be approved of by the Provincial Councils concerned and registered with Central Council'.

The most important motion of all and the most debated at the 1913 Congress was proposed by Harry, 'That the maximum number of players shall be fifteen aside'. John Lalor, Kilkenny, seconded the motion which had a rough passage. J. J. Walsh of Cork, another IRB member, moved an amendment 'that the seventeen aside team be retained for hurling, but that the maximum number of footballers be 14'. Much debate followed and then two divisions of voting took place until it was decided that 15 players be the maximum and 13 the minimum. The reduction of players made the game more open, more strenuous and more active for the players but also more attractive to watch. [22]

Hurling and Volunteers

The Dublin of the first decade of the new century contrasted between the wealthy shopping and landlord class and the very poor who lived in dreadful conditions. Parents and often up to eight children existed in the one room.

Catherine Boland was now fifty-five years of age and her family was reared. The income that the children were bringing into the Boland home from their combined jobs encouraged them to change residence to a more open environment in Marino Crescent, Clontarf. They rented a large three-storey house with a spacious basement in a curved row of twenty-six houses. The Bolands lived almost in the middle of the curve, No. 15 – the houses were joined and they all had skylights opening off the roofs.[1] An RIC man lived in one of the houses in the row and although the Boland family had a different political viewpoint to him they lived on good terms.[2]

Jim Larkin came to Dublin and set about forming an Irish union of workers which he called the Irish Transport and General Workers' Union. A federation of four hundred Dublin employers, organised by William Martin Murphy, refused employment to members of Larkin's union. Men employed in the Dublin Tramway Co., also controlled by Murphy were asked to sign a pledge that they would resign their membership of the Irish Transport and General Workers' Union and if they were not then members that they would never join it. When they refused, hundreds of tram workers were immediately locked out. This led to the 1913 Dublin Workers' Strike. All the Boland family were fully behind the workers. They were all trade union men and Gerry had a trade union book. Harry and Kathleen, in sympathy with the workers, refused to board a tram no matter how long the journey they had to make on foot. They also refused to buy any items of food, clothing or merchandise from any firm that was locking out workers: 'we were all Labour, as most of us were workers and sons of workers'.[3] The strike led to public meetings of union members at which the police batoned workers causing the death of two men and one woman.

Then came the meeting in Sackville Street when Jim Larkin,

dressed in a long black coat and wearing a beard, appeared at the balcony window of the Imperial Hotel and said a few words to the crowd. The three Boland brothers, Gerry, Harry and Ned were in the crowd.[4] The police attacked without warning, indiscriminately batoning the people to the ground and kicking them when they were prostrate. They pursued those who escaped into lanes and side streets wielding their batons mercilessly and beating those they caught. Harry was strong and so was his brother Ned. The Bolands fought their way out through the police cordon. Ned, who later on trained professional boxers in Dublin, was fearless and between him, Harry and Gerry, they floored two policemen who came at them as they burst through with their fists flying. Six hundred people, mostly workers, were later admitted to hospitals in Dublin for treatment.

Pádraig Pearse wrote in *Irish Freedom:*

> I may be wrong but I do hold it a most terrible sin that there should be landless men in this island of waste yet fertile valleys and that there should be breadless men in the city where great fortunes are made and enjoyed.[5]

Harry joined the Volunteers at the inaugural meeting at the Rotunda and Gerry and Ned enrolled also.[6] Women formed Cumann na mBan. To Harry membership of the new Volunteer force meant an increased work-load and a dual role. He had been re-elected as chairman of Dublin County Board on 19 October. He also changed hurling clubs and transferred to Faughs, a prominent senior hurling team. Faughs reached the 1914 Dublin County Senior Hurling Final against Collegians – a team which was made up mostly of UCD university students. Harry played in the full-back position and had a good game before a record crowd. Faughs won easily and Harry acquired his first Dublin senior hurling medal. Faughs easily beat Davis hurling club in the Dublin Senior Hurling League four weeks later and again Harry received praise for his many long clearances from the full-back line.

Harry was asked by John Tynan, to be bestman at his marriage to Cis Meagher, Cloncourse, Ballaghmore. John now had his own farm at Rockview House, Borris-in-Ossory.They were married in Dublin and after the church ceremony the photographer set up the usual scene where the bridegroom and bride, followed by the bestman and bridesmaid, were to emerge from the open church door and halt outside for a photograph to be taken. The people gathered outside would at the same time throw confetti on the married couple just before the photographer clicked his camera. The group lined up inside the church but just before they began the walk-out, Harry whispered to John, the bridegroom, 'Let's change places, just for the laugh'. A quick word all round and they all agreed. The church door opened and they made a majestic exit with Harry arm-in-arm with the bride and a wide grin on his beaming face. The crowd laughed heartily but they still shook confetti on the 'new' bridegroom. Then they cheered tumultuously when Harry kissed the bride.[7]

Meanwhile Erskine Childers had been in France and Belgium and finally in Hamburg where he purchased 1,500 second-hand Mauser rifles and 49,000 rounds of ammunition to arm the Volunteers. He brought the cargo into the small harbour of Howth in his yacht, the *Asgard*, on 26 July, 1914. The Irish Volunteers marched to Howth that morning under Thomas McDonagh, Bulmer Hobson and Cathal Brugha. Pat McGinley was a crewman on the *Asgard*. He described their entry into the small fishing harbour of Howth in north County Dublin:

> The weather was bad and as we were crashing the harbour, I happened to look up at the other end of the round pier and I saw the Volunteers coming down and I told Mr Childers, 'There they are, they are coming down' ... Erskine Childers was a real good seaman. We got the guns out to the Volunteers in short time.[8]

Harry was not with the Volunteers that day as only the officers were aware beforehand of the reason they were marching to Howth and he was in Dungarvan visiting the Frahers.

On 3 August, in the House of Commons, the British government announced their decision to declare war on Germany. John Redmond, leader of the Irish Party assured the English government that the Volunteers, on whose executive Redmond had twenty-five nominees, would guard Ireland's shores against German invasion. The following day the United Kingdom of Great Britain and Ireland officially entered the war. Shortly afterwards the Home Rule Act received the royal assent and was put on the statute book but its operation was postponed until after the war. Supporters of Redmond regarded this as 'a great triumph for the Irish Party'.[9]

But Redmond's attitude was frowned upon by the more extreme Volunteers and particularly by the IRB. Redmond widened the divide between himself and some young men like Harry when he spoke to Volunteers assembled at Woodenbridge in Co. Wicklow on 20 September. He said that it would be a disgrace for ever to Ireland if Irishmen refrained from fighting 'wherever the firing extends, in defence of right, freedom and religion in this war'. The Volunteers gathered throughout Ireland to consider Redmond's war policy. The number of Volunteers was estimated to be about 180,000 and the vast majority backed Redmond. There was a clear split. Those who followed Redmond took the name of 'National Volunteers' and those who did not want anything to do with England or her war were known as 'Irish Volunteers'.[10] Many of the Irish Volunteers, including Harry, expressed the same ideas as Sir Roger Casement articulated in a letter published in Ireland and the United States: 'Ireland has no blood to give to any land, to any cause, but that of Ireland'.[11] Harry felt 'that a greater and more vital question has arisen from the World War. The men who received the votes of the Irish people to secure Self Government, have endeavoured to harness the people of Ireland to England's war chariot, forgetting that only a freely elected government in a free Ireland can decide the question of peace and war for Ireland'.[12] The top leaders of the IRB inside the Irish Volunteers believed Ireland had suffered many evils at the hands of British administrators down through the years and that this war against Germany was Ireland's opportunity to strike a blow against England for the freedom of Ireland. Tom Clarke, Seán MacDiarmada and the recently recruited Pádraig Pearse were already taking the first steps to organise an armed rising against England. Harry was attending his secret monthly IRB meetings and he heard about plans for a rebellion. Gerry saved his money to buy a gun and he began to toughen himself up for possible hardship in his role as an Irish Volunteer in the event of a rising. For periods he went on strict diets of very little food, practising self-denial so that he could face deprivation if this was required of him at any future date.[13]

Towards the end of 1914, Harry was re-elected as chairman of Dublin County Board GAA for the fourth time. The board revived their cross-country running programme by holding a novices' championship at Larkfield. Garristown won the championship and the board entered a strong team for the All-Ireland Novices Cross-Country Championship. This team won the first team prize for Dublin.

In 1915 Harry had his last season of club hurling with Faughs and on 13 June he lined out to play against Davis in the final of the Dublin Hurling Championship at Croke Park – Faughs won. In November Harry had another superb game when Faughs beat Rapparees in the final of the Dublin Senior Hurling League and this victory ended Harry's club hurling career but he had won two Dublin Senior Hurling Championships and two Senior Hurling Leagues.

On 13 February, 1916 Harry lined out with his native Dublin in the semi-final of the Wolfe Tone Memorial Hurling tie between Kilkenny and Dublin. Harry hurled well in his old position of full-back.[14] Dublin beat Kilkenny to qualify for the Leinster Hurling Wolfe Tone Memorial Final against Leix – this semi-final was Harry's last competitive game of hurling in Ireland and his last hurling game with his native Dublin.[15]

Tommie Moore, a top-class Leix hurler with Faughs and winner of two All-Ireland senior hurling medals with Dublin, said Harry 'was a fine hurler and he could have been a real inter-county star but you'd never know when you had him. He'd hardly train at all. He was too busy with other things – national things.'[16]

From Fairview to the GPO

Harry arrived home later than he had expected from the GAA Congress which was held in the City Hall on Easter Sunday, 1916. His mother noticed that he was more subdued than usual. When she spoke to him he seemed to look straight ahead into the distance as if he had not heard what she was saying. 'Maybe he had a tough day at the congress,' she thought to herself.

Then Harry spoke in a grave tone. 'I have to go out with the Volunteers, mother – soon.'

'Where?' asked Catherine Boland.

'The other boys are going. It is serious.'

'Who are they?' asked Catherine.

'Jack Shouldice, Frank Shouldice and many others.'

Jack and Frank Shouldice were GAA friends of Harry. Jack was an All-Ireland footballer. On his way home from congress he had told Harry that the Military Council of the Republican forces, without MacNeill's authority as Chief-of-Staff of the Irish Volunteers, had decided to go ahead with their planned insurrection on the following morning, Easter Monday.

Catherine looked at Harry with tears in her eyes. 'Go, in the name of God,' she said softly. 'Your poor father would haunt you if you did not do the right thing.'

She was trying to put up a brave face.

'The only thing, I am worrying about is how you will manage,' replied Harry.

'I managed after your father's death, when you were all babies, and I can manage again. I am in a better position now than I was then.'[1]

Tom Hunter was the commandant of the 2nd battalion. He spent Easter Sunday night at Fr Mathew Park in Fairview getting military and medical stores in order. He gave fresh orders orally on Easter Monday morning at 7.30am for the mobilisation of his battalion. He led the men of the 2nd Battalion who came earliest on that Monday morning to the west side of St Stephen's Green near the College of Surgeons. Those who came late to Fr Mathew Park were kept there to load the military and medical supplies on to horse lorries that would take them to St Stephen's Green. These military stores included ammunition and some guns. Seán Russell, an officer in the Fairview Volunteers, came late to Fr Mathew Park as also did Harry and his brother, Ned. Gerry, on the other hand, had married and now lived in Crooksling and on Easter Monday he cycled into town with his gun.[2]

Leo Henderson's company of Volunteers were amongst those detailed to escort the lorries carrying the supplies to St Stephen's Green. Enniscorthy-born Captain Thomas Weafer, was in charge of this operation. Commandant Hunter arrived in St Stephen's Green, lined up his men and reported to Brigade-Commandant Thomas McDonagh. McDonagh told Hunter the 2nd Battalion was moving out straight away to take over Jacob's Biscuit Factory less than a quarter of a mile away. McDonagh noticed that the turn out from the 2nd Battalion was smaller than he expected. Hunter told him that about 100 Volunteers were still in Fr Mathew Park loading the military and medical stores.[3] McDonagh moved out to occupy Jacob's as he was scheduled. Gerry Boland arrived on his bicycle and joined his fellow 2nd Battalion Volunteers in occupying Jacob's biscuit factory.

Outside Liberty Hall in the city centre what seemed to be an armed parade of units of Irish Volunteers and Citizen Army and the Kimmage garrison was held. Many of the men, about 150 in all, believed that they were going out on ordinary manoeuvres. Because of Eoin MacNeill's countermanding order the number of men was less than expected. They carried Lee Enfields, Mauser pistols, even pikes, bayonets and sabres. Only one quarter of them wore uniforms. The others wore only leggings or bandoliers to show that they were soldiers. At five minutes to twelve the men were lined up. Then Pádraig Pearse, James Connolly and Joseph Mary Plunkett came out of Liberty Hall, all uniformed with Pearse and Plunkett carrying swords in their hip scabbards. They moved to the front line, Connolly in the centre. At twelve o'clock James Connolly gave the order 'Column Attention! Quick March!' They moved off at a quick marching pace. 'Left, right. Left right,' re-echoed through the almost deserted streets. They came out of Lower Abbey Street, wheeled to the right and advanced. When they were directly opposite the GPO, James Connolly then gave the order, 'Left Wheel – GPO Charge'.[4] The Irish Republican forces broke ranks and rushed into the GPO. They ejected staff and customers and took over the building. One elderly man moaned as he was

25

being ejected, 'What's the world comin' to at all when a decent man can't buy a penny stamp in comfort and peace in the chief post office in the capital city of his country'. Members of the Irish Volunteers and Citizen Army took down the Union Jack from the flagpole on the roof of the GPO and put up instead two flags – one a green flag with a golden harp in the centre and Irish Republic written across it and the other a Tricolour of green, white and orange.[5]

Simultaneously members of the new Irish Republican forces occupied buildings in other parts of Dublin. Later that afternoon, P. H. Pearse, Commandant-in-Chief, came to the steps of the GPO and read the proclamation of the Irish Republic:

> We hereby proclaim the Irish Republic as a Sovereign Independent State, and we pledge our lives and the lives of our comrades-in-arms to the cause of its freedom ...

In Fairview, Captain Thomas Weafer, knowing that action had begun at midday in the centre of Dublin became aware that Fr Mathew Park was in danger of attack from British forces who were in their training camp on Bull Island three miles to the northeast. If they were to seize the park they would capture the stores of the 2nd Battalion and put the 100 Volunteers, under his charge, out of action. He consulted the other officers present, Leo Henderson, Liam Breen, Frank Henderson, Oscar Traynor and Tom Ennis. Oscar Traynor wanted to go immediately into town but Tom Ennis said that they would lose all their stores if they did. They decided to send Tom Ennis and John McDonnell to the GPO to discuss the matter with Pádraig Pearse. Tom Ennis was soon back with a written order from Pearse to bring the men and stores into the GPO. At 3pm the half battalion set off by Ballybough and Summerhill to reach Sackville Street, a journey of about two miles. As they went over the Royal Canal at Clarke's Bridge on the top of Summerhill Parade, scouts from Dollymount reported to Captain Weafer that the British forces from Bull Island were moving in the direction of the city centre also. Just then they heard firing behind them and it was coming from the direction of the Great Northern Railway. Weafer decided to send a detachment under Frank Henderson to Ballybough Bridge and Fairview Strand to block the British from getting into the city centre. He sent a smaller band of Volunteers under Leo Henderson to intercept the British forces at Annesley and Newcomen bridges if they tried to get in by the North Strand Road. He took the main body of about fifty men into the houses near the Royal Canal at the top of Summerhill Parade. When the British forces did not follow, the main body of 2nd Battalion Irish Volunteers re-formed under Captain Weafer and reached the GPO at 4.30pm on that Easter Monday afternoon. The medical supplies they brought with them were later used by the Fairview Cumann na mBan to establish the first-aid station in the GPO. The military stores, mainly made up of ammunition and some guns, were a godsend to the GPO garrison.

Harry was one of the detachment under Captain Frank Henderson who occupied Gilbey's, Wine Branch Depot, in Fairview Strand near the junction with Richmond Road. Fairview Strand was a continuation of Ballybough Road with the top of it facing out towards the northern railway line between Dublin and Belfast. These rails ran over sloblands that stretched out for about 200 yards. A parapet, reinforced by an embankment, propped up the railway line. All was quiet for a time but then the British troops from Bull Island training camp under Major H. F. Somerville of the School of Musketry advanced and went into the area stretching from Fairview Strand to Annesley Bridge and Wharf Road (now East Wall Road). The Irish Volunteers in corner houses on North Strand, in Spring Garden Street, Annesley Place and in Leinster Avenue opened fire on the British advance guard crossing Annesley Bridge. During the fight the Volunteers put the British machine gun out of action. Those British soldiers who succeeded in rushing down Wharf Road came under fire from Volunteers in Leinster Avenue through an open space between the two roads.[6] The main enemy force came under fire from Volunteers 200 yards to the north of the bridge. They retreated under cover into the streets around, including Fairview Strand. Here they came under fire from Frank Henderson's group for about 20 minutes. Harry Colley, one of the Fairview Volunteers, was wounded badly near the insurgents' barricade of sandbags at Annesley Bridge.[7] One British soldier was mortally wounded in this exchange of fire.[8] The British forces were determined to maintain control of the Great Northern Railway line to Belfast and to advance with more of their forces into the city centre. The Volunteers were attempting to hold off British troops coming from Bull Island for as long as they could.

James Connolly got a report that there was firing in Fairview and he sent 30 riflemen under Seán T. O'Kelly to reinforce the Volunteers. They marched as far as Annesley Bridge where they set up headquarters at the Drumcondra side of that bridge in the fertiliser factory of the Dublin and Wicklow Company. They also occupied the offices of the same company at North Strand corner and they erected barricades nearby. There was no fighting going on at that time but O'Kelly sent scouts to find out what had caused the earlier gun battle. The scouts found armed Volunteers looking out from the windows of houses near Fairview Strand. These Volunteers told them that there had been an engagement shortly before that with British troops who had tried to advance into the city across Annesley Bridge. Seán T. sent a messenger back to the GPO to report that everything was under control in Fairview. After a short time the courier returned to him with an order to return with his 30 riflemen to the GPO.[9]

Later on that Monday evening Kathleen Boland made her way from her home in Clontarf to see Harry in Gilbey's. There was no firing since early afternoon in Fairview but still she took cover by stooping down and edging along by the walls of the houses. Frank Henderson opened the door of the wine store and Kathleen entered bringing some food. This group in Gilbey's feared they might run out of ammunition. Volunteer Flynn who lived in nearby Ballybough told Kathleen that he had a bag of ammunition in his house which he did not have time to collect. Kathleen volunteered to collect it and bring it to him. She also knew that her friend Ena Shouldice, who was in lodgings at Addison Road nearby, but who was out of town on holidays, had some ammunition locked in a trunk. Kathleen who had a key to the house went and broke open the trunk. She got about ten packets of .303 rifle ammunition and brought it to Gilbey's along with Vol. Flynn's bagful.[10]

British forces now knew that there was a concentration of insurgents in positions extending along Ballybough Road, Fairview Strand and Annesley Bridge. During Easter Monday night Major H. F. Somerville, unaware to the Volunteers, brought up more reinforcements from Bull Island and slipped them past Fairview in the darkness, travelling by foot on the northern railway line. He brought his men into the city where he captured the Custom House, Amiens Street Station, the North Wall railway terminus and thus secured the important dock area.[11]

A party of 2nd Battalion Volunteers tried to blow up the

northern railway line across the Tolka River just before dawn on Tuesday, but the explosives failed to do enough damage. They then ripped up tracks further up the northern line. At 2pm a strong military force in an armoured train pushed out from Amiens Street Station to repair the line. Again the insurgents at Annesley Road and Fairview Strand fired at them. They pinned them down for a while, but the British fought bravely. A section of them went to repair the rails while the rest took the offensive against the insurgents and fought their way across the sloblands and in between the streets and avenues of Fairview trying to dislodge the insurrectionists. They retreated when their companions had repaired the rails but they left some of their men behind who surrendered to the Volunteers.[12] During this fighting Harry's group in Gilbey's captured one of the British soldiers – Sergeant Henry, a machine gun instructor at the British camp on Bull Island and Harry took charge of him. The British suffered casualties on the railway embankment and the Volunteers captured rifles and ammunition.[13]

· Kathleen Boland managed to get to Gilbey's again on Tuesday evening to see if she could do anything to help but Harry told her to go home and not to come back as she would be of more help at home.[14]

With only about 60 insurgents in the Fairview district there was the imminent danger that they would be cut off between troops coming out from Amiens Street Station and other forces advancing from the Bull Island direction. Extra troops came in from the Curragh by the Great Northern Line that evening. Captain Weafer, who had gone ahead to the GPO with the battalion's military stores the day before, was worried about his men in Fairview. He had only intended that they fight a rearguard action to give him time to get in with his important stores to the GPO. Now that he was involved in the fighting in Sackville Street he realised that he could lose 60 active 2nd Battalion Volunteers by allowing them to be cut off in Fairview. He consulted James Connolly and Connolly knew from reports that the British were now in possession of the Amiens Street Station – North Strand sectors. They were converging on Drumcondra and coming in on the Malahide and Howth Roads. Connolly issued an order to the Fairview Volunteers directing them to get into Sackville Street as soon as possible and strengthen the garrisons of the Irish Republican forces close to the GPO.[15]

Captain Frank Henderson got the order in Gilbey's. They had to bring Sergeant Henry, their prisoner, with them. The khaki uniform of their prisoner helped to get them past the British machine gunner at Clonliffe Road within whose sights they passed. Sergeant Henry was 'whinging' when he was not released and Harry and others commandeered a cab into which they bundled the prisoner and they drove quickly out of Fairview Strand towards the city centre. It was near midnight when most of these Volunteers reached Sackville Street.

The *Times History of the War* records that the attempts of the rebels 'to control communications to the west and the south and the north had come to nothing at King's Bridge, at Broadstone and at Amiens Street'. But they admitted that the Volunteers 'strangled the Great Northern Line to some extent by their command of the Fairview district, an old Larkinite stronghold'.[16]

LIVED TO SEE AN IRISH REPUBLIC

The 60 Fairview Volunteers arrived in Sackville Street in the centre of Dublin a little before midnight on that Tuesday evening. James Connolly was watching for their arrival and he shouted to the GPO garrison to let them in.[1] Peter Carpenter 'was part of a group with Oscar Traynor and Seán Russell and Harry Boland who reported first to the GPO'.[2]

When Harry arrived in the GPO he had Sergeant Henry with him. He was sent to report to The O'Rahilly who was in charge of the custody of prisoners in rooms on the top floor of the building where the food stores were also kept and the cooking done. Henry protested to O'Rahilly at his detention and wanted to know what was to happen to him. The O'Rahilly told him that the policy of the leaders of the insurrection was to treat captured British soldiers as prisoners of war. Amongst some other British captives whom Harry saw was Private William Richardson, a British soldier in the Connaught Rangers as well as a Dublin Fusilier.

Harry was then told to report to his colleagues from Fairview. These Volunteers were divided into three groups and James Connolly issued instructions to them. Harry was detailed to go with a group to occupy the Metropole Hotel which was within a block of shops and offices between Prince's Street North and Middle Abbey Street, and facing out on Sackville Street. Harry's youngest brother Ned, was in a group sent to the Imperial Hotel on the opposite side of Sackville Street.[3]

James Connolly put Lieutenant Oscar Traynor in charge of Harry's group in the Metropole. Seán Russell, Peter Carpenter and Charles Saurin, all from the Fairview district, swept into the hotel. Both Connolly and Pearse believed that the British would in the end charge into Sackville Street and fight a close battle with the insurgents. Connolly looked on the Metropole Hotel as an outpost which the British would have to take first before capturing the GPO. Frank Thornton was in charge of the company of men in the Imperial Hotel. He was a Louth man who had come from Liverpool to join his comrades in Ireland in the Rising just like the London-based Michael Collins had done.

On Wednesday morning Sackville Street came under attack

from sniper and machine gun fire coming from the roofs of the Rotunda, the Custom House and Trinity College. Every time Harry saw an armed khaki-clad figure dash from one street to another he fired. Later that day Harry saw Noel Lemass dash from the Imperial Hotel and race across the wide expanse of Sackville Street with a despatch for the GPO. Bullets hit the pavement in front and behind him but still he made it to the post office unscathed. Noel had to return to the Imperial Hotel with the answer. Harry watched from his perch at the Metropole Hotel window as Noel dodged across again, zig-zagging as much as he could from the machine gunners and the snipers. Harry uttered a short curse when he saw Noel fall as he reached the footpath and put his two hands to his leg where he was apparently wounded. Then he saw two Volunteer figures as they ran from the Imperial Hotel to grab hold of Noel and drag him towards the hotel door. But he sat bolt upright when he saw that the big six foot Volunteer dragging Noel towards the door was his brother Ned! The other man was Jack Whelan. He saw the two men successfully pull Noel Lemass to safety and breathed a sigh of relief when they all got safely inside the hotel door.[4]

Mid-afternoon on Wednesday Harry heard a frightening whistling noise overhead followed by the loud boom. He heard the sound of breaking glass. The walls shook and so did his nerves. Machine guns opened from the tower of the fire station and the roof of the Tivoli Theatre. He could see bullets ricocheting off the tram lines and hitting the portico of the GPO. Noise, rifle-shots, machine guns surrounded him. Harry caught an occasional flash of a British soldier rushing from one barricade to another and this gave him a target to aim and fire at.

James Connolly had put Captain Weafer in charge of the Reis building and the Hibernian Bank on the opposite side of Sackville Street to the Metropole Hotel and the GPO but closer to the Liffey. He lost no time in building a great barricade of furniture and newsprint at the top of Lower Abbey Street to protect Sackville Street from a possible British sortie from that direction. On Wednesday afternoon the British peppered this position with machine gun bullets ripping clouds of mortar from the Hibernian Bank. The insurgents counter-fired and Captain Weafer toppled over and collapsed on the floor – he had been shot through the lung. Weafer's body was never recovered as his remains were burned in the fire which engulfed the Hibernian Bank.

During Wednesday night and Thursday morning Oscar Traynor told his men in the Metropole Hotel to tunnel through the block as far as Manfield's, boot and shoe manufacturers, on the corner of Middle Abbey Street. Thursday morning was a superb spring day. For years after weather like this would be described by Dubliners as 'good insurrection weather'. At ten o'clock a British shell made a direct hit on the *Irish Times* printing office in Lower Abbey Street, setting fire to newsprint rolls in the building. Sparks from the flames got to the barricade. It went on fire and the flames spread to Wynn's Hotel on the south side of the street. Connolly, fearing that this was the beginning of the British attack which would come up Sackville Street sent a further 20 men to the Metropole Hotel to reinforce Oscar Traynor's garrison. Harry was one of a group who had broken through the corner wall of Manfield's and into Middle Abbey Street as far as Eason's. They could now see down as far as Westmoreland and D'Olier Streets. British military began to penetrate into Sackville Street from Lower Abbey Street, but they were stopped in their tracks by rifle fire from Oscar Traynor, Seán Russell, Harry and the other Fairview Volunteers in the Metropole and Manfield's. The Metropole outpost fired so effectively that they halted any military advance up Sackville Street for the time being.[5]

By mid afternoon on Thursday the fire on the other side of Sackville Street was advancing along from shop to shop until it was almost in line with the GPO. The British told the Dublin Fire Brigade that they could not provide cover for them to tackle the fire so they were unable to move in with their hoses and fire fighting equipment. The blazing inferno was getting out of control.

British shells were now getting the range of the GPO. Harry was in the Metropole Hotel when he heard the now familiar noise of an approaching shell which seemed like it was directly over his head. Then he heard the slates on the roof of the hotel crashing down. Oscar Traynor shouted an order 'Get into Manfield's at once. Move fast' – they crawled through the hole in the wall. The GPO got its first direct artillery hit just then. Flying shrapnel wounded Republican snipers on the roof. James Connolly was in Middle Abbey Street directing a Republican military action when a bullet ricocheted from the pavement and fractured his ankle.

British troops in Dublin now far outnumbered the insurgent

forces. Their military tactics were far superior to those of the in-surrectionists. Using maps and manuals, they planned for the gradual siege of Sackville Street. Companies of Sherwood Foresters closed off every possible outlet of escape for the GPO garrison. The fires along the other side of Sackville Street kept on spreading northwards. It was dark that Thursday evening when Hoyte's and Son, oil and painting warehouse, went up in flames. Oil drums exploded. There was a danger that the fire could spread across the street to the GPO.

Throughout the night machine-gun and rifle fire raked through Sackville Street. The flames from the fires generated such a glow that Harry and the Fairview group got no sleep that night. His heart missed a beat as he saw the flames engulf the Imperial Hotel because his brother Ned was there. His heart sank when some men made their escape and he did not see Ned among them. Minutes later the flames burst out through the windows. He heard a crash and a grinding roar and then the building was gone. But had Ned gone down with it? He wasn't given time to brood.

Two more shells landed on the roof of the Metropole Hotel almost over his head. The British were making another attack up Lower Abbey Street. Oscar Traynor, Harry and their 30 or so companions in the Metropole and Manfield's fired rapidly in the enemy's direction – trying to halt their advance.

In the faint light of dawn on Friday they saw the military creeping furtively across the bridge and taking cover in the debris of Sackville Street. General Sir John Maxwell who had been appointed General Commanding-in-Chief of the British forces in Ireland during the week of the Rising wrote to his wife that morning, 'The Sinn Féiners are all over Ireland: when we have done with them in Dublin we will have to clear the outstations – in Dublin we have them surrounded'.[6]

In mid-afternoon the British began to hit the GPO with incendiary bombs. The roof caught fire. Men passed buckets of water along a line in a race to stem the flames. Slates and plaster fell to the floor underneath, injuring some Volunteers. A second incendiary shell hit the portico in the front of the post office. Flames and sparks worked their way down to the cellars where the Irish Republican forces had stored their home-made explosives.[7] At this stage Pearse, Connolly, and Plunkett realised that the GPO was doomed and the only alternative was to evacuate.

At 7pm Diarmuid Lynch supervised the removal of the home-made bombs and gelignite from the basement. Relays of men stood with lighted candles along a dark passage to guide the Volunteers, carrying the dangerous substances. They put the home-made bombs in a storeroom off Prince's Street courtyard.[8]

Harry was still moving between the Metropole and Manfield's but collapsing roofs, scorching flames and intensive heat pushed the Volunteers back to the Prince's Street corner end. Word came for them to withdraw to the GPO. Oscar Traynor called his group back from all the buildings in this block. Sadly Harry crawled through the wrecked walls, then he dashed with the others across Prince's Street. They got covering fire from their comrades in the GPO and they rushed into the post office.

The O'Rahilly called down the Volunteer snipers from the roof and he motioned to the fire-fighters to desist.[9] It was difficult for them to stop because it meant the battle was lost. Most of them edged their way towards the Henry Street exit. On their way to show that they were still undaunted they sang 'The Soldiers' Song' which had become the popular song of the Republicans during the week.

The prisoners held by the insurgents were now brought up from the basement and given the option of leaving on their own initiative. Private William Richardson told the story of their dash for freedom – when they got into Henry Place, their own British guns were firing down Moore Lane from the Rotunda Hospital. There was an opening in Henry Place and the machine gun's bullets were flying through it. They had to pass by this street gap. 'We rushed through – our own side's gunfire playing on us and over us. Some of us got through and some didn't. I saw the Dublin Fusilier topple over'.[10] The Dublin Fusilier was shot through the head by fire from his own Sherwood Foresters. Sergeant Henry, who was captured by Harry earlier in the week, got away unscathed.

The main body of the insurgents now retreated from the doomed GPO. They had received news from Vol. John McLoughlin that there were British troops with a machine gun at the top of Moore Street. This group, led by McLoughlin and Michael Collins with a drawn revolver, rushed into Henry Place just twenty-five yards across from the Henry Street post office exit. They dashed into this lane which went straight down for seventy-five yards but then turned to the left at a right angle for Moore Street. No trouble for the first seventy-five yards but then they turned into the second line of the right-angled exit. Thirty-five yards up was the gap where the Dublin Fusilier prisoner had been killed a short time before. Some Irish Republican soldiers ran across – others hesitated and doubled back causing a build up. Volunteer McLoughlin who showed great military initiative ordered them to search for materials to make a sheltering barricade across the gap. Some insurgents found an old motor van in a nearby yard, pushed it across and this gave some protection to the running fugitives as they dashed across.

Harry had come into the GPO just before the main evacuation. As his comrades moved towards the Henry Street exit to get ready to evacuate, he doubled back to help Diarmuid Lynch who had not finished his work in making the home-made bombs safe. Both remained in the storeroom in Prince's Street to finish the work and were not aware that the evacuation had been completed while they were in the outside storeroom. When they ran back through the collapsing GPO, they could not see anybody through the thick smoke. As they ran, they avoided falling beams and collapsing walls. They groped their way towards the red glow of light in Henry Street. Harry was a short distance ahead of Diarmuid Lynch when he reached the exit door. Even Pádraig Pearse had left before them although he thought he was the last man to leave.[11]

Jim Humphreys was scared in his public house at the lower end of Henry Street. Right across from his window he saw the Republican forces evacuate the GPO. Flames were leaping from the roof of the post office. He decided that it was time for him to 'abandon ship'. He opened his front door and came out onto the street. Just then Harry was staggering out from the Henry Street door of the post office. He recognised Jim as he was a GAA man and Harry had paid the odd visit to Jim's public house.

'Jim,' Harry shouted. 'Go back in or you'll be shot.'

Humphreys recognised Harry and went back into the house. 'Harry saved my life that day'.[12]

Harry had to get out of Henry Street. He looked down Henry Place and saw Pádraig Pearse just turning the right angled bend seventy-five yards ahead of him. Harry sprinted down. When he turned the corner, he saw Pearse slip and fall just where the protective barricade had been pushed across the gap. However, he quickly jumped to his feet again. Now it was Harry's turn to cross the gap which was still being raked with British bullets. He ducked down below the old motor van and ran and got safely across as did Diarmuid Lynch who was following close behind him. In less that ten seconds they were at the entrance to Moore Street. Pádraig Pearse went into Cogan's, a green grocery shop on the corner of Moore Street. Boland and Lynch slipped into the hallway of the same house. Connolly, Plunkett, Clarke and Mac-Diarmada were also in Cogan's. At dawn on Saturday morning Pearse asked a group of the Republicans to bore through the walls towards Great Britain Street. The whole party moved forward through the hole in the walls until they came to Hanlon's fish shop at No. 16 Moore Street. James Connolly was in terrible pain as his foot was becoming gangrenous. Here the leaders at one last council of war decided to try out one final plan to break through the British cordon. However, Pearse feared that he would lose many of the men in this last charge and just as preparations were afoot for this last push an incident happened in Moore Street that decided Pearse against further military action.

Robert Dillon who had a public house in Moore Street left his premises with his wife and daughter when it went on fire from a burning piece of timber from the GPO. They walked behind a white flag but the British opened fire on them from Great Britain Street and they all died before Pearse's eyes.[13] Soon after that Pádraig Pearse surrendered unconditionally to General Lowe 'to prevent the further slaughter of Dublin citizens and in the hope of saving the lives of his followers then surrounded and hopelessly outnumbered'. James Connolly surrendered because he could not bear 'to see his brave boys burned to death'.

Seán MacDiarmada rounded up most of the men in the lanes and warehouses around Moore Street. He marshalled the fit men into ranks in the middle of the street. Amongst them was the disappointed sad figure of Harry Boland. They marched slowly into Henry Street and then to the right-hand side of Sackville Street. The area was silent as they passed a war-torn scene of collapsed and smouldering buildings. They marched to within a hundred yards of the military drawn up at the Parnell monument. They halted, advanced five paces and laid down their arms.

As they marched to the grounds of the Rotunda Hospital they were heartened by the fact that they had put up a good fight. The enemy who outnumbered them by almost twenty to one, had artillery and military equipment that far outclassed the Howth rifles of the Republican forces. Private William Richardson told an *Evening Herald* reporter the 'like of the bombardment we were under that Friday night in the GPO, I never experienced. I never heard the like and I hope to God I never may have to go through the like again'.[14]

A Prisoner after 1916

Retribution by the British was harsh and swift. The war was on in Europe and the Irish Revolution and everyone connected with it had to be put down quickly. General Sir John Maxwell was not one for kid glove methods.

From the Rotunda Harry was marched with the other prisoners to Richmond Barracks in Inchicore. On their way large groups of people stood on the pavements and jeered them. 'Shoot them! Bayonet them!' they called out to the soldiers who were escorting them. Many of the prisoners felt safer when they arrived at the barracks and got off the streets.

Harry was close to the gates of Richmond Barracks when he was recognised by Mary Byrne who used to work for the Boland family when they were in Wexford Street. He spoke quickly to her as he passed, 'Tell my mother that I'm in Richmond Barracks. I'm well.' Mary walked all the way to Clontarf with the message. Kathleen, Harry's sister, tried to see him in Richmond Barracks. She did not get in to see him but outside she met Fr Augustine and Fr Albert, remarkable priests who ministered to the insurgents. They assured Kathleen that she could give any message she had for Harry to them and they would bring it to him.[1]

In Richmond Barracks Sergeant Henry, the prisoner whom Harry arrested during the Rising, was brought along to pick out any of the Republican soldiers he could identify. He saw Harry in the line. With glee on his face he approached him and pointed him out. Then looking Harry straight in the eyes he half smiled and said, 'He who laughs last, laughs best'. Harry smirked back, 'Yes, chum, I am laughing. I am not cringing like you were when I took you prisoner'.[2] He was separated from the main body of Irish prisoners and told that he was to be court-martialled.

On 3 May the executions began. Thirteen leaders were executed in great haste. The trial of the two remaining signatories of the Proclamation, James Connolly and Seán MacDiarmada took place on 9 May and both were sentenced to death. On 11 May, John Dillon of the Irish Parliamentary Party made an impassioned plea in the British House of Commons to Mr Asquith, the British Prime Minister to stop the executions 'This series of executions is doing more harm than any Englishman in this House can possibly fathom'.[3]

Harry was brought before a British court-martial on 11 May 1916. The charge against him was 'of taking part in armed rebellion and waging war against His Majesty, the King, such act being of such nature as to be prejudicial to the Defence of the Realm and being done with the intention and for the purpose of assisting the enemy (Germany)'.[4] Witnesses were brought to testify against him. Sergeant Henry identified him as his captor. Harry was sentenced to ten years' penal servitude (with five years' remission).[5]

Frank Thornton described what happened after their court-martial that day: 'Seán MacDiarmada ... walked with difficulty with the aid of a stick ... and one of the first acts of his escort when we were ordered to fall-in for our march to Kilmainham, was to take the stick and immediately Harry Boland came to his rescue and put his arm around him'. Thornton went on to explain that even at this stage the executions were changing the attitudes of the people towards the participants in the Rising: 'The open trams passing by always brought a cheer from somebody, even though rifles were pointed at the offender on every occasion. Old men stood at the street corners and saluted, despite being pushed around'. Seán MacDiarmada was resigned to his fate and he turned around and said to the others: 'I'll be shot, and it will be a bad day for Ireland that I'm not. You fellows will get an opportunity, even if in years to come, to follow on where we left off'.[6] Seán Mac-Diarmada was in fact shot with James Connolly at 4am the next morning. Those were the last shots of the 1916 Insurrection.

Harry, Frank Thornton and other sentenced prisoners were transferred to Mountjoy and spent a week there. While Harry was in Mountjoy Prison his mother and his sister Kathleen came to see him. His mother, who thought it might be some advantage to Harry if she protested his innocence, said to him, 'Wasn't it an extraordinary thing to arrest you, and you only coming from the races!' But Harry said, 'Ah, no, mother. I was not coming from the races. I went out to strike a blow against the bloody British empire'. Kathleen told him that his younger brother, Ned, was safe and at home in Marino Crescent.[7] Harry was delighted because he had not heard Ned had escaped. He also knew now that his mother and Kathleen would have someone to care for them during his own absence.

The sentenced prisoners who had been court-martialled were

treated more harshly than those internees, including Gerry Boland and Michael Collins, who earlier had been marched to the North Wall in Dublin and sent without trial to Frongoch. The sentenced prisoners who included Harry were destined for the toughest criminal prisons in England. After four or five days in Mountjoy, they were brought down in Black Marias to the North Wall, to be shipped to an unknown destination because the authorities would not reveal the name of the prison to which they were being sent. In this party were Harry, Frank Thornton, Éamon de Valera, Tom Ashe, Dr Richard Hayes, Frank and Jim Lawless of Swords, Jack McArdle (Liberty Hall), Con O'Donovan a university student from West Cork, Gerald Crofts the singer and Professor Peadar Slattery from Pádraig Pearse's school, St Enda's.[8]

When the boat was sailing down the Liffey, Gerald Crofts raised his fine singing voice and though he was 'down below' his rich clear notes reached the brisk morning air as he sang, 'Oh! The last glimpse of Erin'.[9] As yet Harry 'was only a rank-and-file man of the Dublin Brigade'[10] but from this date on his status in the whole national movement rose. The *Irish Independent* printed his photograph on the 13 May 1916, beside Kerry-born Tom Ashe, because he was already well-known in GAA circles, had participated in the 1916 Rising and was sentenced to 10 years' penal servitude (with five years' remission).

Tom Jones in his *Whitehall Diary* describes the effect the 1916 executions had on American opinion: 'The numerous executions had made a profound impression on the Irish in America and were exploited there to the full. T. M. Healy says: "A Requiem Mass was said in every church, by order of the bishops, for the men shot. The 'funerals' got up for the Dublin dead in April were attended by millions in the USA".'[11]

Harry denied that he or the other insurgents were motivated by pro-German sympathies:

We went out in Easter Week, not to fight for Germany but to fight for Ireland. Not as rebels but as insurgents for we spoke for a nation and if we thought well of it, we were quite justified in allying ourselves with our enemy's enemy. Fr O'Flanagan put it very nicely when he told the story of the cat and the mouse. A mouse ran out on the street and a cat pursued it. Then a dog pounced on the cat and of course the mouse was pro dog ... We were like that mouse. We were not pro-Germans.[12]

When they arrived in England they were taken in lorries through a desolate area of rocks and moorlands before they reached Dartmoor Prison. The governor, doctor, chief warder and a strong force of warders, each of them with a baton swinging by a leather thong from their right wrists, were waiting for them. When the doctor had examined each of them they were issued with old prison clothes, khaki in colour, that had been worn by previous convicts. They were then finger-printed, photographed and issued with a prison number which in Harry's case was Q 90. This number was stamped on his boots, shirts, on the left sleeve of his drab prison uniform and on the black shield on the front of his forage cap. He was known as Prisoner Q 90 instead of by name.[13] A report from Dartmoor Prison, dated 16 May 1916, described the arrival there of the Irish prisoners and how the prison authorities planned to deal with them: 'The 38 prisoners are being kept apart from the other convicts and are being split up and the arrangement amounts to star-class segregation'.[14]

The prisoners continued to arrive until the number came to eighty. Wexford journalist Robert Brennan, who had taken part in the 1916 Rising in Enniscorthy, described his first day in Dartmoor Prison in his book, *Allegiance*. He said that he heard the cheerful voice of Harry just outside his cell:

> He was replying to a warder who was giving him orders regarding the polishing of the steel rail of the staircase. As he started to polish Harry began to sing. The warder was shocked. 'Silence!' he barked
> 'What's up?' asked Harry.
> 'You're not supposed to sing here.'
> 'That's funny,' said Harry. 'I was only singing to myself.'
> 'Well, you can't sing here.'
> A few minutes later Harry began to whistle.
> 'Whistling's not allowed either,' barked the warder.
> 'Why not?'
> 'Because it's the rule.'
> 'Well, it's a rotten rule and someone should tell the Governor so.'
> Harry was told to go back to his cell because the warder could not listen to him any longer.[15]

Prisoner Q 90 was described in Dartmoor Prison as 29 years of age, with no previous convictions whose occupation was tailor's cutter. He was put in charge of a fatigue party with Con O'Donovan serving breakfast on one of the Irish prisoners' landings. The food was bad, the water was full of iron and the men developed very bad teeth. Harry and Frank Thornton suffered from bad toothaches and swollen jaws. One morning when they both went to the doctor's office with this complaint he looked into their mouths and then ordered two warders to grab them, hold them down in ordinary chairs and then, without any local anaesthetic, extracted an aching back tooth from each of their mouths. For ten days afterwards they were unable to talk and they felt as if they were lock-jawed.

The rules in Dartmoor were very strict. Talking, as in Harry's earlier experience, was strictly forbidden at work and at exercise. For exercise the prisoners had to walk around in a ring in the prison yard and keep a distance of two paces between each of them. It wasn't long before they learned the art of ventriloquism but not all became experts in the skill and some were caught and the punishment was one or two days on bread and water.[16]

Éamon de Valera and Tom Ashe were continually making representations to the governor on behalf of all the prisoners – that they should be treated as prisoners of war. Dev, Dr Richard Hayes and Desmond Fitzgerald[17] were removed from Dartmoor and sent to Maidstone because the 'governor was afraid that they would organise a revolt in the prison and they were exercising a bad influence on the others'.[18] The Irish prisoners, including Harry, reacted to their transfer by organising passive resistance in the prison. They worked on the mail bags in the prison workshop until they were about half completed and then they ripped them up and started all over again. The prison staff became frustrated with all this insubordination. Daily routine had become more difficult for them since the Irish prisoners arrived. In Dartmoor some Irish prisoners were held in solitary confinement every day of the week on a diet of bread and water. The more severe the punishments, the more determined the prisoners became to start a wholesale prison revolt. Stories of the harsh treatment of Irish prisoners in Dartmoor Prison began to filter through to Ireland. Alfie Byrne, Dublin MP, made forceful representation to the Home Office for special treatment for Irish prisoners.

Ned Boland and a family friend, Doran, went to see Harry in Dartmoor but they were only allowed to see him for a quarter of an hour. They found him in fairly good spirits and his mother and sister Kathleen were glad to hear that he was in good health.[19]

Harry's brother, Gerry, had been interned at Frongoch with Michael Collins. Michael sent out a report from Frongoch complaining about conditions. Gerry disagreed with Collins as he felt that the Irish internees there were getting the same rations as the soldiers at the front and that they could not expect better than that. Even when Joe O'Connor, MP of the Irish Party, visited Frongoch, Gerry refused to sign the report saying that he had a young bride, a mother and a young sister at home and he did not want them to be distressed over prison conditions that seemed fair to him. This was the first of many personality clashes between Gerry and Collins. They could never meet without an argument. Later on Gerry continually warned his brother, Harry, about his friendship with Collins, saying that Harry would 'regret the day he brought that fellow (Collins) into the organisation'.[20]

Untried prisoners in the internment camp at Frongoch were released at Christmas 1916, but not sentenced Irish prisoners like Harry. The Irish prisoners in Dartmoor heard on the 5 December 1916 that the prison authorities were transferring them to another prison. The prison commission in the Home Office, decided after protracted representations, that the 'Irish Rebel Convicts' should be collected together in a special prison – Lewes Prison, outside London. The Home Office statement listed improved privileges which the prisoners would be allowed:

> These new privileges provide that they shall be located in a prison specially laid apart for them, that they shall be allowed monthly letters and visits, that they shall be allowed daily while at exercise to converse with each other and that facilities for writing on other than political matters shall be granted under certain conditions.[21]

The prisoners were removed to Lewes Gaol in chains on 21 December 1916.[2] Major R. A. Marriott, the governor of Lewes Prison, was lenient with the prisoners at first. They began to organise themselves and they chose a committee to act for them with Éamon de Valera as Commandant, Tom Ashe as Vice-Commandant and Tom Hunter as Adjutant. In the first week of March, Patrick Kelly, one of the prisoners, was sent to the punishment cell and put on bread and water for talking during work. Dev ordered all the prisoners to refuse to work. Governor Marriott, very upset, spoke to De Valera and Kelly was discharged from his punishment.

The prison commission in the Home Office did not agree with

the leniency of Governor Marriott and J. R. Farewell, inspector of prisons, was sent to Lewes. The probability of a long battle between the prison authorities and the prisoners loomed. Harry was determined to fight for better jail conditions with Dev. Farewell warned the prisoners when he spoke to them of the consequences of combined insubordination:

> You must understand that any man guilty of the offence of combination to resist authority will be at once transferred to another prison. If any other report comes to the governor against any person found talking at labour, it will entail forfeiture by that prisoner of talking at exercise.[23]

De Valera declared another strike, which ended on the 17 April when the prison governor received a letter from the prison commission in the Home Office saying that the Secretary of State was prepared, after careful consideration, to allow the privilege of talking while at work on condition that 'either the output of work or the discipline of the establishment is not adversely affected'.[24] The Irish prisoners had won a small concession and to Harry it was a major victory. It gave them confidence in the leadership of Dev.

There was a by-election in Longford on 9 May 1916 and the idea arose, in Longford first, of selecting Joseph McGuinness, one of the Lewes prisoners, as a candidate. Michael Collins conveyed the message to McGuinness through the prison chaplain. Joe McGuinness spoke to Éamonn Duggan, Piaras Béaslaí, Éamon de Valera, Thomas Ashe, Diarmuid Lynch, Seán McGarry and Harry about whether he should stand or not. They all thought, including Joe McGuinness, that it would be better if he did not go forward as a candidate – except Thomas Ashe and Harry who liked the idea.[25] De Valera got this message out of the prison: 'As regards the contesting of elections question, it is so extremely dangerous from several points of view that most of us here consider it very unwise'.[26] The reason they opposed the selection of prisoners as candidates in elections at this stage was because they thought they should have nothing at all to do with the British parliament – not even to contest British elections. They were also afraid that if McGuinness were defeated it would also be seen as a defeat for the men of 1916 – as they were locked up in prison they were unaware of the great change in people's attitudes outside.

Their advice was ignored by Michael Collins and others working in Longford. They fought the election on the abstentionist policy of Sinn Féin, so if McGuinness were elected he would not attend the British parliament at Westminster. All subsequent by-elections were contested on this principle. During this by-election Michael Collins stayed in the Greville Arms Hotel, Granard, run by the four Kiernan sisters and their brother, Larry. As well as owning the hotel the Kiernan family were proprietors of a bar, grocery, hardware, bakery and undertaking business. It was then that he first met the attractive Kitty Kiernan but it was Helen, Kitty's sister, who first 'took his eye'.

Harry, in the company of three other prisoners, 'lifted' a copy of the *Independent* newspaper from the chaplain's office desk and brought the news to the prisoners that Joe McGuinness had won the Longford by-election. Joe, the new MP, was grabbed, lifted up and carried shoulder high around the prison yard. His election excited the prisoners as they prepared for a bigger battle. The Irish Nation League, formed in Ireland after the 1916 Rising, was pressing for prisoner-of-war treatment for Irish prisoners. In Lewes, Dev was thinking along similar lines, but before starting out on such a battle he wanted to see if there was support at home for such a fight. He got word out to Republican supporters in Dublin suggesting that if they were prepared to back the bid for prisoner-of-war status they should send a telegram to Lewes to Harry telling him that his uncle had died – the chaplain broke the sad news to Harry and offered to say a Requiem Mass for a dear departed uncle![27]

On Whit Monday, 28 May 1917, Éamon de Valera, on behalf of the other prisoners, served a notice on the principal warder that the Irish prisoners demanded prisoner-of-war status:

> The Irish people demand that we be made prisoners-of-war. Until the government declares our status as such we refuse to do any labour except those services directly necessary for ourselves, e.g., cooking, laundry, etc.[28]

Then the Irish prisoners left their work stations and went quietly back to their cells. They were kept confined to their cells until the end of the week. They were deemed to have lost all privileges. The prison authorities offered to allow them out to exercise in small groups, provided they walked in silence, and in convict manner – but nobody broke ranks and took the offer.

Dev expecting the prison authorities to let them out to Mass the following Sunday, issued a written order to the Irish prisoners instructing them what to do after they left the prison chapel:

> No man is to go into his cell again. Keep perfect order. The idea is to com-
> pel them to bring in the military if we can ... If we are still in our cells with-
> out exercise on Monday break the panes in the upper parts of the win-
> dows. Reason to get more air. The cells are the Black Hole of Calcutta. If
> we get out on Sunday, try to stuff the locks with buttons, etc., or strain the
> hinges so that they cannot be locked again.[29]

They were indeed in their cells on Monday because some un-
thinking prisoner dropped the written order in the bathroom and
a warder picked it up. Major Marriott, the governor, gave orders
that the prisoners would only be allowed to attend Mass on Sunday provided that each gave an undertaking he would proceed to
and from the chapel in a quiet and orderly manner. About 50 prisoners would not give such undertaking – in spite of every effort
made by the chaplain. This chaplain thought that no real Irish Catholic would have contemplated rebellion after Mass and Holy
Communion but he considered De Valera a 'half-breed' capable of
any enormity. The following day Dev sent another note to the governor saying that 'if we are confined in this manner' they would be
compelled to take steps of their own to secure a proper supply of
fresh air. The governor did not react to De Valera's note and the
prisoners went ahead, according to the prison report, and 'broke
their windows and did a good deal of shouting and singing and
amused themselves by passing notes by means of pieces of string'.
The second night the prisoners broke the spyholes, the third night
the lamp screens and then the gas box glass. All this destruction
was accompanied by much hullabaloo and cheering. The report
on the riot said that 'the shouting and the singing could be heard
beyond the prison walls and as much of the shouting is in Gaelic
it sounds like howling'.[30]

Colonel Winn was instructed by the Home Office to go to
Lewes to arrange for the immediate removal of De Valera and
other ringleaders to Maidstone Prison. Harry was named as one of
the ringleaders and was to be taken by motor car, dressed in
prison dress and under such restraint as might be deemed necessary. On arrival at Maidstone Prison he was to be informed that
his special privileges were forfeited and he would be subject to the
ordinary rules of penal servitude. His privilege of sending special
letters and of having extra visits would also be cancelled. He would

be badged and treated as a star class convict in Maidstone.

On 6 June, Col Winn reported to the Home Office that Dev and Tom Hunter had been conveyed to Maidstone. De Valera said that 'it would make no difference where he was taken as he would refuse to work' Then Winn reported that 'Boland and Duggan have just gone off in two cars to Maidstone. Boland said he had done nothing criminal. For as long as he was degraded by being treated as a criminal, he declined to obey the orders of the administration. He resisted violently on being handcuffed and had to be carried to the car glorying in the fact that it took more than three men to carry him. On being brought from his cell he had shouted out something as he came along the hall. Boland made some remark as the car drove off. Col Winn described Boland as a 'truculent member of the Irish prisoners'. Robert Brennan, imprisoned in the same block as Harry, remembers him being carried down the hall yelling 'Keep the flag flying' and all the prisoners gave him a big cheer.[31] The escort who took Harry to Maidstone reported that 'Boland tried to attract attention while passing through Lewes, but no one seemed to take any notice, and he was quiet all the remainder of the way'.[32] Harry was quiet because he had not been trying to attract attention but to deliver a message home about the treatment they were getting. Before he left the prison he had written a letter on both sides of a piece of toilet paper with a fountain pen. In the struggle with the four warders to handcuff him they had not succeeded in searching him and he smuggled the message out. During the journey through Lewes he suddenly stood up, put his hands out and flung the letter through the window.This piece of paper was picked up on the street by a young girl who brought it home to her English mother. She sent the note to Catherine Boland because 'I too have two sons doing their bit'. In his letter Harry outlined the harsh treatment and the reason that they had wrecked the jail:[33]

> Our leaders were removed on Tuesday, mid-day ... We have sworn to do no work, nor obey any order whatsoever, until the government treat us as soldiers. We fought a clean, fair fight, and should be treated as honourable men, not criminals. Mother, do not worry too much, with God's help I will keep my health, my spirits are high. Good-bye.[34]

When Harry arrived at Maidstone he said that he 'would make a fight for it' and would not obey orders. Col Winn told the Maidstone governor that certain men like Boland were becoming more prominent by these actions and they hoped to gain kudos with their 'so-called military Volunteers in Ireland'. Colonel Winn was in Lewes after the removal of the ringleaders and he reported that the staff there was much relieved:

> It is quite a new experience in prison life to have howling going on, punctuated by crashing of bed boards against the doors and window smashing ... Dr Cook, the medical officer looks a little drawn, and has, no doubt, felt the strain. In fact, this may be said of all, and the chief warden (Banes) told me last night that all the officers were feeling it, owing to the uncertainty of what might happen next.[35]

Shortly after the ringleaders had been removed from Lewes, the bulk of the remaining prisoners were taken to Maidstone, Parkhurst and Portland gaols but some remained on in Lewes. Before Éamon de Valera was forcibly removed, he asked the prisoners to continue their protest for political treatment in whatever new prison they were lodged. He expected them to endure whatever loss of privileges they would suffer but strongly advised against the hunger strike weapon.[36] Harry was prepared to observe the rigid code of prison indiscipline worked out by Dev. Every order given by the prison officers was ignored. Repeated appearances before the governor for punishment took the form of bouts of solitary confinement on bread and water

Meanwhile news filtered through to Ireland about prison conditions. Kathleen Boland brought the letter Harry had dropped on the street in Lewes to the offices of the Irish Prisoners' National Aid and she showed it to the permanent secretary, Michael Collins, and Michael Staines. On Sunday, 10 June a protest meeting was held in Beresford Place, Dublin. The British authorities banned the meeting but a huge crowd attended. Count Plunkett and Cathal Brugha addressed the meeting. Harry's letter was read out. When the police attempted to arrest the speakers the crowd surged forward and Inspector Mills was killed with a blow from a hurley stick. Count Plunkett and Cathal Brugha were arrested.

Lloyd George wanted American support for his war effort and he thought an Irish Convention would persuade Americans that he was intent on solving the Irish problem. But he also knew the idea would not work unless he released the prisoners. A letter from Lord Derby on the 15 June to Stamfordham stated:

> The king will no doubt have seen from the minutes of the War Cabinet
> the recent discussion on the subject of the Irish prisoners and the decision
> after the fullest consideration to grant an amnesty.[37]

On the same day, Bonar Law, the Chancellor of the Exchequer, announced that all the 1916 prisoners would be released 'with a view to creating a favourable atmosphere for the Irish Convention'. The king issued the following command, 'Now know ye, we in consideration of some circumstances humbly presented unto us, are graciously pleased to extend our Grace and Mercy unto the said prisoners and to pardon and remit unto them the remainder of their said sentences'.[38]

On the evening of 16 June all Irish prisoners were transferred to Pentonville Prison for civilian clothes. After that they travelled by train to Holyhead and De Valera marched them on to the first class compartments of the ship. Harry was up on the deck to get the first glimpse of Ireland as the bright sun lit up the blue Wicklow Mountains on the horizon. He had left Ireland as a rank and file member in the Irish freedom movement but he returned as a leader.

A crowd gathered in the Boland house when they heard the news that Harry was coming home. They stayed up all night preparing and in the morning they walked in all the way from Clontarf to Westland Row as the trams had not started to run before they left. At Westland Row the prisoners received a tumultuous welcome home from thousands of people. Kathleen Boland was in the crowd waving her flag.

De Valera was the hero of the hour. Harry had come to know Dev very well in prison and he had great admiration for him. Boland and De Valera had also learned that passive resistance, properly operated, could achieve political aims.

THE GERMAN PLOT

The released prisoners were ushered to a meeting in Exchequer Hall, Exchequer Street. Here they signed a proclamation on Irish linen addressed to the president and the congress of the United States pointing out the right of the Irish people to defend themselves against external aggression. The message quoting from President Wilson's recent address to Russia read, 'No people must be forced under a sovereignty under which it does not wish to live'. Patrick McCartan, a member of the IRB, was waiting to take the signed linen scroll with him to the United States.

Harry looked well after his imprisonment. He had lost weight and he was slim, elegant and nearly six feet tall. His face was square rather than long but taut as he had no extra flab. His hair though thinning slightly was still ample and low on his forehead. He had clear blue eyes, a long narrow nose and a pointed chin. Celebrations over, Harry had to get his life together again. He was still chairman of the Dublin County Board GAA, even though he was in prison since Easter 1916, the county board and the delegates at the annual Dublin convention had insisted on keeping him in office. His position as tailor with Todd, Burns and Co. Ltd., Mary Street, had been filled in his absence as the company had expected Harry would be in prison for five years and they had employed someone else to carry on his work.

Harry began to frequent Vaughan's Hotel in Parnell Square and he often met Michael Collins there. They got to know each other really well and the two of them were matched in many respects. Michael had heard of Harry's truculence in British prisons and how it had taken four warders to hold him down. Harry was sociable and generous, the type of man with whom Collins was comfortable. Mrs Vaughan, a Clare woman, owned the hotel which was situated on what was at that time the 'quiet' side of Parnell Square, away form the traffic of Sackville Street. Collins' boisterous pals at this time were Harry, Diarmuid Lynch, Diarmuid O'Hegarty, Fionán Lynch and Piaras Béaslaí.[1]

But there were many people in the national movement who did not like Michael Collins. Robert Brennan thought 'he was ruthless with friend and foe' and that Collins 'had great faith in the secret conclaves of the few, as if he despised the intelligence of the many.' He wrote of a visit he paid to the Boland home in Marino Crescent a few weeks after they were released from prison. He found that Gerry and Harry were sharply divided on the question of Mick Collins. Gerry said that he was a 'braggart and a bully':

'He's nothing of the kind,' said Harry.
'You haven't seen as much of him as I have,' said Gerry. 'In the camp, if he didn't win all the jumps, he'd break up the match'.[2]

Harry was not long home from prison when Éamon de Valera was elected MP for East Clare with a huge majority over the Irish Party's nominee, P. J. Lynch. Released prisoners were recruited by IRB leaders who knew them in prison and were aware of their worth. This recruiting drive was led by Collins, Diarmuid Lynch, Harry and Seán Ó Muirthile who regularly met in Vaughan's. Collins was organising the IRB to be what he described as 'a force on practical lines and headed by realists'. Of 1916 he said 'I think the Rising was bungled terribly costing many a good life. It seemed at first to be well organised, but afterwards became subjected to panic decisions'.[3] The Collins' IRB Vaughan's Hotel group, including Harry, shared this view.

Harry's whole political career changed after the Sinn Féin Ard-Fheis in the Mansion House on Thursday and Friday, 25 and 26 October, 1917. When Arthur Griffith had founded Sinn Féin, his policy was to establish an independent Irish parliament but 'linked to Britain through the person of a joint monarch'.[4] But the Easter Rising came and the insurgents proclaimed the Irish Republic and now all the groups which shared the spirit of 1916 – the Irish Volunteers, the Irish Citizen Army, the IRB, the Gaelic League, the Liberty Clubs, Irish Nation League and Sinn Féin – wanted an umbrella movement under which all could move forward together. A provisional committee was formed to go into the matter and seek to hammer out a compromise between Griffith's monarchism and those who stood by the 1916 proclamation. This was difficult and, but for De Valera's presence on this committee, a split might have taken place. A compromise was worked out between the Republican elements represented by Cathal Brugha, Michael Collins and Rory O'Connor and the traditional Sinn Féin element under Arthur Griffith and Darrell Figgis, with Dev acting in the middle to bring the two sides together. This allowed the provisional committee to draw up a new constitution for Sinn Féin encompassing the differing views and the committee arranged an Ard-Fheis to discuss the new constitution and to elect officers and an executive committee. Harry was passionately interested in this development and wanted to serve on the executive of the new organisation.

The constitution of Sinn Féin as proposed by the executive stated in the second clause: 'Sinn Féin aims at securing the International recognition of Ireland as an independent Irish Republic. Having achieved that status the Irish people may by referendum freely choose their own form of government'. This was the compromise Dev had drafted to get Cathal Brugha and Arthur Griffith to accept the proposed constitution and it glossed over the contentious subject matter without defining whether the aim of Sinn Féin was to set up an Irish Republic or be satisfied with something less. This new constitution was approved by the Ard-Fheis.

The next item on the agenda was the election of the president of Sinn Féin. Many commentators had predicted a split in the organisation as three names were proposed – Arthur Griffith, founder of Sinn Féin, Éamon de Valera and Count Plunkett, Sinn Féin MP for North Roscommon and father of the executed 1916 leader, Joseph Mary Plunkett. Count Plunkett withdrew his name 'in favour of Mr de Valera, the man who fought for them in Easter Week'. There was a big murmur of surprise in the packed hall when Arthur Griffith said: 'I told Mr de Valera that I would propose him instead of myself'. Éamon de Valera was then unanimously elected president of Sinn Féin. The Ard-Fheis moved on to the election of a Sinn Féin executive of 24 members. When this item was announced, a delegate from London, Mr Martin, drew attention to the fact that there was canvassing for certain names. He asked the Ard-Fheis to condemn this line of action. Fr Michael O'Flanagan said that there were two lists circulated and his name appeared on both without his permission – 'One of the lists represented the desires of what might be called the extreme right of the movement and the other the desires of the extreme left' – and he asked the delegates to vote only for men whom they knew.[5]

What had happened was that Darrell Figgis had led the campaign for Arthur Griffith and moderate Sinn Féin members by issuing a list of names to his supporters and Michael Collins had canvassed for De Valera and he also issued a typed page to all IRB members listing candidates that they were expected to support for the executive. Harry's name was on the list that Collins sent out to the IRB members.

Voting took place before the Ard-Fheis adjourned for tea but the result was not announced until the next day's sitting when a very popular Sinn Féin figure, Dan McCarthy, announced the result. Harry was elected in tenth place obtaining 448 votes. A big surprise was that his friend and backer, Michael Collins, barely made the executive with only 340 votes.

On Sunday, 28 October Harry was in Croke Park as chairman of Dublin County Board to cheer on his own county hurling team, Dublin, who were meeting the reigning All-Ireland champions, Tipperary, in the All-Ireland Hurling final. While they were training for the All-Ireland final, he pucked the sliotar around with them and was an unofficial substitute on the team. He knew all the hurlers on the panel of players – six were from his old team, Faughs and seven were from Collegians, a team made up of university students, who had won the previous Dublin county championship. Tipperary were very confident of victory but the Dublin team caused a big surprise by winning comfortably.[6] Johnny Leahy, one of the stars on that Tipperary team that day, told Seán O'Donovan later, 'we came up to beat the school boys but got the hell of a drop'.[7] Because Harry was an unofficial substitute for the winning team and due to his previous long record of hurling with Dublin, the County Board presented him with a special All-Ireland medal.[8]

Harry was working for Sinn Féin but he was also becoming prominent in the IRB. De Valera and Brugha were not members of the IRB and Dev tried to get Harry to discontinue his membership of the secret organisation. Harry ignored his advice. He had no steady income, though he was an excellent tailor's cutter, and needed to sort out his private life. Two county teams, Wexford and Dublin, unknown to Harry, arranged to play a testimonial football match for him. In very inclement weather the game was played in Croke Park on Sunday, 11 November. Three thousand people attended and Dublin won by two points.[9] Harry wanted to buy a premises in 64 Middle Abbey Street, Dublin to set up his own tailoring and outfitting business and the receipts from this benefit match helped him to complete the purchase.

The National Aid Association, the organisation set up to help the survivors of the 1916 Rising and the dependents of those killed and executed (Michael Collins was now secretary), asked the GAA to help out by playing hurling and football matches to raise funds. Harry approached the central council of the GAA to enlist their help. Marcus de Búrca in his book *The GAA, A History* describes Harry's work in organising national aid in the GAA:

In 1917 the central council, where Harry Boland was now an influential figure, made the GAA the principal source of finance for national aid. A special sub-committee chaired by Boland sponsored inter-county hurling and football tournaments for national aid funds ...[10]

Harry was very active in all the by-elections in 1918. The Irish Party leader, John Redmond, died on 6 March and John Dillon succeeded him as chairman of the Irish Parliamentary Party so a by-election took place in Waterford City. The Redmond family was respected and very well liked in Waterford City. The Irish Party selected John Redmond's son, Captain Willie Redmond as their candidate. Sinn Féin put up a popular local figure, Dr Vincent White. Polling day was the 22 March and Willie Redmond won by 1,242 votes to 764. Early in April the Irish Parliamentary Party had another victory over Sinn Féin in East Tyrone where its candidate Thomas Harbison defeated Seán Milroy comfortably.

In late March Michael Collins brought Harry to Longford and they stayed in the Kiernan family hotel in Granard. Like most single fellows of around thirty years of age they were out for a bit of fun and staying in the Greville Arms Hotel for the night they felt safe. They started up a bit of light revelry and the Kiernan sisters joined in the frivolity. They all did their party pieces and had a good sing-song. Harry was attracted to vivacious good-looking Kitty while Collins was attempting to win the affections of the equally appealing and delightful Helen. The night ended all too quickly but there was an invitation and an immediate acceptance for a return visit.

Harry was active on the Sinn Féin executive when another by-election fell due in King's County (Offaly). The party executive chose Patrick McCartan as their candidate. Due to the conscription crisis, John Dillon, leader of the Irish Party, decided the party would not contest the election so McCartan was returned unopposed.

Michael Collins began to organise his intelligence network between sympathisers inside Dublin Castle and his own secret contacts outside the castle. The political section of the 'G' Division of the Dublin Metropolitan Police watched all the movements of the principal Dublin activists in Irish national movements wherever they went and they gathered files on the most important Sinn Féin, Irish Volunteer, Cumann na mBan and IRB members. But some of the 'G' men were Irish and had sympathy with the Irish political leaders. Ned Broy worked in a secret department of the castle where vital information passed through his hands and he began to send information to Michael Collins through a Sinn Féiner, Michael Foley, whom he knew, and these reports warned Collins of impending round-ups. Thomas Gay, a librarian in the Corporation Library in Capel Street, knew another young detective, Joe Kavanagh, who worked in the castle and he passed vital information on to Gay. Harry's new tailoring shop was not far from Capel Street and Gay found it convenient to drop into the shop as he passed going to and from work and slipped notes to Boland. The notes went straight to Michael Collins.

On 12 April the police arrested a Galwayman, Joseph Dowling, and they discovered he was a member of Casement's former Irish Brigade in Germany. He had come ashore in a collapsible German boat but had mistakenly landed on an island rather than on the mainland. The British government suspected he had been sent by the Germans to get in touch with Sinn Féin and the Volunteers but the Sinn Féin party knew nothing about Dowling.[11] It was enough to give the British government an excuse for charging the Sinn Féin leaders with entering into 'treasonable communication with the German enemy'.

On Wednesday, 15 May, Ned Broy sent Collins a list of people the British were planning to arrest. On Friday evening Joe Kavanagh went to Thomas Gay in the Dublin Corporation library with another warning about a series of raids on the houses of prominent Sinn Féiners in Dublin that night. Gay went immediately to Harry in his tailoring shop with this message and Boland lost no time and got in touch with Michael Collins. Collins sent out warnings to all on the list that Broy had given him. That night there was a meeting of the Executive of the Irish Volunteers at Parnell Square. Michael Collins again warned all those present, whose names were on Broy's list, of the proposed castle 'round-up' that night. The conscription fight was still on and De Valera was reluctant to go 'on the run' as it would made his work very difficult. Piaras

Béaslaí, who was present at this meeting described what De Valera did:

> There was, however, a general consensus of opinion that De Valera should avoid all possible danger of arrest by staying in Dublin that night instead of returning to his house in Greystones. De Valera was reluctant to agree to this, but in view of the strong representations made to him by other members, he seemed inclined to consent to stay. At the conclusion of the meeting, however, he again announced his intention of returning home to Greystones. He did so and was arrested at Greystones.[12]

Arthur Griffith was also aware of the impending detective raid and, though not at this meeting, he came to the same decision as De Valera. The whole operation was designed to take all prominent Sinn Féin leaders out of circulation all over the country. As well as Éamon de Valera and Arthur Griffith, Count Plunkett, W. T. Cosgrave, Darrell Figgis, Joseph McGuinness, Seán Milroy, Countess Markievicz, Mrs Tom Clarke and many others were arrested. They were brought to a gunboat at Kingstown (Dún Laoghaire) and interned in various English prisons. De Valera was held in Lincoln Prison and the women were detained in Holloway.

When the Volunteer executive meeting finished, Collins, Boland and Duggan went over to Vaughan's Hotel for a drink and stayed there until well after midnight when they started to cycle home. Collins was staying at 44 Mountjoy Street and as he came close to his lodgings, he saw a military lorry and some soldiers in the street. He turned aside and cycled after Duggan who lived in Drumcondra and told him the raids were on. Harry cycled in a different direction and when he arrived home his mother and Kathleen told him that the military had raided. Harry slept the night in his own home near the skylight in the attic in case the British returned. Collins cycled to Clontarf where Seán McGarry, an IRB member and secretary of the Volunteers, lived, but he was too late – Seán had been arrested. Michael stayed in this house for the night knowing it was safe because the military had left earlier with their quarry.

Broy was angry at how little care the Sinn Féiners had taken after he had put himself in danger by getting the warning information out to them:

> I had a list of the suspects who were to have been arrested. Forty-eight hours before the correct date I handed on the list ... I was brought to the

castle and put on the phone. I listened to an account of the arrests that were being made. I was cursing for none of them seemed to have got out of the ring ... On the phone I received information about De Valera going to the station for the Greystones train and then news of his arrest came in. 'They are cods these Sinn Féiners,' I said, 'they don't mean anything. They won't trust a source.[13]

Most of the political leaders of the Irish independence movement had gone in one giant swoop. But Boland, Collins and Cathal Brugha were still free. Harry took the political side under his wing and Collins took on the organisation of the Volunteers. They were the closest of friends and now the two of them were propelled centre stage.

BOLAND FILLS THE GAP

The arrests of many of the executive of Sinn Féin left Fr Michael
O'Flanagan, a Vice-President, in charge of the whole movement.
Michael Collins concentrated on re-organising the Volunteers in
case it came to a head-on collision with the British over conscription and he did not attend meetings of the Sinn Féin ruling body
for a period. Harry took over the duties of Secretary of Sinn Féin
with Alderman Tom Kelly as his acting co-secretary and his experience in the administrative side of the GAA was of tremendous
benefit to him. He was a member of the IRB for many years and
now he became a member of the Supreme Council, filling the va-
cancy created by the arrest of Seán McGarry.[1]

Harry had to be careful to avoid being arrested – he took to a
bicycle, like Collins, but, unlike him, he disguised himself with a
false moustache and wore spectacles as he travelled from Marino
Crescent, Clontarf to Sinn Féin Headquarters in 6 Harcourt Street.
He noticed that detectives were watching the front door of the
Sinn Féin offices the whole time. Apparently they did not know
that there was a back entrance which he used. He used this disguise for a few months but he changed it when he heard that a
stranger told a friend of his, 'I saw a man passing on a bicycle, with
spectacles with no glass in them. I wonder who he was'.[2]

He slept at home in Marino Crescent as he felt safe there – he
knew the area very well and had looked at ways to make a quick
get away from the house. The house was in a curved row of three-
storey houses, all attached together, stretching from the Howth
Road across to the Malahide Road.[3] Harry, or any other Volunteers, who stayed the night slept in the top storey room that had a
skylight opening on to the roof and a step-ladder and table. Across
the top of the roofs, there was a hollow between the two sets of
chimineys that formed a valley which gave complete cover. During
one raid around this time Harry, Jack Shouldice and another Volunteer were sheltering in the house. Kathleen was awakened out
of her sleep by loud knocking on the front door and she knew
there was a raid on. She jumped out of bed to stall the RIC raiding
party to give Harry and his companions a chance of getting away.
She described the raid:

The police were in charge of Inspector Love and Sergeant Smith, who was afterwards shot. On this occasion, when the knock came to the door, I shouted through the window that there were only women in the house and the raiders would have to give us time to get dressed. In the meantime, the four Volunteers, including Harry, got out in their pyjamas through the skylight and along the valley of the roofs of the houses of the Crescent, and got down through the skylight of the last house. The people of the house, called McGraths, had no sympathy with our way to thinking and actually had members in the British army and navy. They kept them there and the daughter came to our house later for the clothes of the Volunteers, who hurriedly dressed in McGrath's and got away.[4]

The runaways passed over the roof of an RIC man's house.[5] The Bolands rented the house from Mr Jennings, a Baptist, and Sergeant Smith went to him hoping he could persuade the landlord to evict the Bolands from their house:

'Do you know that Mrs Boland keeps a bunch of rebels in her house regularly,' he asked Mr Jennings.
The landlord did not react.
'Mrs Boland is a decent woman,' he replied. 'She pays her rent regularly, and I knew her husband and he was a decent man too. Outside of that I don't know anything about the family.'

Mr Jennings, instead, passed on word to Mrs Boland to tell her family that Sergeant Smith and the RIC were watching their house.[6]

In June Arthur Griffith, a prisoner in Gloucester Jail, agreed to contest a by-election in East Cavan. Harry worked hard at organising the Sinn Féin election machine – every Sinn Féiner was drafted into East Cavan by Harry and his co-workers. They canvassed from early in the morning to last light. The Hibernians were strong in East Cavan and they marched to support popular local Irish Party candidate, O'Hanlon. Fr Michael O'Flanagan spoke as often as six times a day for Sinn Féin. Eventually Griffith beat O'Hanlon, by 3,785 votes to 2,581. The British government saw from the results that the Irish people were still behind Sinn Féin at the polls and they were determined to get rid of this threatening menace. In the first week of July they issued a proclamation declaring that Sinn Féin, the Volunteers, Cumann na mBan, and the Gaelic League were suppressed on the grounds that these associations encouraged and helped persons to commit crimes. Persons calling or attending meetings of these organisations were liable to arrest and prosecution. The following day British military headquarters issued another order banning the 'holding or taking part in meetings, assemblies, or processions in public places in the whole of Ireland' unless these were authorised by the police. The prohibition applied to sports and athletic meetings as well as feiseanna and open air concerts.

Within a week the RIC went to work, especially in rural districts, by breaking up hurling and football games and sports meetings because the GAA committees refused to seek official permits to play. In some cases the RIC were so diligent that they dug up and carried away goal-posts. A special meeting of the central council, attended by the secretaries of the Munster Council, the Athletics Council, the Dublin County Board and by the Dublin Board chairman, Harry Boland, held on 20 July, decided to assert their members' rights to play games without permission or permit. It was decided that on Sunday, 4 August, all clubs all over the country would arrange to play a hurling or football match at the same time in the afternoon and clubs or boards would not apply for permits for these games and if any member or unit of the association sought a permit, they would face automatic suspension from the GAA.

The fourth of August was called Gaelic Sunday and at 3pm almost 100,000 people lined out with senior, junior and club teams all over the country. In the Dublin area, under Harry, 24 matches were played. British troops and police ringed Croke Park to prevent anyone entering. The female section of the Dublin GAA, with the approval of Harry Boland, decided to entertain the bored looking British troops by playing a camogie match on the road outside.[7] Not one arrest was made because neither the police nor the British army had the resources to cover so many venues at the same time.

Following on the success of Gaelic Sunday, Harry persuaded the Sinn Féin executive to hold passive resistance meetings all over the country on 15 August to again challenge the English government. Just as in the case of the GAA matches, the local Sinn Féin Cumann organised an outdoor meeting and any local Sinn Féiner who could put a few words together addressed the meeting. He also read a statement from Sinn Féin headquarters protesting against the ban and stating that it would not be recognised or obeyed by the organisation. People met together in every townland or parish – in all about 1,500 meetings were held and each meeting only lasted fifteen minutes. The police did not interfere but later they went to the homes of the speakers and arrested them. Many were charged and sentenced to long terms of imprisonment.

The English government realised that their conscription policy was not likely to work in Ireland so they decided to set up a recruiting council with the task of getting 50,000 Irishmen into the British army before the 1 October. The more notable members of the council, Capt. Stephen Gwynn, MP, Col Arthur Lynch, MP, and Capt. James O'Grady, MP decided to hold a recruiting rally in Kildare Place, Dublin on 24 August. Thousands attended the first meeting – some had just followed the marching bands, others were there because they believed in the cause, and a great many others came hoping for a stormy meeting which would provide a good bit of excitement and entertainment. Col Lynch was the principal speaker. There was the odd interjection from a heckler: 'Why not stop in Ireland and share our dangers?' There was cheering at this but no great reaction. Col Lynch did not reply until the cheers died down. Then he shouted, 'Stop in Ireland and share your cowardice!' – the whole meeting erupted and fell apart.[8] Harry and Michael Collins were at the fringe of the crowd. They saw Frank Gallagher and Joe Stanley at the front just below the platform and they asked them to come and see them. Harry and Mick thought that these meetings should be captured for Sinn Féin and their plan was for Sinn Féiners like Gallagher and Stanley to watch for an opportunity when the recruiting speakers were addressing the crowd and then to get up on the platform and read a letter or ask a question.[9]

Another recruiting meeting was held later and Col Lynch again spoke. The crowd kept on interrupting and he could not be heard and as he was leaving he went over to the pressmen and summarised his speech. But Frank Gallagher and Joe Stanley jumped on the platform and took over the meeting. There was a huge cheer from the crowd – so loud that the journalists could not hear Col Lynch. Joe Stanley spoke first, then Frank Gallagher and as Gallagher looked down he recognised a few 'G' men just under the platform. Then he saw that a big number of RIC men were approaching the platform in a cordon. He could see a man with a jet-black moustache pushing his way hurriedly through the crowd in the direction of the platform. Gallagher kept on talking though by now his flow of words had slowed and his speech began to falter.

The man with the moustache stopped just behind the RIC cordon. Gallagher looked again and he could see that the man was winking his left eye – Harry – in disguise. He shouted out, 'Gallagher, jump, over the cordon, quick.' Frank jumped without thinking and hands grasped him as he came down. He felt himself being passed bodily over the heads of the crowd and back towards the edge of the meeting. When he came to his feet, Harry was standing beside him. 'Frank, get home as quick as you can,' he whispered. The platform was crowded with RIC men searching the crowd to find him.[10]

It was decided to hold the Sinn Féin annual Ard-Fheis in the Mansion House, Dublin on Tuesday, 29 October. A large number of delegates attended although the platform party looked very much depleted, because of all the arrests, since the previous year. The acting-president, Fr Michael O'Flanagan chaired the Ard-Fheis. Harry, Michael Collins, Piaras Béaslaí, J. J. Walsh, Pádraic Ó Máille entered the Ard-Fheis by the back door very early in the morning as they were under police surveillance and liable to arrest at any time. Harry, in his capacity as acting-secretary of Sinn Féin, read the reports of their work. He said the comprehensive scheme laid down by Éamon de Valera at the previous Ard-Fheis had been broken by the 'German Plot' arrests. However, since then they had confined their work to four vital points: organisation, elections, propaganda and food. Harry said that an early election 'was on the cards' and that Sinn Féin would do extremely well in these elections. The Director of Elections, Robert Brennan, said that the party had done a canvas which showed that in some constituencies Sinn Féin candidates would poll at least ten times more than the Irish Party.

Éamon de Valera was again unanimously elected President and Fr O'Flanagan and Arthur Griffith were re-elected Vice-Presidents. Harry and Ald. Thomas Kelly were elected as secretaries. Late on Wednesday night the Ard-Fheis adjourned until the next day and as Michael Collins looked out the window, he saw that the detectives still waited outside the front door, looking for wanted men. He passed on the word and Harry, J. J. Walsh, Pádraic Ó Máille and Piaras Béaslaí stayed behind playing cards and around midnight the detectives left. The wanted men then went home and returned at an early hour the next morning for the second part of the Ard-Fheis. Seán Forest, objected to the negotiations carried on

between the Standing Committee and the Labour Party about parliamentary seats. He said that since Sinn Féin was the dominant
political party in Ireland, it was not up to them to go to any section
but for others to come to Sinn Féin. Harry replied on behalf of the
standing committee:

> We marched shoulder to shoulder with Labour to establish the Irish
> Republic and the standing committee held that we should now march
> shoulder to shoulder to accomplish the same end. We cannot afford in
> this election to antagonise Labour. The standing committee has decided
> that in the event of a Labour candidate signing a pledge to work for the
> establishment of an independent Irish Republic and that he would ab-
> stain from attending the English Parliament, they would advise the
> Comhairle Ceanntair to stand down and give all the support at their dis-
> posal to the Labour candidate.

Seán T. O'Kelly, though he supported Harry, felt that it would be
best if Labour would agree to stand aside and let the election be
fought on the clean issue of Ireland versus England. Mrs Sheehy-
Skeffington said that the bodies of Pearse and Connolly were in
the same grave – in quicklime. It was decided to leave the relationship between Labour and Sinn Féin in the coming election in
the hands of the standing committee.[11]

Harry read a letter from Mr T. Finnegan, Belfast, describing
the atrocious conditions in Belfast Prison under which 111 Republican prisoners, suffering from the deadly 1918 influenza, were
being held. Austin Stack was one of these prisoners. Then a telegram arrived from McEntee, 'three men moved to workhouse
hospital; condition very grave; pneumonia. It is imperative something must be done'.[12] Harry proposed that the entire meeting
should march to College Green and hold an open-air meeting in
protest against the treatment of the prisoners. When his motion
had been accepted he realised the danger of what he had proposed – the detectives outside would move in to arrest the wanted
men, including Michael Collins, Piaras Béaslaí and himself. He
went over to Collins and said, 'I'm going with them, Mick'. Collins
retorted, 'So am I,' but he looked at Boland with a frown, 'For the
Lord's sake, Harry, will you stop and look ahead before you act
next time'. Collins then handed any secret papers he had to Tom
Cullen. Béaslaí went looking for Dick Mulcahy who convinced
Collins not to go. Harry still felt he could not back out of it but
Mulcahy, as Chief-of-Staff of the Volunteers, gave him a direct order

not to go and so he stayed in the Mansion House. The other delegates marched to College Green where they held a huge meeting. The Dublin Castle detectives did not attempt to interfere because of the large crowd.[13]

It was decided that the new executive should be composed only of persons who were not in prison at the time, as otherwise the governing body of Sinn Féin could consist of prisoners who could not act at that critical time just before a general election. Michael Collins said, when the voting results were announced, that Cathal Brugha should have come higher in the voting result. 'There he is half-crippled with English bullets, away from the meeting because he is doing work that they would never dare to think of, and they vote for Mr X and Mrs Y and leave Cathal near the bottom of the list'.[14] Cathal got 419 votes and was well ahead of Collins himself who had only obtained 361 but this was enough to get him on the executive.[15]

The delegates returned to every corner of Ireland encouraged by what they had seen at the Ard-Fheis organised and conducted by replacements for the prominent Sinn Féin leaders in prison. They were told going home to get their cumainn ready for what promised to be one of the most important elections ever held in Ireland. Harry had the onerous responsibility, as secretary of Sinn Féin, of getting a majority result for Sinn Féin.

BOLAND WINS SOUTH ROSCOMMON

The First World War ended on 11 November and Lloyd George, thinking the moment opportune, decided to go to the polls. Thomas Johnson addressing a special session of the Irish Trade Union Congress and Labour Party in November 1918 referred to the end of the war and the proposed Peace Conference which would supersede it and how these factors had influenced the Labour Party:

> The grand inquest about to be opened has for a jury the nations of the world; the verdict will be given according to the weight of evidence adduced, and that will depend upon the degree of unanimity marked at the polls on the demand for self-determination ... Your executive believes that the workers of Ireland join earnestly in the desire, that they would willingly sacrifice for a brief period their aspirations towards political power if thereby the fortunes of the nation can be enhanced.

A vote was taken and the executive's resolution was passed by 96 votes to 23, and this had a major impact on later events.[1]

Harry believed that the danger of his arrest had ended and as he was working on the details of the election in Sinn Féin headquarters in Harcourt Street with Piaras Béaslaí he announced his decision to change tactics.

'I'm finished with the bicycle and the back door,' he said confidently. 'I'm fed up of going around like that. I'll walk out the front door tonight.'

He walked briskly out and Béaslaí went on with his work. Ten minutes later Harry burst through the door, breathless and panting. He rested for a minute with his hand on his chair and he bent slightly forward to catch his breath as if he had finished a 400 yards race.

'Béaslaí,' gasped Harry, 'when I went out the front door, the two detectives watching outside made a dash to grab me. I made a burst and got away from them. I nearly broke the world record.'

Piaras Béaslaí laughed but wondered if Harry had been followed.

'How, in Heaven's name did you get back here?'

'I outpaced them, I got down through the lanes to the back door. None of them saw where I went.'[2]

After this Harry took more care.

The ending of the war was celebrated in Dublin and mobs filled the streets flying Union Jacks. Harry thought they might attack Sinn Féin Headquarters in Harcourt Street that evening. He gathered a band of Volunteers from the 3rd Battalion and armed them with sticks and knuckle-dusters, collected a stock of stones, dismissed the staff and prepared to defend the building against all-comers. The attack turned out to be worse than expected – there were many soldiers on leave in the mob and they outnumbered the defenders in the Sinn Féin rooms. At one stage the Volunters feared for their lives when showers of stones broke the windows and blazing cloths were thrown through the broken glass. The building started to go on fire but then Harry's men quenched it as the mob began to howl and shout threats and the thirty Volunteers used their sticks when the attackers came within close range. They saved the building and forced the mob to retreat.[3] Next morning the Sinn Féin headquarters looked as if it had been caught in a blitz and Dubliners who passed had sympathy for the Sinn Féin workers who defended it.

The following day as Robert Brennan was trying to restore order to his files, scattered all over the floor, Seamus O'Kelly came in. Seamus, editor of the *Leinster Leader* in Naas, had volunteered to help Sinn Féin after the arrest of Arthur Griffith by acting as temporary editor of Griffith's paper. O'Kelly had a heart complaint and doctors had warned him not to take on any extra workload. As he was coming through Grafton Street that morning he said that the Union Jacks were flying so low from top windows that they brushed against his face as he passed. 'I thought I'd never again see the like of that in Dublin after 1916'. Harry came bustling in and, acting out the part, he gave a vivid account of the close encounters in the attack the night before. Seamus enjoyed Harry's discription but then Robert Brennan noticed O'Kelly making an unsteady sidelong movement and grasping the side of the table for support. He staggered sideways again. Harry rushed over and caught him in his arms as he fell towards the floor. He was unconscious and his breathing was heavy. The ambulance came and took him to hospital where he died that night.[4]

Mick Collins often joined Harry in the office and they were

very determined that only 'fighting' men should be selected as candidates throughout the country.[5] There were conservative members in Sinn Féin who looked on Boland and Collins as 'two wild young men' but the pair were ruthless as well. They went carefully through the likely candidates in each constituency and eliminated all except staunch Republicans. A lot of the constituencies wanted a prominent Sinn Féiner as their candidate and many of the comhairlí (councils) pressed the national executive to allow them to put forward De Valera. This gave Harry and Mick Collins their chance to name a substitute who was a strong Republican and almost invariably an IRB member. It was surprising that Harry did not stand for the constituency of Clontarf where he lived. The Sinn Féin organisation nominated him but the election committee decided that he should stand in South Roscommon – the county from which his family originated and where he still had family connections. Richard Mulcahy was nominated for Clontarf. He attributed his selection to 'Collins and the IRB element'.[6]

The Sinn Féin executive asked Fr Michael O'Flanagan, Harry and Robert Brennan to submit separate drafts of what each of them would consider a good Sinn Féin election manifesto. Harry criticised the Irish Party and their policy of advising the young men of Ireland to fight with England in the World War. He explained what Sinn Féin stood for and what it proposed to achieve:

> Sinn Féin is not a political party. Sinn Féin is the natural successor of that great body of the Irish nation, that never, through the long and bloody struggle, surrendered the right of Ireland to absolute independence.

A paragraph of his draft was based on the 1916 Proclamation of the Irish Republic and was quoted in the official Sinn Féin manifesto and there is no doubt but that Harry was a moderate socialist at heart:

> Sinn Féin stands by the Proclamation of the Provisional Government of Easter 1916, reasserting the inalienable right of the Irish nation to sovereign independence, reaffirming the determination of the Irish people to achieve it, and guaranteeing within the independent nation equal rights and equal opportunities to all its citizens.[7]

However it was mainly the draft submitted by Robert Brennan which was adopted by the Sinn Féin Executive. After the election De Valera spoke to Robert Brennan about the manifesto:

'You made it strong,' said Dev, 'I wouldn't have gone so far.'
  'Why not? Because of the voters?'
  'Yes. I was afraid it might frighten them.'[8]

On the 20 November, three weeks before the general election, the Sinn Féin Headquarters was raided and Robert Brennan was arrested and taken to Gloucester Jail in England. He was a big loss to the election campaign.[9] Harry was not on the premises at the time. James O'Mara took over as director of elections.

Harry went electioneering in South Roscommon at the end of November. John P. Hayden, outgoing Irish Party MP, opposed him for the seat. Michael Collins had found out, through his intelligence network, that the British government had issued an order that 'wanted men' should not be arrested if they were speaking as candidates in their own constituency. The order prohibiting the holding of public meetings without a permit was also withdrawn for the duration of the election.[10] Harry was escorted from his hotel in Roscommon town to the fixed meeting place by a procession with bands and banners, headed by a contingent of mounted men. Harry did not mince his words in his election address:

> I don't ask you to vote for men but for the Irish Republic. The greatest events in Irish history were the Rising of 1916 and the North Roscommon Election last year.

He was not a fan of Daniel O'Connell and he hated the thought of Ireland being partitioned:

> O'Connell sowed the seeds of the last ninety years ... Then the old Gaelic tongue was spoken and the old Gaelic learning was our pride ... To what has constitutionalism brought us from Repeal to Home Rule and from Home Rule to Partition. Partition! Is Ulster, our Ulster, to be handed over. Ulster, our Ulster, Ulster of the Gaelic tongue, of Patrick and Bridget and O'Neill. Never! Never!

Then he emphasised again that his goal was an Irish Republic, though he pointed out that he thought this aspiration could be achieved through the peace conference. He was not insular in outlook because he referred to the countries of Europe and stated that he felt an affinity with them:

> We were in the Gaelic League and in the GAA, in the Irish industrial movement and all the time we were planning our Irish Republic ... We

believe in new times, new men, new ideas. In 1914 there was only one Republic in Europe; today there are thirty-two. When we spoke of the Republic we were called rainbow chasers. Well, the people of Europe have caught the rainbow and Ireland will catch it too – at the peace conference.[11]

The sitting Irish Party MP for South Roscommon, John P. Hayden, made every effort to defend his seat and spoke at many meetings. At a poorly attended meeting in the centre of the constituency he pointed out the achievements of the Irish Party:

The Irish Party has brought the country from poverty to prosperity, got decent houses for the farm labourers, and secured many benefits for Irishmen of all classes. We have forced the British government to recognise Ireland's right to self-government.

He criticised the abstentionist policy of Sinn Féin and the impossible demands they were making on the British government:

Is Ireland, pending the restoration of her National Right to Self-Government, to have any representation in the House of Commons except the followers of Sir Edward Carson? Sinn Féin is jeopardising Ireland's claim to freedom by putting forward the impossible demand for an Irish Republic.

Mr Hayden claimed 'he had the manhood and womanhood of Ireland behind him'.[12] But Harry's tour through the constituency was well supported and was already looking like a triumphal march. For the 1918 general election women had secured the franchise and women over the age of thirty could now vote and could stand for parliament.

Polling day was the 14 December. The weather helped Sinn Féin in their last canvassing push. It was the mildest December for many years and polling day was spring-like. Sinn Féin had seen every voter twice or three times.[13] There was a relatively good turnout of 69% of the electorate considering that there was an epidemic of the deadly 1918 flu at the time.

Twenty-five Sinn Féin candidates were automatically returned from constituencies where no one stood against them. Michael Collins was one of these Sinn Féin MPs as he was returned for Cork South without a contest. There was a long wait over Christmas until 28 December before the votes were counted to facilitate the gathering of votes from absent Irish soldiers in the

British army. Harry had prepared Sinn Féin Headquarters for the announcement of the election results. Crowds gathered outside the offices from early afternoon and he had arranged for a notice board to be fixed outside the second-floor window. As each result was phoned or wired in from the counting centres, the victor's name and the details of the count were written on it. Boland came to the window and as silence fell on the crowd he called out – 'Countess Markievicz is in'; 'Seán T. has been elected', 'Alderman Tom Kelly beat them both in Stephen's Green', Pierce McCan wins East Tipperary'. The crowd cheered loudly and heartily and then Paddy Sheehan emerged after a pause and cried 'Harry Boland wins South Roscommon'. There was another burst of applause. Harry appeared to announce another result, but the cheers were so loud he did not get a chance to speak for some time.[14]

Sinn Féin had done remarkably well except in four counties Antrim, Down, Armagh and Derry where Unionists had a majority over Sinn Féin and Nationalists combined but the Unionists were in a minority in Fermanagh and Tyrone. Sinn Féin won 73 seats out of the overall total of 105. The Irish Party defeated Sinn Féin in two constituencies, Waterford City where Captain William Redmond was returned with a majority of 500 votes and in Belfast (Falls) where Joe Devlin easily out-polled Éamon de Valera who was already returned unopposed for East Clare. Unionists won 26 seats – 25 of them in Ulster and one in the Dublin (Rathmines) constituency where Sir Maurice Dockrell polled more than the combined Sinn Féin and Nationalist vote.

In twelve constituencies Sinn Féin captured over 50% of the total electorate: Limerick East; South Tipperary; Leitrim; South Galway; Longford; West Wicklow; South Kilkenny; Waterford County; Westmeath; Queen's County; South Kildare; South Sligo.

Harry polled well defeating his rival by a majority of almost 6,500 votes, getting 48% support of the total electorate and 72% of the votes cast – the thirteenth best performance for Sinn Féin in Ireland. Sinn Féin celebrated but two factors went unnoticed in the euphoria of victory – the elected candidates were made up of many different interests, moderates like Griffith and Eoin MacNeill, socialists like Liam Mellows, Republicans such as Cathal Brugha, and IRB members like Michael Collins and Harry. Éamon de Valera did not fit comfortably into any group but his function seemed to be to knit the whole coalition of interests together into the one unit.

The other factor was that in the twenty-six county area which was eventually to form the jurisdiction of the new Dáil, almost 200,000 people or nearly 33% of those who had cast their votes, voted against the establishment of an Irish Republic.

On the 2 January Harry Boland and Ald. Tom Kelly issued invitations from the Sinn Féin Headquarters in Harcourt Street to all the MPs to attend a private meeting in the Mansion House on Tuesday, 7 January. Count Plunkett, the senior member, chaired the meeting and it was decided to invite all MPs [Unionist, Irish Party, Nationalist or Sinn Féin representatives] to the opening session of Dáil Éireann.

Harry and Seán T. O'Kelly contacted Thomas Johnson of the Labour Party, inviting him to submit a draft proposal on the attitude that Dáil Éireann should adopt towards the welfare of Irish citizens and particularly towards the well-being of children and the elderly.[15]

On the same day, 21 January 1919, as Dáil Éireann was established two policemen were killed by armed men while they were escorting gelignite from Tipperary Town to Soloheadbeg quarry about three miles away. The attack happened between 12.30pm and 1pm before Dáil Éireann assembled.[16] This ambush in Soloheadbeg is regarded as the start of the Irish War of Independence.

Neither Harry nor Michael Collins was in Dáil Éireann, although others answered the roll call for them and they were officially marked present. They were on the boat to England to perform a special undercover job.

THE PROFESSOR DECAMPED

It was from inside Lincoln Prison that the first move in an escape bid started. Michael Lennon was speaking to his fellow prisoner Peter De Loughry one day and asked Peter did he think there was any possible way to escape from Lincoln Prison. De Loughry thought that there was only one way of escaping and that was 'to open the door and walk out'. He noticed that, unlike most prisons, there was a small door in the prison wall leading from one of the exercise grounds out to the farm. He was an expert on locks as he worked on them regularly as the owner of a large iron foundry in Kilkenny. He decided to study the locking system in the prison and discovered that one master key, with a slight variance, would open all locks as all were based on the one unlocking formula. Shortly afterwards he consulted Seán McGarry about the scheme and Seán agreed that the plan should be further investigated. The idea developed in their minds and they spoke about whom they should 'spring' and whose escape would have the most effect on public feeling outside the prison:

> We agreed that if anybody was to escape from the prison, De Valera should be the man, on account of the position he held in the Sinn Féin organisation, and the effect it would have on our sympathisers outside. Once we had got to this stage McGarry and I went to De Valera and put the plan before him. He seemed at first to think the matter of escape was impossible but when we convinced him that there was a reasonable chance of success he became enthusiastic ...[1]

Much work had to be done on the inside and on the outside. De Valera 'borrowed' the chaplain's master key while serving Mass and made an impression of it in candle wax which he had warmed with the heat of his own body. Seán Milroy reproduced this impression on a comic Christmas card and sent it to Mrs Seán McGarry but she did not know that she was to get in touch with Michael Collins and there was disappointment in the prison when they did not get a reply. On Christmas Eve De Valera composed another letter which John O'Mahony wrote to Fr Kavanagh, a curate in Leeds. He got in touch with Paddy O'Donoghue of Manchester who was working as a secret agent for Collins in England and he brought the message across to Ireland and met Collins in

Mrs McGarry's house. Con Collins was there with Michael Collins and between them they interpreted the contents.[2] Once this was done they got busy in Dublin. Collins roped Harry in to help as Harry had spent part of his youth visiting his father's relations in Manchester and was familiar with the city.

Harry asked his brother, Gerry, a fitter by trade, to make keys to the pattern of the one that was sent out on the Christmas card. Gerry got three blocks and cut out one. Shortly afterwards Harry and Mick Collins went over to Manchester where they stayed with Harry's aunt, Lily Boland.[3] She lived in Tipping Street, Ardwick, Manchester[4] and it was from there that Harry and Mick prepared the final plans to attempt to rescue De Valera.

Harry arranged for Gerry's key to be sent into the prison in a cake,[5] but this key did not fit the locks. Paddy O'Donoghue got a friend of his who worked in a Manchester firm of locksmiths to make a second key but again it failed to work.[6] Harry made a third attempt to supply the required key but this did not work either. Fresh directions came out of the prison – they were to send in a rough-casted blank with files to help Peter de Loughry to work on the key from inside. While Collins and Boland were thinking about ways to get the blank key into the gaol they got a message from Ireland that solved their problem. On 23 January Kilkenny Corporation had elected Peter de Loughry as Mayor of Kilkenny.[7] The occasion was worthy of celebration and Kathleen Talty, an Irish schoolteacher, baked and iced a cake with greetings to the new Mayor of Kilkenny. She put a rough-casted blank key and two small files into the cake[8] and delivered it addressed to Councillor Peter de Loughry, Mayor of Kilkenny.[9] He worked on the rough-casted blank and said it was a difficult frustrating job as he had to work in silence at night time with the two files and a stout pen-knife but he persisted until his new key opened all the locks in the prison.[10] Word came to Collins and Boland that everything was ready. Then Seán Etchingham recently elected MP for East Wicklow, was released from prison because he was seriously ill. He returned to Dublin bringing with him last minute details of the proposed prison breakout. As soon as Collins heard that Etchingham was in Dublin, he rushed back from England to consult with him – all parts of the plan were then fitted together.[11]

The escape was fixed for 3 February. It was arranged that Seán Milroy and Seán McGarry would make the escape bid with

De Valera. Harry and Collins completed their arrangements. One of the last things Harry did was to get a fur coat for De Valera from the second-hand clothing shop of Seamus Barrett, an old Fenian in Manchester and a friend of his father, Jim.[12] Two other Irishmen living in Manchester helped them – Paddy O'Donoghue and Frank Kelly.

Harry, Collins and Frank Kelly arrived at the barbed wire entanglements around the prison at 7.30pm on the night of the escape. They cut their way through but Frank Kelly got separated from them in the darkness.[13] Boland and Collins lay down in the field facing the jail at 7.40pm – the appointed time. Harry raised his torch and switched it on. Dev was thrilled to see the signal at the upstairs window of the prison. He waited for it to disappear but it lingered for much longer than he expected. In the field Harry cursed his luck because the switch of his torch locked and he could not turn it off so he stuffed it, still lighting, into his pocket and the beam died. De Valera gave a sigh of relief and returned the signal – he struck a match and lit four matches held together in his other hand and Collins and Boland saw the flare in the prison window.[14] Everything was ready.

Collins and Harry advanced furtively in the darkness towards the small door in the prison wall. Dev took out the master key that he had tied to his braces and together with Milroy and McGarry set off down the stony passageways. Each door opened and De Valera closed each one behind him to obliterate all clues as to how they had got out. They came to what they thought was the back door but when they opened it they found there was another locked iron gate before them.[15]

Harry and Michael were at the iron gate already. Collins carried a duplicate key and put it into the lock but when he tried to turn the key, it broke in the lock. De Valera, Milroy and McGarry approached the iron gate. Boland and Collins could see their shadows inside. Harry described to Piaras Béaslaí the awful feeling of suspense that gripped him after all the weeks of preparation:

> Collins said, in a heart-broken tone, 'I've broken a key in the lock, Dev'. De Valera uttered an ejaculation and tried to thrust his own key into the lock from the other side. By an extraordinary piece of luck he succeeded in pushing out the broken key with his own, and opening the gate.[16]

The gate was rusty and made a hollow grinding noise as it opened.

The five of them darted across the wide field. Boland and Collins had cut the barbed wire so they got through the fencing quickly. But then they were forced to stop as they were beside the Wragby Road and many soldiers from the nearby military hospital were locked in fond embraces with their girlfriends near the hospital gates. Harry was wearing the fur coat he got for De Valera and he exchanged De Valera's thin raincoat for the fur. Dev pulled up the fur collar around his neck, Harry put his arm around him and they looked like lovers out for a walk. Harry greeted the other courting couples as he passed them with 'Cheerio mates' in the Manchester accent with which he was familiar. They walked along the Wragby Road towards Lincoln where Paddy O'Donoghue had a taxi reserved and waiting outside the Adam and Eve Inn.[17] Collins and Boland parted company with them here and caught a train to London. O'Donoghue and the three escaped prisoners drove twenty-five miles to Worksop. Fintan Murphy had another taxi waiting on the Sheffield Road that brought them to Sheffield. Then Liam McMahon, a businessman, took them to Manchester in his own car. Milroy and McGarry were put up by McMahon. De Valera was taken to the presbytery of Fr Charles O'Mahony in Manchester. When he arrived there he was only five minutes behind the planned schedule.[18] The breakout had taken five and a half hours.

Next day Harry returned to Manchester and Collins went to Liverpool having transacted IRB business in London. With the help of Neill Kerr, one of his secret agents on the Liverpool shipping line, he got back to Ireland although it was risky because detectives were watching the Liverpool boats for the escapees. It was the following day before prison authorities discovered the back door leading to the field was open. The Press Association's Lincoln correspondent reported:

> De Valera and his friends in escaping from Lincoln Prison, have left nothing behind but some footprints in a field. The police are left like men trying to judge the whereabouts of an aeroplane by its starting track ... With five hours' start and the night hindering pursuit there is little doubt that the fugitives are in whatever part of the British Isles they choose to be.[19]

De Valera was reported to be in Paris and even in Skibbereen but he never moved outside Manchester until Collins and Boland had arranged a safe departure for him to Ireland. Harry stayed over there and co-operated with Paddy O'Donoghue, Kathleen Talty and Mary Healy in concealing De Valera. Two weeks after his escape Collins arranged, through Neill Kerr, to get Dev back by boat to Ireland from Liverpool. He landed safely in Dublin in the early hours of the 20 February. Harry took him to the home of Robert Farnan in Merrion Square. He was interviewed by an American journalist who was amazed to find the fugitive in rubber-soled carpet slippers being served sandwiches on a tray and having tea from a silver tea service.

Harry and Michael were searching for an alternative 'safe house' and they moved De Valera for one night to the Dublin Whiskey Distillery premises owned by Denis Lynch in the north side of the city. Harry then brought Dev to Fr Michael Curran who took him to the gatekeeper's lodge in the grounds of the archbishop of Dublin. Though Fr Curran was Archbishop Walsh's private secretary, the archbishop was unaware of the presence of De Valera at the top of his avenue.[20] The Irish people were delighted about the way De Valera and his accomplices had out-foxed the British. When Peter de Loughry was released from gaol, E. T. Keane, editor of the *Kilkenny People*, a man of sharp wit with a clever turn of phrase, greeted him at the welcome home parade. He referred to the ten months that the recently elected mayor had spent in Lincoln Prison:

> Our mayor has got a certain amount of education in England. However much that might be a cause for regret, I think there is some satisfaction in the fact that his professor was De Valera. You heard our new mayor speak to-night with amazing fluency and eloquence in our native tongue and it struck me when I heard him speak in the language of the Gael that this was De Valera's work. Alas, he did not have an opportunity of completing his education because (may I say unhappily) his professor decamped.[21]

De Valera decided to go to America to bring Irish-American pressure to bear on President Wilson to push Ireland's claim at the Peace Conference.[22] Collins did not agree with him and told De Valera that he thought that the best place for the leader of Sinn Féin was in Ireland. Collins' only interest in America was to procure more arms to fight the British. This was the first manifestation of conflict between Collins and Dev. Harry knew that De Valera was sticking to his decision, as a close friendship was developing between them. De Valera's decision came as a surprise to many others, not least to the GHQ staff of the Irish Volunteers – whose president he was. They felt that Dev's departure would be disastrous and that the Irish people might misunderstand his motives. When this view was expressed at a meeting Collins said, 'I told him so, but you know what it is to try to argue with Dev. He says he has thought it all out while in prison, and that he feels that the one place where he can be useful to Ireland is in America'.[23]

SPECIAL ENVOY TO AMERICA

While Éamon de Valera was in Lincoln Prison and while he was in hiding, he spent a considerable time deciding how best to push forward Ireland's claim to complete independence. He believed, like many in Sinn Féin, that a plan of passive resistance was best at this time.

In February Sinn Féin set up eleven departments intending to appoint a director to each department; units to deal with elections, organisation, the Irish language, industries, trade and commerce, national finance, public health, foreign affairs and land cultivation. When Harry settled back into Dáil activities, he became a member of a sub-committee to devise a plan for co-operation in 'land acquisition and working' and it was of particular significance in the South Roscommon constituency he represented. Fr O'Flanagan believed in the survival of the small farmer and he recommended that farmers should come together to acquire new farming technology and arrange a type of co-operative society. This sub-committee was to recommend a land policy which would be discussed by the Ard-Chomhairle of Sinn Féin as part of an all-round agricultural programme for the organisation. They, on the suggestion of Michael Collins, also investigated a plan for a co-operative bank to be set up to help young farmers purchase and equip their farms.[1]

Kitty Kiernan invited Harry and Michael Collins to Granard for the weekend in March 1919. She said that her sister Maud, who was the keeper of the accounts in the family business, had a friend visiting her:

> Will yourself and Mick come down here for the weekend? Maud's friend is here and we would all like to see you again ... Please don't disappoint![2]

Harry and Michael went to Granard for the weekend and this was Harry's second visit. He was becoming infatuated with Kitty and he went for walks in the countryside with her – but Collins was never far away.

Before Seán McGarry had been arrested he had been president of the Supreme Council of the IRB. Harry took his place on the Supreme Council and shortly after he became president. The IRB did not disband after the establishment of Dáil Éireann although Cathal Brugha, then Minister for Defence, thought that its existence was no longer needed. Collins and Boland believed the IRB had important work to do still.

Boland and Collins organised other prison escapes. Patrick Fleming, from the Swan, Co. Leix, was in Mountjoy Jail, sentenced to five years' penal servitude by court-martial for attempting to buy arms and ammunition from an English soldier. He refused to allow the prison authorities to treat him as a common criminal in Maryborough Prison.The British tried everything to subdue Fleming, they even constructed a special cell of what they considered to be unbreakable materials to thwart the prisoner's protests. But they failed and were forced to grant him political status in Mountjoy Jail. Fleming was not satisfied with small mercies and with outside help from Peadar Clancy, Dick McKee and Rory O'Connor, Michael Collins and Harry, he planned and executed an escape, not only for himself, but also for twenty other prisoners. Tomas Ó Maoileoin, from Westmeath, was one of the escapees:

> We ran along the canal. Someone gave me a bicycle. I went with J. J. Walsh to Jones' Road where I spent the night in O'Toole's. Mick Collins and Harry Boland came in. My clothes were in a bad state. Without a word, Boland who was a tailor, took a tape from his pocket and measured me. 'I'll have you right in a couple of days.' And sure enough a fine suit arrived at O'Toole's a short time after.[3]

Dáil Éireann had not met since 22 January 1919. Many of the deputies who were 'faoi ghlas ag Gallaibh' (in British Jails) for the inaugural meeting were now free to attend. As at the first meeting, only Sinn Féin members were present – the Unionists and the Irish Party MPs were attending the Westminster parliament in London but they were roughly 30% of the total number of elected representatives. Fifty-two deputies attended the Dáil on 1 April. Cathal Brugha had been acting as Príomh-Aire since January but as Éamon De Valera was free again, Brugha proposed him for Príomh-Aire and he was elected unanimously. At the meeting of the Dáil on 2 April, Dev nominated his cabinet of seven ministers: Arthur Griffith was in charge of Home Affairs; Cathal Brugha, Minister for Defence; Count Plunkett, Foreign Affairs, Eoin MacNeill, Industries; Michael Collins, Finance; William T. Cosgrave, Local Government and Countess Markievicz, Minister for Labour.[4]

At the session of Dáil Éireann on 10 April, De Valera showed that his programme was clearly a strategy of passive resistance. He concentrated on three approaches, sending representatives to Paris to the Peace Conference and to the League of Nations, dispatching a number of accredited ambassadors and consuls to other countries and issuing a Bond Loan to be offered at home and abroad:

> In order to secure for our own *de jure* government, and for the Irish Republic which the Irish people have willed to set up, the necessary international recognition, we shall send at once our accredited representatives to Paris to the Peace Conference and to the League of Nations ... We shall send also to other countries a number of duly accredited ambassadors and consuls to see that the position of Ireland is understood as it truly is ... It is obvious that the work of our government cannot be carried on without funds. The Minister of Finance is accordingly preparing a prospectus, which will be shortly published, for the issue of a loan of one million sterling – £500,000 to be offered to the public for immediate subscription, £250,000 at home and £250,000 abroad, in bonds of such amounts as to meet the needs of the small subscriber.[5]

He spoke about President Wilson of the USA and his self-determination principles based 'upon the consent of the governed' and he appealed for Wilson to stand by these policies as they applied to Irish independence:

> If President Wilson does not stand by his principles the Irish race will stand by them, and if no other people will lead the way the Irish people will do so and see that justice and right is done ...[6]

Dev referred to the goal that Dáil Éireann had in mind – the establishment of an Irish Republic:

> The Irish Republic was the aim of Wolfe Tone and the United Irishmen, in which the Protestants of the north were foremost. The Irish Republic was the dream of Emmet; it was the central aim of the men of '48; it was the aim of the men of '67, and of those who proclaimed the Irish Republic in 1916, and to that only we give allegiance. We are the trustees of the faith of these men, and we promise them that we will never betray that trust.[7]

He spoke about physical force and the new role of the Volunteers:

> The Irish Volunteers are the last reserve. I have always held the same attitude in regard to physical force ... Certainly I am not going to tie my right or left hand behind my back when dealing with such a tyrant as the

British government. If the British government were to keep me in jail until such time as I was going to say I would renounce the Irish Volunteers, then I would be still in jail ... The Irish Volunteers has now the national government behind them and no moral sanction further is needed.[8]

Harry was still Collins' friend but his ideas were being influenced by De Valera's concepts. His attitude towards the 'G' men, who were constantly following Collins, Béaslaí and him around and spying on their movements, was stiffening. They were so familiar to him now that he knew their names and he ruffled them by calling out their names when he saw them lurking in the shadows: 'Hello, Wharton! Hi there, Hoey! Good night to you, Smyth!'[9]

He often stayed at Vaughan's Hotel, Parnell Square with Collins and Béaslaí as this building had so far escaped the notice of the 'G' men. The three of them frequently shared the same bedroom. They never went to bed early – seldom before two o'clock in the morning and they spent most of the midnight hours talking.[10] One night the three of them became involved in an intense discussion about the comparative effectiveness of passive resistance or physical force methods to win Irish freedom. Harry championed passive resistance as the most effective weapon. He maintained that the man who gave up his life for an ideal without using force was the better man.

'Be Jepers!' retorted Collins. ''Tis late in your life you're preaching that doctrine.'

'I know,' said Boland, 'that I'm not able to live up to it, but the man with an idea is better than the man with a gun.'

Béaslaí said that there was no reason why the man with the idea should not also use a gun in defence of his idea against another gunman. Michael joined in and defended Béaslaí's point of view. But Harry still argued that to resort to force lowered the quality of the principle.[11]

He attended his last GAA Congress on Easter Sunday, 20 April 1919. He seconded a recommendation of the Cork County Board 'that the Central Council start inter-provincial school and college competitions in hurling and football commencing this year'.[12] Although these did not start straight away, the idea was planted. The decision to suspend members of the GAA who took the oath of allegiance was passed by a vote of 50 to 31 after a tense, emotional and heated debate. During his speech in support of the motion, Harry claimed that 'the Gaelic Athletic Association owed its position to the fact that it had always drawn the line between the garrison and the Gael'.[13]

Then it was announced that only two names had been put forward for the office of president – Harry and the then holder of the post, Alderman James Nowlan of Kilkenny.[14] Harry refused to go forward because he felt he might soon be leaving Ireland and secrecy prevented him from explaining.[15]

At the end of April 1919 Éamon de Valera asked Harry to go to the USA on a special mission. Dev chose Harry for this assignment for a few reasons – one of which was that 'our personal relations were of the closest'. He explained why he wanted Harry to go to America:

> ... I sent Harry Boland to America because of a message given to me that there was a split amongst our friends in America which was likely to do the helpful movement there considerable harm ... Fr Edmund O'Shea of Philadelphia, was, I think, the person who brought the message. The dispute arose about the disposal of funds which had been raised in the 'Victory Drive' following the Philadelphia Convention of, I think, February, 1919. Mr Boland's mission was to investigate the situation, try to bring the parties together, and bring about unity.[16]

On the 30 April Dev appointed Harry as a special envoy from the elected government of the Irish Republic to the government and people of the United States and granted him all the privileges and authorities of right which appertained to that office.[17]

Harry accepted the post although he had mixed feelings about leaving Ireland. He began to make preparations straight away for his long, secret and concealed journey across the Atlantic.

DISUNITY IN AMERICA

Not many knew of Harry's departure and the few who did, were only told about it at the last minute. Michael Collins regretted that their great friendship and teamwork, which had been so effective, was about to suffer a temporary interruption. Collins arranged a farewell party for Harry at Vaughan's hotel. Only a few trusted friends were invited.[1] Speeches were made and songs were sung.[2]

Harry left a manager in charge of his tailoring and outfitting business in 64 Middle Abbey Street, but he would not do as well in the shop as Harry had been doing.[3]

The morning after the farewell party, Harry left for England where he stayed in Manchester with his Aunt Lily before travelling on to Liverpool.[4] With the help of Neill Kerr, Harry was smuggled as a fireman on the White Star steamer, *Celtic*, bound for New York port.[5] On the journey across, he had sore, chafed hands as he was inexperienced in handling the rough shovel required to stoke up the ship's furnace. He reached New York without detection and safely disembarked about 11 May.

Jim McGee and Jim Gleeson[6] met him and brought him straight to Diarmuid Lynch – an old friend. Diarmuid became the Sinn Féin Food Director but was arrested in the spring of 1918 and because he was an American citizen he was deported to the USA.[7] He was appointed National Secretary to the Friends of Irish Freedom movement at the Second Irish Race Convention in New York on the 18 May 1918.[8] In the general election in Ireland later that year, Diarmuid was returned unopposed as Sinn Féin MP for Cork South-East.

Harry stayed with Diarmuid for two days and they discussed the differences that had arisen between the Irish American leaders on matters of policy and tactics.[9] The chief protagonists in the conflict were John Devoy and Judge Daniel Cohalan against Joe McGarrity and Patrick McCartan. In America the organisation corresponding to the IRB was named Clan-na-Gael and John Devoy was secretary. The clan had a newspaper of its own, the *Gaelic American*, and Devoy was the editor. After the abortive Fenian rising of 1867, Devoy had served a term of penal servitude in English jails and when he was released he went to New York. The Clan-na-Gael leaders called together an Irish Race Convention in New York on 4 March, 1916. From this convention of about 2,000 delegates from many Irish American organisations all over America, the Friends of Irish Freedom Association was founded. Its object was to 'encourage and assist any movement that will tend to bring about the national independence of Ireland'.[10]

Judge Daniel Cohalan was the son of Cork emigrants. He was a member of the clan but not on the executive. He was very active in American politics and he opposed Wilson's presidential nomination at the Democratic Party's convention in Baltimore, Maryland in 1912 and backed his Republican Party opponent, Charles Evans Hughes, when Wilson stood for a second term.[11] Wilson never forgave Cohalan and never co-operated with him.

A native of Carrickmore, Co. Tyrone Joseph McGarrity went to America when he was sixteen years of age, he did well in Philadelphia and he became a wealthy man. When he became a member of Clan-na-Gael, he organised the Philadelphia branch, and in 1904 he was elected as the district officer in that city. From then on he was one of the chief men in the Irish Revolutionary movement in the USA.

Patrick McCartan qualified in Ireland as a doctor. When the sentenced 1916 prisoners, including Harry, were released from prison they signed a proclamation on Irish linen addressed to the President and the Congress of the United States and McCartan went to America to present the inscribed cloth to President Wilson.[12] He failed to see Wilson but handed the signed fabric to the president's secretary who advised his assistant secretary 'to file it and not reply'.[13] McCartan stayed on in the USA as the envoy of the Supreme Council of the IRB.[14] In March 1918 McGarrity founded a new Republican weekly newspaper, the *Irish Press,* and Patrick McCartan was the editor.[15]

Liam Mellows was also prominent in Irish American circles at this time. He had been asked to go to America by the Supreme Council of the IRB after he had escaped capture following the 1916 Rising

Differences had surfaced amongst the Irish American leaders. Mellows, McCartan and McGarrity wanted recognition of the Irish Republic proclaimed in 1916. John Devoy and Judge Cohalan were speaking in terms of 'self-determination' – that was the phrase used by President Wilson in regard to the independence of small nations and they thought it gave them a better chance of communicating with him. But it was the method of the disposal of the Irish Victory Fund which caused the biggest dissension – when Joseph McGarrity proposed the collection of these funds at the February Irish Race Convention in Philadelphia, the resolution did not specify when, where or for what purposes these funds should be spent. But on the 1 May 1919, a circular was sent out from the headquarters of the Friends of Irish Freedom, specifying that most of the money collected would be spent in America educating the public on the justice of the Irish cause – rather than being spent in Ireland to help Dáil Éireann. It was signed by Rev Peter E. Magennis, National President, and Diarmuid Lynch, National Secretary, Friends of Irish Freedom.[16] The circular surprised many, particularly Liam Mellows and Patrick McCartan, who were Sinn Féin TDs representing Ireland in the USA, and expected the money would be sent to Ireland to help Dáil Éireann. McGarrity, who first proposed the Victory Fund thought the same – Gavan Duffy, the representative of Dáil Éireann in Paris, had written to McGarrity saying that there were men elected to the Dáil who did not have sufficient money to pay their train fare from their constituencies to attend Dáil meetings in Dublin.

Harry's job was to unite the rival factions in this feud. 'I wish to work in harmony,' he said to Diarmuid Lynch.

'Things are very serious here,' answered Lynch.

Harry was listening to Diarmuid because he regarded him as a very old and trusted friend. But he began to doubt his impartiality when Lynch told him that he thought a British spy had got hold of Patrick McCartan and Joe McGarrity; and that while Harry would find McGarrity very decent, he would want to look out for McCartan.

'Isn't that very extraordinary,' Boland remarked. 'For I have letters from home confirming Dr McCartan in his position.'

Harry asked Diarmuid about Liam Mellows, his health and his whereabouts.

'I don't know where Liam is lately – anyway his manner seems to be very odd lately.'

Harry had great respect for Mellows and thought that he was one of the best men who ever stood up in any great cause.[17]

'Look Diarmuid,' Harry said, 'there are not huge differences between you'.

Diarmuid then proposed to Harry that he should call a conference of Devoy, McCartan, Cohalan, McGarrity and five or six other men prominent in the Friends of Irish Freedom Association.[18] At a meeting on his third day in America, Harry met Judge Daniel Cohalan, John Devoy, Hugh Montague, Richard Dalton and many members of Clan-na-Gael and the Friends of Irish Freedom in the New York area. Harry had come to America as envoy of the established Republic, delegated by Dáil Éireann, and he had brought credentials from the IRB which entitled him to sit in with the Clan-na-Gael executive. This was not a clan executive meeting but an introductory meeting for Harry to the New York area and Judge Cohalan took the chair. He was a forceful speaker and an expert in handling public meetings. He began by asking each one at the meeting to introduce himself and to give his qualifications and academic records. He first gave an account of his own *curriculum vitae*. Harry was uneasy about this procedure. How different it was to Dublin. Most of the men in the IRB in Ireland were not men of property or eminent lawyers and judges but men who had answered the call to arms and came to prominence fighting behind barricades.[19] He wanted to impress this fact on his American friends. Judge Cohalan's eyes moved to Harry's place at the table.

'We have Mr Boland with us from Dublin, Ireland to tell us what to do,' said Judge Cohalan. 'Now, Mr Boland will give us an account of his academic qualifications.'

Harry looked around at the neatly dressed, affluent men around him at the conference table. He was not going to go along with this type of pomposity.

'My university number is Q 90'.

A voice from the meeting asked him to explain.

'My university was Dartmoor Prison, England and for the record my prison number was Q 90'.[20]

Harry had a list from Ireland – things that they wanted done immediately – and he was only speaking to the meeting for three minutes when Judge Cohalan interrupted him and referred to politics in America.

'Mr Boland the time has come in this country for a third party. The Irish people are good politicians but poor strategists. The time has come when a third party must be created in America – our party – and we must take our rightful place in the United States.

When that is brought about, we will order Canada off this hemisphere, build a navy and lick Great Britain and in that way Ireland will be free.'

'That's all right, Judge,' answered Boland. 'But before you are halfway through that dream, we'll be either free men or dead men in Ireland, and we want your help, and we want it now'.[21]

Harry then went to Philadelphia to talk to McGarrity and McCartan. Dr McCartan was the envoy of the Irish Republic in Washington but he had never received any credentials from Dáil Éireann to support his position. John Devoy looked with disfavour on McCartan and considered him as an unauthorised person pursuing a policy of opposition to Cohalan and himself. When Boland arrived as special envoy McCartan thought Devoy had complained him to Dáil Éireann and that Harry was sent to replace him.

McGarrity brought Harry to the house owned by a sister of McCartan. Harry handed McCartan his new credentials. McCartan read them – as envoy of the Republic of Ireland, his duty was to secure recognition of the Republic. He then handed the document back to Harry.

'Keep this until you understand conditions here. Then if you deem it wise you can give it to me'.

Harry looked surprised. He had sympathy for McCartan.

'They are yours, and I hand them to you now in accordance with my instructions'.

McCartan had felt isolated before Harry arrived and now he felt that Harry would do a better job in ensuring unity in the USA.

'The stand we made for recognition of the Irish Republic has aroused great bitterness in Devoy and Cohalan,' McCartan said.

'You have made a fine stand,' Boland assured him, 'and you have a great name at home.'

McCartan felt a lot better with this assurance and thought that Harry, through the clan, might influence Devoy to ask for recognition of the Republic.[22]

Harry showed McGarrity and McCartan his own credentials. McGarrity explained to Boland how the whole American organisation worked and he told him that the Clan-na-Gael executive was in charge. He advised Harry to call on John Devoy and ask him to call the clan executive to a meeting. Devoy was now in his seventies, very deaf and easily irritated. He trusted Judge Cohalan absolutely and took his advice in political matters. Devoy welcomed Harry and received him well. He agreed to call the Clan-na-Gael executive meeting.

Harry sent his first report back to Éamon de Valera before this meeting was held. He gave an account of what he had done since he arrived and he was optimistic that he could settle the differences between the two groups:

> I have seen many groups since my arrival and I hope to bring them together early next week ... Most opportune that I got here at this moment as I may be able to harmonise the little differences that have arisen on policy, finance, etc. ... you need not be uneasy regarding Paris as all the cost of your delegation will be borne form here ...[23]

John Devoy kept his word and the Clan-na-Gael executive meeting met in the third week of May 1919. When the question of how the Irish Victory Fund should be spent was raised, some speakers said that Judge Cohalan had specified that it should be spent 'for educational propaganda in America' and that the Philadelphia Convention did not question that interpretation. McGarrity pleaded for support for the struggling Irish Republic. Harry explained that he, as an Irish representative, did not want to be part of a row in America and said that it was essential that unity should endure but that they must have money for Dáil Éireann. He looked for $250,000 for a start.[24] Harry said:

> I was witness to what I consider a most disgraceful performance ... the meeting ended up after fourteen hours with one man calling the secretary a liar, and the secretary calling him a traitor.[25]

A decision was made to come together again on the following Wednesday.

Harry decided to put off pressing for the Bond Drive for the moment because he felt if he did so straight away it would reduce his chances of getting a substantial amount of money from the Irish Victory Fund for Dáil Éireann.[26]

At the Wednesday meeting Harry said he knew that most of the subscribers had given the money for Ireland. The people at home would take a dim view of Clan-na-Gael and the Friends of Irish Freedom if they did not get a decent share of the Irish Victory Fund. The meeting went on for four hours and it ended by deciding that 25% of the $2,000,000 should be sent to Dáil Éireann –

without prejudice to further appeals. They also decided to send $50,000 to Ireland within a few weeks and the balance would be available by August. Judge Cohalan reluctantly agreed to this arrangement. In Harry's written report of the meeting he said 'the judge held that it is essential that the money be spent here (in America) and he had a comprehensive scheme for linking up the race so that they might be a power in American politics'.[27] When Harry had heard the views of the members of Clan-na-Gael and the Friends of Irish Freedom he came to the conclusion that Joe McGarrity was the man 'who thought in the same terms as the men back home in Ireland'.

He wrote a second comprehensive report for Dev describing the situation among the Irish Americans in Clan-na-Gael and the Friends of Irish Freedom and assured Dev that 'today the Irish in America are powerful and with this big organisation, have no un-easiness, that Ireland will be forgotten'. Harry referred to the 'Teachtaí Dáil Annseo' (the TDs here) and their reaction to the situation: McCartan had not got on well with Cohalan or Devoy; Liam Mellows was fed up and was anxious to go home; Diarmuid Lynch was doing well as National Secretary of the Friends of Irish Freedom. He spoke about his own position and he was confident he could smooth over the tensions. In this paragraph he used his own name 'Boland' instead of the pronoun 'I':

> Boland must remain here for some time as he is in with every one ... Boland regrets this as he hoped to be home by the end of June. 'Tis but in vain for soldiers to complain.

He described how he hoped to live in America while he was doing his job as Special Envoy – no salary or allowance was given to him, even to pay his expenses:

> On receipt of the $50,000 dollars, send back for McCartan and me, £500 as we must be independent. I have to do the heavy when I come out, dress suit, etc.

Harry's lenghty report was written in neat, legible, nicely-styled, long-hand script as he had no secretary – but his report was de-tailed and complete, mixed with good humour and good sense. His last paragraph to Dev was amusing. He referred to John Hayden whom he defeated in the South Roscommon constituency in the 1918 General Election and how he described Harry: 'In conclusion the writer asks you to forgive any grammatical errors, ill spelling, punctuation or any other defect your professional eye may spot, remembering that as Mr Hayden said, "I'm only a tramp tailor".'[28]

Patrick McCartan requested a meeting of the four Dáil deputies then in America and pointed out that the vital difference between the Devoy–Cohalan policy of seeking self-determination and his own strategy of seeking recognition of the established Irish Republic had caused a deep personal rift between Devoy, Cohalan and himself. He said Dáil Éireann needed an envoy who would be able to unite all the factions to secure recognition and felt that he was not the one to do it. He said he could best serve Ireland by leaving the United States.[29]

Then quite unexpectedly Harry received a note from Éamon de Valera:

> On my arrival in New York Harbour ... Will tell you idea when we meet. Am anxious to travel to Rochester tonight – Hope it can be managed. Want to see you before I meet anybody. I learnt a number of things since you left dealing with the matter you came to investigate. If you are watched here better not come to see me but travel to Rochester tomorrow or as soon as you can.[30]

Dev had arrived unannounced in New York on 11 June 1919 to begin his stay in America .

I FEEL AT HOME AT THIS WORK

Harry had not expected Éamon de Valera in New York – in fact no one in New York knew about his coming and no one was near the harbour to meet him. Dev had left Ireland in a hurry. Mrs de Valera's birthday was on Sunday, 1 June. De Valera had cancelled all appointments for that day as he had been in prison and away from his wife, Sinéad, for her last four birthdays. That morning Michael Collins had a visit from a Liverpool seaman named Dick O'Neill who told him that arrangements had been made to smuggle De Valera as a stowaway to America on board the SS *Lapland* which was due to sail. They both went immediately to Greystones to explain the situation to De Valera. Within half an hour Dev was preparing to leave home to start his journey to Liverpool to board the ship as a newly signed-on seaman.

When the ship arrived in New York, Dick O'Neill and Barney Downes, the two seamen who had accompanied Dev on the journey across the Atlantic, contacted Harry. Accompanied by Joe Mc-Garrity he set off for the harbour and at 11.30pm met Éamon de Valera.[1]

Éamon de Valera went to Rochester to meet his mother, then Catherine Wheelwright. Éamon's father had died when he was two and a half years old and his mother then married Charles Wheelwright. In her second marriage she had one son, Tom, and he became a Redemptorist priest. When Dev called, Catherine was sixty-three years of age – still an active and handsome woman.

Harry visited Dev in Rochester and in the few days before De Valera appeared openly before the American public they discussed the situation. Harry had already sent two comprehensive reports to Dev but they had not arrived in Ireland before he left. They left Rochester in a hurry to avoid newsmen and went to Philadelphia;[2] then on to Baltimore where they paid an unannounced courtesy visit on Cardinal Gibbons and 'they spoke about many matters but never once mentioned the Irish situation'.[3] From Baltimore they drove the sixty miles to Washington on an unofficial visit and met many senators there including Senator Borah.

Dev met Patrick McCartan who began to report on his difficulties with Devoy and Cohalan and had just told him that his big problem with them was that Cohalan had tried to reduce Ireland's claim from recognition of a Republic to one for self-determination. When De Valera interrupted and said that 'self-determination was a very good policy', McCartan got so much of a shock that he went no further.

McGarrity told De Valera that he should speak in America as President of the Irish Republic. De Valera pointed out that he was not President of the Irish Republic but Chairman of the Dáil. McGarrity said it was the same thing and that their publicity had painted an image of him as President in the minds and hearts of the American people.[4]

Dáil Éireann met in Dublin on 17 June, 1919 and Arthur Griffith said that 'the president has, by and with the advice of the ministry, gone on a mission abroad, particulars of which will be communicated to the Dáil before the conclusion of the session'.[5] The deputy speaker read a letter from Éamon de Valera in which he declared: 'I hereby appoint the Secretary for Home Affairs, Art Ó Gríobhtha, as Deputy-President in my absence'.[6] When the Dáil met on 19 June Arthur Griffith proposed that a payment of £156 per annum be paid to Harry's family while he was in America on official work for the Dáil and the payment was unanimously approved.[7]

On 17 June, McGarrity drove Harry to Atlantic City to the Convention of the American Federation of Labour. Thomas Rock had been sent by Devoy to present a resolution on self-determination for Ireland. McGarrity was angry when he read Rock's resolution and took it from him and tore it up. McGarrity used his influence with Billy Boyle, a prominent Labour delegate from Philadelphia, to get important delegates to the convention to speak to Harry who urged them to support McGarrity's resolution which included, as part of it, recognition of the Irish Republic. Boland impressed them because he was a 'man from the actual struggle just over from Ireland'. McGarrity's resolution was the one adopted by the convention:

That the Senate of the United States earnestly request the Peace Commission at Versailles to endeavour to secure Edward de Valera, Arthur Griffith, and Count Noble Plunkett a hearing before said Peace Conference in order that they present the case of Ireland, and be it further resolved that the Congress of the United States recognise the present Irish Republic.[8]

Delighted Harry hurried back to report this achievement to De Valera but his news did not delight De Valera as Dev, at this stage, was keeping his options open – the problem of the unionists in the north-eastern corner of Ireland had yet to be resolved. He felt that some concessions might yet have to be offered to the unionists in the north-east to avoid the country being partitioned and he was also trying to foster a spirit of unity among the Irish Americans.

On 21 June Harry appeared at the Waldorf-Astoria Hotel in New York and took up a position in the lobby to give an important statement to the American press. He announced that Éamon de Valera, President of the Sinn Féin Irish Republic had arrived in America and said the President would arrive at the hotel the next day and hold a reception for his friends. Mr de Valera had no intention of 'meddling in American politics' but wanted to secure international recognition for Ireland. Shortly after making the announcement Harry disappeared from the Waldorf.[9]

He came to the Waldorf-Astoria again the next day and this time he was accompanied by several friends, including Miss Martin who was connected with the Friends of Irish Freedom. A *New York Times* reporter described Harry's arrival:

> De Valera's advance emissary, Harry J. Boland, the Sinn Féin member of parliament for South Roscommon, brushed into the lobby of the Waldorf yesterday accompanied by several friends. Boland is of medium height, powerfully built, and rather soft-spoken except when Great Britain and a free Ireland are mentioned. Then his broad thick hands close, his chin is thrust forward, and he isn't soft spoken at all.[10]

President de Valera did not appear and Harry said that De Valera wished to remain in seclusion until he had finished a statement he wanted to issue the following night. He forecast that 'his chief' would step into the presidential suite at the Waldorf at 5.30pm the following day. Then Harry went on to explain the reason for Dev's visit to the USA:

> He decided with the approval of his cabinet to come to America to plead the cause of Ireland before this great Republic ... He wished to get in touch with official America and float a bond issue of the Irish Republic.[11]

At 5.45pm on Monday, 23 June, De Valera's car swung into Thirty-third Street from Fifth Avenue and parked at the Waldorf-Astoria. Outside the hotel there was a crowd of 300 people who cheered De

Valera – mainly made up of members of Clan-na-Gael and Friends of Irish Freedom. John Devoy was in the hotel and Judge Cohalan had come with Dev. De Valera began by saying, 'From today I am in America as the official head of the Republic established by the will of the Irish people, in accordance with the principles of self-determination'. He was trying to satisfy both the McGarrity–McCartan group by his reference to the Republic and the Devoy–Cohalan faction by mentioning 'the principles of self-determination'. President de Valera's main theme was that the Americans, nurtured in liberty, had always been liberty's most consistent champions. They had heard the cries of the people of Poland, Greece, Hungary and the Latin race of the American continent and had helped them by backing up their claims to independence – Ireland hoped for the same help from America in seeking Irish freedom.

After De Valera's speech reporters asked Harry about the plans of 'Professor de Valera' and he said that another visit to Washington, this time 'officially', was likely.[12] Later on that evening as De Valera, McGarrity, Mellows and McCartan drove through Central Park, De Valera suddenly chuckled to himself: 'I wonder what Griffith will say when he reads that I came out in the press as President of the Republic'.[13]

Heartening news came from Chicago the following day. De Pauw University had conferred the honorary degree of Bachelor of Laws upon Dr de Valera and telegraphed the degree to him at the Waldorf-Astoria. 'We are hoping the President of the Irish Republic will be in Chicago soon', said the Irish American priest, Fr Francis McCabe. 'When he comes we will give him the welcome he deserves'.[14]

The Irish mission had to organise themselves into a working unit when Éamon de Valera had come out in public with his campaign. They were using the Friends of Irish Freedom offices as their headquarters and they needed somebody to do their secretarial work. Diarmuid Lynch recommended Kathleen O'Connell, a native of Kerry, for the job. She became a very trusted member of their staff and she described her duties in the Irish mission:

> I was the only Irish born girl in the office of the Friends of Irish Freedom – they were mostly Irish Americans on the staff. I took dictation from Mr Boland a few times. I typed confidential communications for the President ... these included communications with the cabinet of Dáil Éireann, with Michael Collins, the Minister for Defence, Cathal Brugha and Mr

Griffith ... Quite a lot of the work related to military matters because Mr Boland was the American delegate from the IRB and he was in constant communication with Mr Collins ... Harry Boland was also Secretary to the President at that time.[15]

Harry was representing the Supreme Council of the IRB in the activities of Clan-na-Gael in the USA and was trying to supply the IRA with weapons to defend Dáil Éireann and the established Irish Republic. The American State Department could not raise legal objection against negotiations by De Valera for the promotion of Ireland's independence. However if Harry made any effort to equip a military force in Ireland with weapons from America he would be liable for arrest under the neutrality law because he would be using American territory for setting up military expeditions against a friendly country.

The efforts to procure a hearing of Ireland's case for independence before the Peace Conference in Paris failed. President Wilson said that there was an agreement among the Committee of the Big Four in Versailles that no small nation should appear before it without the unanimous consent of the whole committee and England had vetoed the hearing of Ireland's claim. All future efforts to have Ireland's case heard at the Peace Conference were fruitless. The Treaty of Versailles was signed on 27 June and closed a chapter on Dáil Éireann's effort to seek a hearing of its case.

De Valera made his first public appearance outside New York in Boston on 28 June. The President received a tumultuous greeting when he stepped off his train at the South Station. The following day he addressed a mass meeting of 70,000 people at Fenway Park. Harry described this reception when he wrote to his mother:

At Boston the president received a reception unequalled in the history of America. Men who have toured America with many of America's presidents say that they have never witnessed so many people at a meeting as that which greeted us at Boston.[16]

Éamon de Valera spoke about the Treaty of Versailles which had been designed to end all wars. He was pessimistic about it and forecast that it would give twenty new wars instead. He advised that a 'just League of Nations, founded on the only basis on which it can be just – the equality of right amongst nations, small no less than great' could save democracy.

Dev, Harry and the other members of the Irish mission were

not against the principle of the League of Nations but they opposed the League established in Versailles because Article Ten guaranteed to respect and keep in existence the then boundaries of the member nations. This meant that the Irish Republic would never gain recognition from any member state of this League. The League of Nations still had to be ratified in the USA but President Wilson was preparing to campaign in favour of it.

Harry spoke out against Article Ten because it ignored the fact that a big majority of Irish people wanted freedom:

> The present form of the League of Nations covenant would condemn Ireland to perpetual slavery. I am especially opposed to Article Ten, which will guarantee the territorial entirety of Great Britain, thus preventing Ireland from becoming free. This ignored the fact that seventy-three Sinn Féin delegates who voted to make Professor de Valera President of the Irish Republic represented five-sixths of the Irish population.[17]

Harry wrote to his mother and told her that he thoroughly enjoyed his tour and was in good health. But he was not fully happy with himself:

> The only trouble I have in my mind is that I may be wanted in Ireland. England is evidently in a very bad temper and may use the mailed fist even more strongly than at present. I will never forgive myself if anything happens while I am away ... I feel at home at this work and am gaining every day some new stunt which will be of service to me.[18]

Diarmuid Ó hÉigeartaigh, Secretary to the government, wrote to Harry about Dáil Éireann business on 12 July. He hoped that Harry, on behalf of Dáil Éireann, would proceed without delay with the flotation of the Loan as they would need money to carry out their reconstruction programme in Ireland. The main planks in this programme were outlined including the establishment of a consular service abroad to foster trade; the re-afforestation of Ireland; the development of the Irish sea fisheries; the establishment of a national civil service, and the provision of proper housing for the Irish people. The amusing last paragraph of this letter shows the high esteem in which Harry was held:

> If you have become 'Dr Boland' or any other such exalted personage before this reaches you, please excuse our not having addressed you properly. The Secretary for Finance sends his compliments and good wishes as so do I.[19]

Dev asked Harry to remain in New York (as he continued his tour to San Francisco and Butte, Montana) to prepare the bond issue. Harry had little co-operation from the Friends of Irish Freedom members and he found banks reluctant to agree to accept the money because the Irish Republic was not officially recognised, lawyers claimed the bond issue was illegal. He was also looking for suitable offices to rent as headquarters.[20]

On 29 July Harry sent a cablegram to Arthur Griffith telling him how well President De Valera was doing on his tour of the mid and western cities of the USA:

> Chicago, San Francisco, Butte, and all the western cities greeted President de Valera with civic honours. Resolutions adopted calling on congress to recognise Irish Republic. Hundred thousand people attended each meeting.[21]

Griffith acknowledged Boland's cablegram on 1 August, 'The Irish nation deeply appreciates the enthusiasm of the American people for the cause of justice and freedom in Ireland'.[22]

When Dev returned he asked McGarrity to join with them in organising the Bond Drive. McGarrity consulted W. J. A. Maloney – an Edinburgh medical doctor who was a professor in a medical faculty in New York University. He believed that Bond Certificates could be exchanged for actual bonds when the Irish Republic received recognition. McGarrity consulted a New York lawyer friend, Martin Conboy, who thought the scheme would be legal, but he told De Valera to get a second opinion. De Valera consulted a rising young New York lawyer and politician, Franklin D. Roosevelt, and he confirmed Conboy's legal opinion.[23] Soon afterwards, with the help of Dr Maloney, a bank was secured to accept the money from the sales of Irish Bond Certificates and offices for the headquarters were obtained on Fifth Avenue.

Dr Maloney drafted a Bond Certificate to circumvent the legal snares and had thousands of application forms for the certificates printed and ready for the public to sign. On 23 August it was announced in the press that the American Commission on Irish Independence had been set up to carry out the work of floating a loan for $10,000,000 for the Republic of Ireland. Frank P. Walsh was named as Chairman and Harry as Secretary.[24]

ON TOUR IN AMERICA

Left New York for Philadelphia. Raining. Met by thousands at North Philadelphia. Mounted escort and 300 motors all decorated. Went to Independence Hall where mayor's deputy welcomed Dev in the name of city. Visited Barry's monument. Banquet in evening. Spoke at banquet. Next day evening parade of city to Opera House, great welcome and procession 2 miles long. Hall full and overflow of 30,000 ... Philadelphia gave great send off ... Joe McGarrity a great soul.[1]

These were the notes Harry wrote in his diary for 1 and 2 October – the first two days of Éamon de Valera's grand tour of American cities. In every city they visited they formed a Bond Committee to direct a canvas for subscriptions. On 10 September the British executive in Ireland had suppressed the Dáil and from then on it was essential for Harry, Dev and his party to try even harder to get recognition in America for the outlawed Dáil Éireann.

The hall for the meeting in Pittsburg was packed once again and Dev, Frank Walsh and Harry addressed the meeting. Though Harry was satisfied the way everything went he wrote in his diary 'Boys at home more capable to organise than any I have met here so far'.[2]

They stopped at Louisville and Harry described it as the land of 'dark soil, lovely women, fast horses and dry whiskey'. 'The lovely women' reminded Harry of the attractive girl in Granard and when he reached Cincinnati, Ohio, he wrote to Kitty Kiernan:

A card from Ohio in remembrance. I am off with the chief on the great tour, and I will send you a card as I go along. We are having great meetings and wonderful success. I often think of you, and your happy family, and the pleasant times I had with you. I suppose ye will all have forgotten me by now. Anyway keep a warm corner for me in that gay heart of yours.[3]

After Louisville they took a fast train to Indianapolis where they received a quieter reception than in any other city. They went to meet Governor Goodrich at the state house and the governor was careful not to use any words which might be interpreted as giving recognition to the Irish Republic. The chairman of the local committee of the American Legion, headed a dozen members who attended the governor's reception. The Legion was an organisation representing ex-American soldiers of the First World War and they said they were there 'to observe whether any unpatriotic remarks should be made'. Later one of them said that 'they had not forgotten that De Valera and his followers had stabbed an American ally in the back whenever the opportunity was offered'.[4] De Valera addressed a large meeting in the Tomlinson Hall that night and spoke about English propaganda going ahead of them on their tour: 'They tell the man of Irish blood in America that America is his home and that his whole concern is in America. His position in truth is that of the married man who loves his wife dearly but who still has filial regard for his mother'. Harry closed the meeting with a brief address appealing to all Americans to lend their aid to the efforts of Ireland for independence.[5]

The following evening Dev was the guest of honour at a banquet of the Indianapolis Council of the Knights of Columbanus at the Claypool Hotel. Nearly 700 members of the local branch were present and Dev attacked the League of Nations:

> It is your duty to see that America does not become a member of the League of Nations as it is now proposed ... England has no title to Ireland and you should not recognise her claims to Ireland but if you sign this League of Nations' Covenant as it now stands you would be recognising her title.

The *Indianapolis News* disagreed with Dev and its editorial the following morning said, 'It is unfortunate that De Valera is put forward as spokesman for those who hope for further Irish freedom for he does not represent the 200,000 Irish who fought in the war against Germany'.[6] Harry wrote in his diary, 'Meeting not good. Raining. Evidently one section of the Irish clan ... visit here could have been 20 times better in proper hands'.[7]

From there they drove to South Bend and Notre Dame University in Northern Indiana. On their way a tyre burst and Harry, Seán Nunan and Dev changed the wheel. They arrived at Notre Dame University on the 15 October. They were greeted with a wonderful 'war cry' from the Notre Dame students who were already well-versed in cheering on their 'Fighting Irish' American Football team. Now the chant was: 'University Notre Dame. Rah. Rah. Rah. De Valera, De Valera, De Valera, Rah. Rah. Rah. Boland. Rah Rah. Rah. Republic. Rah. Rah. Rah'.[8] De Valera asked for a half day's holiday for the students and they were delighted. The Irish party went to see the Fr Corby Monument erected by student subscriptions and unveiled on the campus in 1911. Fr Corby was Chaplain Corby of the Union Army who gave general absolution to the Irish Brigade about to enter battle at Gettysburg, 2 July 1863. As Harry left for Detroit he said to Seán Nunan, 'I am fond of Indiana. It's very nice country'.

In Detroit Harry and De Valera succeeded in getting an interview with Henry Ford. Harry thought that Ford was an extraordinary man because he argued with De Valera and his colleagues for three hours about the League of Nations. Ford believed 'that a bad League was better than no League'. He said that De Valera was wrong to condemn the League of Nations.[9]

Three days later they visited the Chippewa Indian Reserve, Spooner, Wisconsin and were entertained by Indian chiefs. They met the medicine man, and watched the Indians in full tribal dress with their feathered headgear dance to their tom-tom beat. Harry and Dev were sitting together on the ground in front of a low stage and they looked very different to the Indians – Harry in a dark neat suit, white shirt, dickey bow, and wide brimmed hat and Dev, wearing a trim over-coat with a white collar and dark tie, held his hat in his hand. The Indians adopted De Valera as a chief of the Chippewa tribe and they named him 'nay, nay, ong, ga be' – meaning 'Dressing Feather'. Harry described this visit as 'their best day so far' and added that 'he loved the Indians'.[10]

The next day at St Paul Harry noted that De Valera made a great speech but that he himself was 'rotten' and added that Seán Nunan and he were 'in bad luck'. Harry was disappointed with the organisation for the Bond Drive in this city – the man in charge arrived for the meeting with the Bond Certificates but had made no arrangements for a bank to accept contributions.

De Valera was not satisfied with the organisation of the Bond Drive in New York or Washington. After a consultation in St Louis on 24 October Harry was asked to return to New York to review the whole planning of the Bond Drive scheme. He was disappointed to be leaving the touring team as he was looking forward to seeing the Rockies and visiting California. ''Tis but in vain for soldiers to complain', Harry said and carried out Dev's instructions.

Back in New York on 29 October he met his brother Ned twice and Ned brought news from home and said Michael Collins was in top form and anxious to meet Harry again.

Harry met J. B. Doyle of the Democratic Party in Philadelphia who told him that the Democrats were considering bringing a resolution before the Senate to recognise the Irish Republic.[11] He met Diarmuid Lynch for lunch in New York on 31 October and Diarmuid made an appointment for Harry to meet Judge Cohalan at nine o'clock that night. Harry called to John Devoy with a note from McGarry in Chicago and asked Devoy to come with him to see Cohalan. They had a long talk with Judge Cohalan and he promised Harry all the help he could give him with the Bond Drive, though he expressed his dissatisfaction with many aspects of the set-up.[12] Harry was better in dealing with John Devoy and Judge Cohalan than Éamon de Valera or any other member of the Irish mission because Devoy respected him. Although it was almost 10.30pm when Harry left the Devoy–Cohalan meeting, he went skating with a lady friend whom he named in his diary as 'Miss Mc'. After that both of them joined a small Halloween Party where he forgot his political worries.[13]

Harry took over the organisation of the Bond Drive in New York in the early days of November. He was very uneasy over the progress made as he felt those in charge while he was on tour with De Valera had 'no idea of detail'. The central office was not yet furnished and some of the voluntary organisers had resigned. He attended a meeting of the Friends of Irish Freedom to discuss the matter: 'Lynch went off like a soda water bottle. Vitriol. Old man (John Devoy) and I square things up. Some hope', he wrote in his diary after the meeting.[14] The *Gaelic American*, 8 November, gave particulars about the loan:

> There has been duly authorised by an Act of Dáil Éireann an issue of $10,000,000 Bond-Certificates of the Republic of Ireland for disposition in America. The Bond-Certificates will be issued as of 1 December, 1919 in denominations of from $10 to $10,000 each ...

The *Gaelic American* editor, John Devoy, said that these details were published in Dr Maloney's *Irish World* newspaper the previous week but did not reach the office of the *Gaelic American* newspaper in time for publication. Devoy complained that the document ought to have reached both papers at the same time. 'It is certain that President de Valera intended it to be printed simultaneously in all Irish weekly papers and that somebody frustrated his intentions. The malicious lie that the editor of the *Gaelic American* and others are hostile to the Loan and are endeavouring to frustrate President de Valera's mission has been industriously circulated through the country', Devoy added.[15]

Harry tried to recruit more volunteer workers for the Bond Drive in the New York area and he was disappointed with the result. He met Judge Cohalan and John Devoy again but he found it difficult to get a united front. He felt tired and worn out so he went to see Dr Maloney who ordered him to take a holiday and recommended the seaside resort of Atlantic City for a few days.[16] Harry went there for three days – 'Salt water baths, skee ball, rifle shooting, theatre' and sitting in the sunshine. When he returned to New York the doctor put him off tobacco but he gradually eased himself into work again.

Éamon de Valera's tour continued. He was meeting opposition in places from former service men who were members of the American Legion. A report from Portland, Oregon said:

> A flag of the 'Irish Republic' was removed here today from the automobile of Éamon de Valera, leader of the Irish Independence Party by request of a party of former service men headed by Ensign A. T. Kurtz. They asked the man in charge of the car to remove the flag, in view of the fact that the United States government did not recognise the Irish Republic. The flag was removed. Mayor George L. Baker issued a statement saying that the use of the flag was objectionable and would not be permitted publicly during the remainder of De Valera's stay here.[17]

Before Harry became ill, James O'Mara, a fellow Sinn Féin TD and a trustee of the National Loan arrived in the USA on the invitation of Éamon de Valera to help in the Bond Drive. O'Mara, managing director of Donnelly's bacon curing in Dublin, had been elected as Sinn Féin TD for South Kilkenny in the 1918 general election.[18] On 5 November O'Mara went to see De Valera who was still on tour and at the end of the month De Valera held a conference on the progress of the loan. It was decided to place James in charge of the Bond Drive and Harry was to return to his old job as secretary to De Valera. Harry had too much to do in handling both jobs, but he was assigned another responsibility – to act as a contact between De Valera–O'Mara and Devoy–Cohalan. Harry accepted the change of job and his only comment on the change was 'Bond Drive shall be accomplished in time. O'Mara in command guarantees success'.[19]

The Irish-American leaders in New York understood O'Mara to be a millionaire and this gave him a high status. O'Mara was generous with his own money and he worked unsparingly to make the Bond Drive a success. The clan in New York sold about $600,000 worth of bonds and Dev and O'Mara were well pleased.[20]

Resolutions were arriving to the USA congress from everywhere De Valera toured, urging the American government to recognise the Irish Republic. Congressman 'Billy' Mason had always been a great supporter of the Irish cause – he belonged to the old American school who sympathised with liberty everywhere.[21] Mason introduced a bill to Congress on 28 May asking the American government to set aside $14,000 to set up a USA diplomatic embassy in Ireland. This money would go to pay the salaries and expenses of a minister and consuls to the Republic of Ireland – an act equivalent to official recognition of Dáil Éireann by the United States.[22] The bill came before the Foreign Affairs committee of Congress on 12 and 13 December and Harry and Dev moved to Washington to be close to the proceedings. Congressman Mason, opening the debate, declared that 'the passage of the bill would make it plain to President Wilson that the people of the United States, acting through their representatives, desire complete recognition of the Irish Republic and wish diplomatic relations established with it'.[23] Others who spoke on behalf of the Irish case were representatives Gallagher of Illinois and Gallivan of Massachusetts, Frank P. Walsh, Mrs Mary McWhorter (National President of the Ladies Auxiliary of the Ancient Order of Hibernians) and Judge Cohalan.[24] Patrick McCartan was present at the hearing and praised the judge highly for the way he presented his case for Ireland on this occasion: 'Quick, decisive, with his facts and figures on his finger tips – he excelled himself'. When Cohalan had finished his presentation McCartan rushed to shake his hand and Cohalan returned a friendly smile. 'The most advanced stage that has yet been arrived at in the struggle of the Irish Republic to win recognition', Joe McGarrity's paper, the *Irish Press* stated.[25]

Harry and Dev took a walk through Central Park and admired the Lincoln Memorial, John Barry's monument and all the historical edifices erected to commemorate American heroes. Dev resented the fact that Judge Cohalan had not consulted them on the Mason bill. Two days after the hearing Harry brought Congressman Mason to see Dev and they chatted for some time on Mason's bill. Afterwards De Valera spoke to Judge Cohalan about the bill and though, in the case of rejection, a compromise had been mentioned on the original resolution for Recognition, De Valera was against watering down the motion in any way.[26]

In mid-December Harry was in the Washington office and De Valera recommended that the filing system in the office should be revamped and he asked Harry to remain behind and undertake the job. The president left Washington and continued on his tour and Harry worked hard in the office but, Harry, a born organiser, was uneasy in his office job. At night he went to the theatre, mostly on his own. On Sunday he walked around Washington, visiting the Catholic University and Rock Creek National Cemetery and admired the wonderful statue over Adams' grave. He said in his diary, 'Have written many letters and met many interesting people' but his thoughts were for Ireland and the events that were happening there.

One line of his diary for 20 December – 'French fired at. Missed'[27] – referred to the ambush on Lord French, the British Lord-Lieutenant in Ireland, as he was driving with an armed escort from Ashtown Railway Station in north Dublin to the Vice-regal Lodge in the Phoenix Park. He and his guards escaped but a young IRA man, Martin Savage, was shot dead.

Harry went to New York on the day before Christmas Eve and Frank P. Walsh invited him to spend Christmas day with his family. Harry had Christmas dinner with them and had 'a happy time'. On St Stephen's Day he met James O'Mara to go over the planned Bond Drive programme. According to Harry, O'Mara 'had things in fine shape'. On the Saturday after Christmas he had a very pleasant meeting with Devoy, the old Fenian spoke to him about James Stephens, a native of Kilkenny and a one time leader of the Fenians, and Col Kelly, a later leader and a relation of the Bolands. He said that 'he could listen all day' to Devoy's old stories. Harry joined De Valera in Washington and both spent New Year's Eve in their new office. Harry felt nostalgic on the last day of the old year:

> The year has been one of great adventure for me ... I feel that Ireland's cause has made wonderful progress. I hope the year we are entering on will see the triumph of Ireland.[28]

He was awakened by the ringing of bells and the sounding of bugles to welcome in the New year of 1920. He got up and wished Dev a happy New Year. Harry found him writing a letter to his wife, Sinéad, and his young children. 'Our first letter of the New Year' Harry said as he toasted his leader.[29]

OH! FOR A GOOD GAME OF HURLING

One afternoon in the middle of winter Harry took a long walk around central Washington. He strolled past the White House, the Library of Congress, the National Archives and the parks were under a carpet of snow and the buildings looked ever whiter than usual. He pulled up the collar of his coat around his neck as the fresh cold white flakes of snow brushed against his face. He sheltered under the high portico of a tall building and looked out at the scene before him. 'Washington is a very beautiful city ... I hope I live to see an Irish embassy here'.[1]

James O'Mara and Seán Nunan called to his office in mid-January. They showed him an advertisement they had placed in the *Gaelic American* announcing the Bond Certificate campaign – informing the Irish American public that every Bond Certificate purchased kept Ireland for the Irish, repeopled the land, harnessed the rivers, put the Irish flag on every sea, abolished the slums, started the looms spinning, drained the bogs and lifted Ireland up.[2] Harry felt that 'James has done wonders on the Bond Drive, it now looks good'.

Harry and De Valera moved back to New York and De Valera received the freedom of the city. The 69th, the Irish Brigade in the American army, was in full uniform and the enthusiasm was wild.[3] An entry of Harry's shows how busy they were: 'Wonderful performance. Five meetings in five hours. Forty miles driving in snow'.[4]

On 5 February Éamon de Valera gave an interview to the *Westminster Gazette*. Harry described the interview as a statement 'on England's security – Good stuff'.[5] There was some opposition in America to Irish independence and De Valera was trying to change this:

> The United Sates by the Monroe Doctrine made provision for its security without depriving the Latin Republics of the South of their independence and their life. The United States safeguarded itself from the possible use of the island of Cuba as a base for an attack by a foreign Power by stipulating: 'that the government of Cuba shall never enter into any treaty with any foreign Power or Powers which will impair or tend to impair the independence of Cuba ...'

De Valera asked why Britain did not make a stipulation like this to safeguard herself against foreign attack as the United States did with Cuba? The people of Ireland far from objecting would co-operate with their whole soul. Dev was speaking about a thirty-two county unpartitioned Ireland and his views raised a storm of protest, especially in the Devoy–Cohalan camp. Patrick McCartan said that none of the members of the Irish mission had been consulted – they had no idea Dev intended to issue a statement and it came as a thunderbolt to them.[6]

The *New York Globe* reprinted the interview on 10 February. John Devoy, Judge Cohalan and their supporters thought De Valera was giving an indication that he was prepared to accept something less than complete sovereignty. John Devoy tore the interview to pieces in the *Gaelic American*:

> Dáil Éireann has the power, but not the right to change the policy and the objectives because its members were elected on a specific mandate to proclaim an independent Irish Republic, entirely separated from England. This aroused the enthusiasm of the Irish in America and loosened their purse strings – and I know them as well as any man living – they would have neither enthusiasm nor money for a so-called free Ireland under an English Monroe Doctrine for the two neighbouring islands.[7]

But John Devoy magnified his argument and declared 'I cannot and will not support him in the radical change of policy which he now proposes'.[8]

Harry defended De Valera's suggestion of a Monroe Doctrine settlement with England. 'Even if he had made a mistake, which I deny, the friendly thing would be to come to him and say, 'We think you were wrong',[9] and he denied Devoy's claim that Dev had lowered the flag. He felt that Devoy was interfering in a matter that concerned the Irish people alone.[10] A week after Harry noted in his diary that Devoy was out for trouble and was using his paper to bring De Valera to heel: 'John, my son, you have your hands full. Shall America dictate? – that's the question. I have no fear of the result. Sorry "Old Man" is firing the balls for Cohalan'.[11]

Thomas J. Lynch, an Irish American, wrote to Éamon de Valera on the 15 February saying that he was wholly, entirely, and absolutely, with the American leaders in opposing De Valera's views on the Monroe Doctrine as applied to Ireland. Harry replied to his letter in very blunt terms. 'I resent you, or any other person, suggesting that a man of President de Valera's record would compromise Ireland's sovereign claim'.[12] Harry was very angry when John Devoy sent the New York district officer of Clan-na-Gael, Larry Rice, to call on him and in Harry's words 'ordered me to leave De Valera there and then and denounce him. If I didn't do that I would be betraying the principles of Wolfe Tone'.[13]

'Sorry I did not kick Larry out. Done the next best thing', was Harry's reaction.[14]

He called to see John Devoy to try and talk calmly to him but they ended up having a fierce row and Harry left about midnight having called a supporter of John Devoy a 'blasted liar'.[15]

A number of the prominent Irish Americans, many of them in the Friends of Irish Freedom, backed De Valera – notably Frank P. Walsh, and J. K. McGuire.[16] The attacks against De Valera in the *Gaelic American* continued and Dev and Harry thought that Judge Cohalan was sheltering behind the pen of John Devoy. They decided that De Valera should write a letter to Judge Cohalan to draw him out into the open:

> I am led to understand that these articles in the *Gaelic American* have your consent and approval. Is that so? ... It is vital that I know exactly how you stand in this matter!

Harry brought the letter to Cohalan and was received with painful silence.[17]

Judge Cohalan replied two days later:

> The *Gaelic American* is edited, as you know, by Mr John Devoy, for whose opinions and convictions I entertain the highest respect. I control neither him nor them ...[18]

Cohalan's reply upset De Valera as he realised it would have been better if he had never written to him, it led to more attacks. Harry reported that the 'Chief not in good form. Nervous indigestion. O'Mara prescribed toast'.[19] Dev realised this conflict could wreck the whole American programme.

John Devoy wrote to John McGarry of Chicago on 26 February and castigated De Valera saying 'he selected the wrong time and the wrong issue for the inevitable row because his judgement was very poor. He was filled with the idea that the great ovations he got in America were for him personally'.

De Valera was afraid of a bad reaction in Ireland so he sent Dr McCartan to Dublin to explain the whole position of the Monroe Doctrine to the cabinet of Dáil Éireann. McCartan reported that the Countess Markievicz said De Valera spoke only for himself and could not commit the Dáil to any course of action unless they voted for it. Count Plunkett and Cathal Brugha were hostile to the proposal, but Collins and Griffith recommended to the others to accept De Valera's explanation.[20]

Harry and De Valera went to a dinner in New York given by Indian representatives and met rajahs, presidents, and Russian revolutionists.[21] Harry got on well with the Russians and met Ludwig Martens and a colleague called Nuorteva. They were representatives of the Russian Socialist Federal Soviet Republic and they too were on a fund-raising mission for their new government. Harry, being a revolutionary with labour sympathies, empathised with his Russian dinner companions. He met Martens and Nuorteva again in Washington on 3 March and they spoke about their mutual national problems.[22]

Then came another body blow. On 1 March, 1920 a letter, to be handed to De Valera, came to Harry from James O'Mara. O'Mara requested Éamon de Valera to relieve him of his duties as director of the Bond Drive in the USA. He also asked him to find a successor to him as trustee of the Dáil Éireann funds and to recommend another Sinn Féin candidate for his seat in South Kilkenny. He showed no animosity to De Valera whom he thanked for all his courtesies to him. He sent a private note to Harry asking him to assure De Valera that the root cause of his resignation went 'away and beyond either the position at the moment or indeed the struggle at all'.[23] Harry felt that 'O'Mara decision very severe blow. Cannot hope to secure his like again. Some serious crisis has overtaken Jim. Hope all will be well'.[24] O'Mara's daughter, Patricia Lavelle writing about her father said that he 'bore the brunt of the controversy about exchanging the initial loan for Bonds', he was anxious 'to return to his bacon factory business in Ireland' and was disappointed that his wife had failed to get a passport to follow him out to America.[25] Harry used all his power as a friend to try to get him to change his mind but he failed and thought that the 'Gaelic American articles doing Bond Drive no good'.[26]

Dev appealed to James O'Mara to reconsider his decision. 'If you leave me now,' he wrote, 'I must cancel the tour (southern states) which would be a serious loss'.[27] He also failed to change O'Mara's mind with this first letter and he wrote to Arthur Griffith later in March saying 'O'Mara will be a tremendous loss, but he seems fixed on resignation. It is purely on private grounds. We have worked in the greatest harmony'. This letter only arrived in Dublin on 14 April. In the meantime De Valera, in the first week of April, had appealed again to O'Mara to reconsider. One line of his letter seemed to sway O'Mara – 'I had dreamed that we would see the end of this mission here together'.[28] James changed his mind after about a month in retirement and resumed his Bond Drive work.

The day before St Patrick's Day Joe McGarrity came from Chicago to New York with the story that John Devoy and his followers were out to 'knife De Valera'. He also brought a copy of the letter that Devoy had written to McGarry on 26 February in which Devoy castigated De Valera saying that his judgement was poor. Harry showed the letter to De Valera who was very angry. They decided to keep the substance of the letter to themselves and to make use of it when it would be to their advantage. That evening Harry went to a meeting of the executive of Clan-na-Gael:

Hell loose. Agree to deputation. Adverse moderate resolution. J. K. McGuire and Joe (McGarrity) steadfast.

This Clan-na-Gael deputation met De Valera the day after St Patrick's Day and said that the Irish Americans should be in sole charge of all political activity in America. De Valera refused to entertain the idea.[29] That evening Harry heard of a 'caucus' meeting to which none of the members of the Irish mission had been invited so he asked Joe McGarrity to remain in New York and go to the meeting.[30] De Valera had been invited to a dinner in his honour in Chicago and was about to leave when Harry discovered that many of the Chicago Clan-na-Gael members were in New York and preparing to attend the secret meeting in the Park Avenue Hotel. McGarrity, suspecting some type of trap, rang Harry to advise him not to allow Dev to travel to Chicago. Both agreed that there was a conspiracy afoot to get De Valera out of New York while this 'caucus' meeting was going on.

McGarrity attended the Park Avenue meeting. Every effort was made by the Chairman to expel him, and when this failed Cohalan went ahead with his case against De Valera. He alleged that De Valera consulted no one, lived in luxurious suites at hotels, wasted money raised to help the down-trodden people of Ireland and spread discord in the ranks of Irish Americans. With his Cuban and Monroe Doctrine he put the Irish people on the side of England and made them possible enemies of the United States if ever there was a war between Britain and the United States for command of the seas. McGarrity countered and demanded that if De Valera was 'under trial' he should be there to defend himself. Cohalan was very surprised when he heard Dev was still in New York and could be contacted. Bishop Turner of Buffalo and Judge Goff, both neutral in this feud, argued that he should be summoned to the meeting. McGarrity telephoned the Waldorf-Astoria and Harry said he would not let Dev go to the meeting – but McGarrity persisted and De Valera went to the meeting with Harry and O'Mara.[31] Before they left the hotel Boland made sure of two things – he checked that they had the copy of the Devoy–McGarry letter and he then put his revolver in his pocket because he feared for Dev's life.[32]

When Dev reached the hotel he gave his version of the hostile treatment he had received from Devoy and Cohalan. Sometimes Cohalan contradicted what he said and at other times Devoy interrupted. Then Dev said that his opponents wanted to oust him and there were cheers, curses, challenges. Boland was anxious about the chief's safety– he was afraid that someone in the audience might take a shot at Dev so he took out his revolver, stood up and shouted over the uproar: 'If any one tries to shoot the president, he'll have to deal with me first.'[33]

When there was no reaction to his challenge he put the revolver back into his pocket.

'Who was trying to oust De Valera?' shouted someone in the crowd.

'John Devoy,' Harry replied.

After a pause when his companion had repeated to him what Harry had said, Devoy (who was almost completely deaf) denied this charge saying that it was a lie.

'John, you wrote a letter to McGarry saying that the president must be sent back to Ireland defeated and discredited.'

'What did Boland say?' shouted Devoy to his companion beside him.

'That you wrote to McGarry saying that De Valera must be

sent back to Ireland defeated and discredited.'

'I never used those words,' said Devoy.[34]

John McGarry from Chicago made a half-hearted effort to agree with Devoy. De Valera pointed to McGarrity.

'Produce the letter, Joe,' he said.

McGarrity plunged his left hand into the inside pocket of his jacket to extract the letter. There was a loud protest from the hall that the letter should not be produced. Shouts followed for peace. Cohalan moved towards Dev, withdrew his charges and shook hands. De Valera responded. Bishop Turner called on everyone to kneel down and pray for reconciliation.[35] The meeting broke up on the understanding that hostility would cease between the two factions from that day on. Boland's reaction was: 'Chief magnificent. Joe great ... Dirty attempts to break chief fails miserably ... Devoy and Cohalan licked'.[36]

But Devoy and Cohalan were by no means 'licked'.

Sandwiched in between all this in-fighting came good news from the American Senate on 18 March 1920. Both De Valera and Cohalan had campaigned against the League of Nations Charter but finally the United States Senate recognised the justice of the Irish case. While discussing the ratification of the Treaty of Versailles, the Senate decided on a reservation in the case of Ireland and passed the following resolution:

> In consenting to the ratification of the Treaty with Germany, the United States adheres to the principle of self-determination and to the resolution of sympathy with the aspiration of the Irish people for a government of their own choice ...

Senator Borah had done good work on behalf of Ireland. The resolution only passed by a margin of two votes.[37] De Valera sent a cable to Arthur Griffith announcing that 'A *Te Deum* should be sung throughout all Ireland ... Our mission has been successful. The principle of self-determination has been formally adopted in an international instrument'.[38] Harry was delighted when he heard the news: 'Senate adopts reservation. Hurrah! Our Washington work aided considerably'.[39] Judge Cohalan said that the resolution came at a very opportune moment and it was 'a notice to England and to all the rest of the world that America is going to continue to be a sovereign state and a guiding star to all people struggling for liberty throughout the world'.[40] Harry celebrated two days later with Jim O'Mara and Seán Nunan. He played poker with his two friends, 'first game of cards since I left Ireland'. Dev might have frowned on his team of ambassadors playing poker – Boland noted that 'the Chief was in Chicago'.[41]

Harry was busy planning De Valera's southern tour. He stayed behind and fixed up the publicity for the trip and Liam Mellows was travelling ahead of De Valera to make prior arrangements for the visit of the president to each city and town. Kathleen O'Connell wrote to Liam saying that 'Harry thinks it advisable that you go to every place marked in the schedule, even tho' we are advised that it not be possible to have a meeting'.[42] Mellows said he would 'go to each place marked on the schedule as suggested. Tonight I leave for Wilmington but Sweeney will stay behind till tomorrow night to take care of publicity and advertising ... I will keep in touch'.[43]

Hopes that the De Valera–Boland v Devoy–Cohalan war would abate suffered a setback on 10 April when James O'Mara, in his capacity as a trustee of the Dáil Loan, wrote to Diarmuid Lynch, Secretary of the Friends of Irish Freedom, requesting a statement of account of the Victory Fund. It had been arranged that 25% of this fund would go to Dáil Éireann and O'Mara felt it was 'only reasonable for the representative of the Government of Ireland to ask for a statement of account, both receipts and expenditure'.[44] Harry was aware of this letter and on 13 April went with O'Mara to see Diarmuid Lynch and had a 'hell of a row'. Harry said that 'Lynch thinks more of Cohalan and Co. than of Ireland. James O'Mara cries off at Lynch in great style. My efforts as peace-maker fail'.[45] The Friends of Irish Freedom replied within a week refusing O'Mara's request for a statement of account. Jim O'Mara got some support for his stance from branches of the Friends of Irish Freedom as demonstrated by this letter from Butte, Montana, '... If I had my way it is not 25% would have been given but 100%'.[46]

De Valera took serious exception to the fact that the request was refused by the Friends of Irish Freedom. He was not satisfied to allow the matter to rest.

Harry received a letter from Michael Collins on 19 April referring to the resignation of James O'Mara as a trustee of the Dáil Loan:

What on earth is wrong with Mr O'Mara? There always seems to be something depressing coming from USA. I cannot tell you how despondent this particular incident has made me ... O'Mara's action, if persisted in, would have a really bad effect here – very much worse than the Gaelic American difference.[47]

But O'Mara had already resumed work with the Irish mission, delay in postage between America and Ireland made the letter out of date but, having read it, Harry and Dev thought that it needed further clarification. Harry, as a close friend of Collins, wished that he could have a long talk with him about the whole American scene and particularly the Devoy—Cohalan problem.

Harry and Dev had met Ludwig Martens and Nuorteva, the representatives of the Socialist Federal Soviet Republic. Éamon de Valera kept his distance but Harry being a representative of the Supreme Council of the IRB kept up contact with the Russians and found that though they were on a fund-raising mission for their new Soviet government, they were not having much success. Martens was under suspicion in America and the police raided his offices. He was known as the unrecognised Bolshevist Ambassador to the United States. The Bolshevist mission was less popular than the Irish mission because the Americans feared the radicalism of the Soviets. McCartan had told De Valera that he thought recognition was possible from Russia, but De Valera rejected the idea at that time as he said he would prefer to secure recognition from the United States first.[48] He thought that if he got recognition from Russia the US government would spurn him. While Éamon de Valera was on tour in the Southern American states Harry met Nuorteva again and the Soviet representative told him that the newly formed Soviet Republic needed hard cash to rebuild their country which had been devastated by years of war and upheaval. The Russian delegation was finding it difficult to pay their personal expenses in America.[49] Harry listened to him because he thought about the chance of making a deal for the recognition of the Irish Republic by the Soviet Republic, and from an IRB point of view he saw the possibility of acquiring arms from them for the IRA in Ireland. Nuorteva wanted $20,000 and the Irish mission had far in excess of that sum in their coffers from the Irish Bond Drive. Nuorteva told Harry that he had some Russian Crown Jewels worth $25,000 to offer in security for a loan of $20,000. Nuorteva took out a cardboard box and showed the contents to Harry: a pendant with a 16-carat diamond and three sapphire and ruby brooches glittered as he took them out of the box to hand them to Harry. Harry could not decide himself – he did not have the authority to sign any cheque from the Bond Drive money – so he visited James O'Mara, a trustee of the Dáil Éireann Loan, and put the proposal to him. They discussed it until midnight and decided to go ahead with the deal. Harry wrote about the decision in hidden terms:

> Visit O'Mara till midnight. Put proposal to him. Enter a new line of ladies' ornaments for security. Reflect on the saying, 'Uneasy lies the head that wears the crown'.[50]

The following day James O'Mara drew the cheque from the Bond Drive account. Seán Nunan was aware of the transaction as well. Harry met 'old Nuorteva' and gave him the cheque.[51] He got the jewels and a receipt, dated 16 April, 1920 and signed by L. Martens, the representative of the Russian Socialist Federal Soviet Republic: 'I hereby acknowledge receipt of twenty thousand dollars ($20, 000) from Mr Harry Boland as a loan to be repaid on demand and return of security rendered'.[52] O'Mara was satisfied, but De Valera was not too happy when he heard about the transaction later:[53]

> Martens and Nuorteva met Harry Boland and James O'Mara and they persuaded them to give a loan of $20,000 on the strength of certain jewels ... De Valera was very annoyed with them for doing this with money he felt they should not lend to anyone else.[54]

O'Mara's wife and daughter, Patricia, arrived in America. Harry and Patricia enjoyed going out together and they spent a day touring Washington – visiting Arlington Cemetery, Arlington House (the home of the Confederate general, Robert E. Lee) and Mount Vernon, where George Washington once lived. Another day Harry took Patricia to a baseball game. He liked it, but coming away from the stadium, he longed 'for a good hurling match'.[55]

Harry received reports from Ireland that the people were showing wonderful courage, the Volunteers had some striking victories and were driving the British garrison from the rural areas into the large towns and cities. He felt that there was a long fight ahead and that it all depended on the courage and resistance of the people. He wanted to organise people from the Irish race all over the world to strike at England everywhere in the final struggle for Irish independence.[56]

BOLAND REPORTS HOME

De Valera was was still angry with the Friends of Irish Freedom refusal to give him a statement of account of the Victory Fund and felt it should be reported to Dáil Éireann. James O'Mara, Dev and Harry decided that Boland should go to Ireland and speak to Dáil Éireann and the Supreme Council of the IRB about all that was happening in America.[1] On the ship Harry passed himself off as a stoker: 'Wonder if all the lies they compel me to tell will count against me in the final tot,' he wrote in his diary. On 29 May 1920, he woke up early to see Dublin Bay before him. As the ship came nearer land, his eyes followed a line on the coast stretching from Sutton to his family home in Marino Crescent, Clontarf.[2] He took the first available hackney as far as Clontarf and then he walked up to his own home in the Crescent.

However there was urgent business. Joe O'Reilly, one of the Squad, arrived soon after – sent by Michael Collins – to drive Harry over to see him as fast as possible. Mick was waiting for him and he came forward to embrace him with open arms:

> Michael comes to meet me and in a second I have the hand of Ireland's ablest man – one who combined wonderful ability with a courage and heart that knows not fear. A genius for organisation, strict disciplinarian and master in this struggle.[3]

Harry gave Mick a full run down on the situation in America. He was looking for Mick's support. They discussed when and where they would convene a meeting of the Supreme Council of the IRB and Harry also told Mick that he wanted to meet the Irish cabinet.

Harry relaxed for the rest of the day. He first went to the new Sinn Féin headquarters in Mount Street and gave the staff there a lively account of his trip across the Atlantic and he told them that he had met Michael Collins soon after arriving.

'And I'm sure ,' said an old friend of his in the office, 'that the first thing he said to you was come and have a ball of malt.'

'You said it, babe,' said Harry in American jargon.

Then Harry asked Robert Brennan if he would come back with him to America.

'We need good men like you over there,' said Harry.

Brennan told him he would go if he were ordered to do so but otherwise he would stay in Ireland. Harry breezed out of the office then like a man in a hurry.[4]

That night he met Michael Collins and Batt O'Connor and many other Sinn Féin and GAA friends. Harry chatted with Paul Cusack from Granard, a Sinn Féiner who had been interned in Frongoch and whom Harry had met on his last visit to Kitty Kiernan in Granard. There had been no further letters between Harry and Kitty since he sent her that card at the beginning of his American tour asking her to keep a warm corner for him in her heart and not having received a reply to his postcard he thought that she had forgotten him. He asked Paul to give Kitty his regards and on 31 May, two days later, Kitty wrote to him from Granard:

> I'd give all I possess to see you again. I was in town last week – if only I had known. Is there any chance of seeing you before you return. I'd do my best if you were keen ... Suppose the idea of you coming here some night is hopeless ... Can you imagine how excited I'd be – I guess you must be some yank now (and I am the same old Kitty). Paul gave me no details only that he met you. I was stunned, you might have sent me a card.

Then she explained why she had not kept up the correspondence with him:

> I got yr (*sic*) nice note from the other side, many thanks. Don't know yr (*sic*) address or I would have written. I was glad your (*sic*) remembered me.

There was no rival for Kitty's love at this time:

> I spent a dull week last week in town – nobody interesting enough! I hope you found Michael well. I never see him ... I thought I'd like to write. But of course I'd much rather see you.[5]

Harry took Kitty at her word and found himself 'walking on air' with the prospect of doing a line with her.

On his fourth day in Ireland, Harry met the Dáil cabinet. He spoke about the activities of the Irish mission in America, referring primarily to the controversy between Dev, Cohalan and Devoy. He was happy when they gave De Valera their full support. Sceilg (Seán Ua Ceallaigh) who was present at the cabinet meeting wrote:

there was a good relationship between the members of the Irish mission and a Russian delegation to the USA. The Russians were seeking a monetary loan from the Irish delegation and Harry said that they offered Russian Crown Jewels as collateral for the loan. He completed the deal. Some of the cabinet laughed at the idea. 'Maybe they are counterfeit jewels', one cabinet member warned.[6]

The following day Harry and Michael Collins drove to Greystones to visit Sinéad de Valera. Harry described Sinéad as a 'wonderful and brave woman who is quite prepared for whatever may come',[7] but she missed her husband as she had the sole responsibility of rearing the children. Harry and Mick played ball with the older children. On their way out Harry suggested to Sinéad that she should come over to America and have a short holiday with her husband.

That night Harry met the Supreme Council of the IRB and he pulled no punches in giving them an account of the hostile attitude of Clan-na-Gael, the *Gaelic American* newspaper, John Devoy and Judge Cohalan to Éamon de Valera and other members of the Irish mission.[8] He said that Judge Cohalan's organisation, the Friends of Irish Freedom, was inextricably linked with John Devoy and Clan-na-Gael. The Supreme Council backed Harry's suggestion that an ultimatum be given to Clan-na-Gael to change its attitude to President de Valera or Clan-na-Gael would be expelled from the IRB. Three days later Harry met Seán Ó Muirthile, Austin Stack, Seán McGarry and Gearóid O'Sullivan, all members of the Supreme Council of the IRB. After this meeting Harry said that the meeting refreshed him 'like a cool plunge after my twelve months away'.[9]

Harry took a day off on Saturday 6 June, and with Michael Collins and his brother, Ned, went out to Howth, crossed by boat to Ireland's Eye, ate barnacles and spoke about the future. Harry discussed his own plan of organising the Irish race all over the world for the last phase in the struggle for freedom and Collins encouraged him to press ahead with his ideas. That night Harry wrote another tribute to Michael Collins in his diary:

Ireland has the man of a generation ... He stands out as the greatest force of the movement.[10]

Michael supported Harry and De Valera in the cabinet and the Supreme Council of the IRB. The Dáil Éireann cabinet meeting of 5

June advised De Valera not to return home as they thought his presence in the USA was of the utmost importance. The cabinet would not object to the president making a tour in South America if he could spare the time for it. They accepted the policy of making the Irish struggle a world wide one and enlisting the help of the Irish everywhere and decided to make diplomatic appointments to Russia, France, Spain, Italy, Austria, Germany, Denmark and Switzerland and to appoint four diplomatic agents to organise and direct Irish opinion around Chicago, New Orleans, San Francisco and Boston. These diplomatic agents would be directed from Washington and they would send a weekly report there and a copy to the Dáil ministry. The cabinet agreed to recommend to the Dáil that a delegation go to Russia – but agreed with Dev's view that the demand for recognition from Russia should wait until it had been given by America. The cabinet also recommended that Thomas Johnson, the Irish Labour Party activist, should be included in the delegation to Russia.[11]

Harry was determined to make a big push for recognition when he returned to America but then he received word from the Irish mission that the Committee of Foreign Affairs of the House of Representatives had reported on the Mason Bill on 28 May. The original bill introduced by Representative Mason asked for a grant of $14,000 to provide salaries for a Minister and Consuls to the Republic of Ireland. This would give virtual recognition but it was defeated – a compromise proposal was passed which said 'in the interest of world peace and international goodwill that the Congress of the United States (the Senate concurring) ... expresses its sympathy with the aspirations of the Irish people for a government of their own choice'.[12]

The Devoy–Cohalan camp claimed credit and their knowledge of American politics and their political contacts did much to nurture the Irish cause. But Éamon de Valera and the other members of the Irish mission also brought pressure on the senators and congressmen as a result of the great rallies they organised in cities all around America. Following these meetings thousands of Irish Americans swamped their political representatives and the Washington State Department with countless cables, telegrams and letters demanding American recognition for the Irish Republic.

Harry accepted Kitty's invitation to visit her in Granard – he drove there with Michael Collins. The three of them went to a ceilí and they had an enjoyable night together. Harry had fallen in love with Kitty and in his letter to her, 17 June, he opened his heart:

> As Paul will have told you, I am hungry to see you again ere I go on the great hike. You will think it very strange of me no doubt, seeing that I have just returned ... if I could only be with you I would indeed try to make you happy. It may be that I will come back soon again from overseas. Please God it may be our lot to win the fight so long waged for freedom ... Yet I long to be in Ireland, more so than ever that I have hopes to win the girl I love best in all the world ...[13]

He left Dublin for America on Wednesday, 23 June:

> Bid good bye to Dublin once more. My mother comes to Abbey Street with Dan Fraher ... A hasty good bye to all my people and run out so that I may not witness the tears of my dear loved mother, the best in the world.[14]

The following day Harry arrived in England and met Neil Kerr who went with him to Southampton, his port of embarkation for New York. He spent another day around Southampton waiting to board his ship and he felt lonely and out of sorts: 'spent the day with sailors around the docks. Drank more beer than I care for – yet keep O.K.'[15] Just before he boarded the ship he sent a farewell telegram to Kitty – 'Goodbye and best love'.[16]

BOLAND PACKED A PUNCH

When Harry arrived in New York, Dev was in San Francisco at the Democratic Convention. He was very tired and went to the Carmelite Priory where his friend, Rev. Peter E. Magennis, looked after him. James O'Mara came to see him and they spoke about the state of Irish affairs in America.[1] During Harry's absence in Ireland the conflict between Cohalan and De Valera had deepened during the Republican Convention in Chicago to choose a candidate for the coming American presidential election. The Irish mission thought that it would be beneficial if they could induce the Republicans to pledge their support for Ireland's case – it was believed that their candidate would win the presidency. However Judge Cohalan and De Valera both arrived at the convention and presented the same case from two different platforms and to avoid the possibility of involving the American Republican Party in dissension between two Irish rival factions, the Republican manifesto contained no Irish plank. When Harry heard this he became angry and immediately took Dev's side. He told O'Mara that he was prepared 'to give them (Devoy and Cohalan) all they wanted and maybe more'. He felt he had the authority of the Supreme Council of the IRB in Dublin to do so.[2]

There were many neutral members of the Friends of Irish Freedom who thought that De Valera's intervention in Chicago was unwise. The Irish in America were now divided further into two distinct camps, the De Valeraites and the Cohalanites and Harry was a firm supporter of De Valera.[3]

The Democratic Party met in San Francisco and as most Irish-Americans voted for the Democrats De Valera had hopes of getting a resolution through at their convention. He put forward a milder resolution than the Chicago one and it was defeated by 665 votes to 402. De Valera was disappointed but was glad about the number of votes cast in favour of his resolution.

Harry and James O'Mara set out for Chicago to meet De Valera at the American Labour Group Convention. On the way Harry read that William Barry had been arrested in Southampton with five secret letters sent by Sinn Féin leaders in the United States to Dáil Éireann ministers in Ireland. Barry was also found to be carrying three automatic revolvers and several hundred rounds of ammunition. Harry, as the representative of the IRB in the US, was organising the transport of guns and ammunition across the Atlantic to the IRA in Ireland and decided that in sending letters to Ireland he should devise a code. With other members of the Irish mission he compiled a secret system for names of Sinn Féin, IRA and Dáil Éireann prominent figures. Michael Collins was known as 'Field', De Valera – 'Phil', McGarrity – 'Phil's Cousin', Devoy –'Oldham', and Cohalan –'Cohen'.

Harry met De Valera in a hotel in Chicago and spent the morning reporting on all that had happened during his visit to Ireland, paying particular attention to the cabinet's views and decisions and the plans the Supreme Council of the IRB had for dealing with John Devoy, Judge Cohalan, Clan-na-Gael and the *Gaelic American* newspaper. He noticed that De Valera was looking very tired and when he mentioned that he had visited his wife, Sinéad, and the children in Greystones, De Valera expressed a wish to see them all.[4]

Dev addressed the Labour Group Convention by invitation and they endorsed a resolution for recognition of the Irish Republic.[5] The British government, knowing that potential damage could be done to the Irish movement in America, published the contents of the five secret letters captured on William Barry. One of these letters, intended for Michael Collins, was written by Seán Nunan, and referred to the fight in America between De Valera and Cohalan and there were references in this letter to Diarmuid Lynch, Secretary of the Friends of Irish Freedom since 1918:[6]

Now, Michael, something should be done about Diarmuid. It is absolutely outrageous that he, a member of the Dáil Éireann, should be supporting those who are opposing in every way the endeavours of the president. I think that it should be put up to him to resign either his seat in the Dáil Éireann or the secretaryship of the FOIF.[7]

The letter had a disastrous effect on Lynch. His attitude, in the conflict between De Valera and the Irish American leaders, had been generally in agreement with Devoy and Cohalan. He had hesitated to resign his Dáil seat because the British government might misinterpret his action as a break in the unity of the Republican government in Ireland. But after Nunan's letter was published he wrote to the people of South-East Cork and resigned as their Sinn Féin TD. He continued as National Secretary of the Friends of Irish Freedom. Harry had real sympathy for Diarmuid:

> Diarmuid Lynch resigns Dáil Éireann because he finds himself unable to agree with De Valera and colleagues. So he quits Dáil Éireann. With deep regret that he should have chosen Sec. FOIF to Dáil Éireann. Diarmuid Lynch proved himself a good man when the call came. I am sorry for him and Mrs Lynch.[8]

Harry wanted to settle peacefully the American dispute between De Valera and his supporters and Cohalan–Devoy: 'I was the one all along who desired peace; I believed it was possible to bring about co-operation'.[9] Seán Nunan said in the letter captured by the British, 'I hope that Harry will be back soon as he is the very, and possibly the only, man to deal with them from the organisational point of view, since they have a very wholesome respect for him'.[10] Harry began to prepare for a meeting with John Devoy and the full executive of Clan-na-Gael. He met Joe McGarrity and Hugh Montague to discuss the situation with them. He went to New Rochelle to meet James K. McGuire and explained the proposals he brought from Ireland. He told him the Supreme Council of the IRB's plan was to have the clan controlled and directed in all matters of policy from Ireland. Harry headed for Atlantic City to meet Patrick McCartan and Joe McGarrity.

Neither of them turned up but Harry waited and had great fun with Seán Nunan along the sea front. He went swimming and relaxed on the sands.[11] He sent a postcard to Kitty: 'Spent a few days here on my way to Philadelphia and Washington. I wish you were along to add another charm to this wonderful place'.[12] He wrote to Kitty again on 12 August. He knew that he was facing a crucial meeting with Clan-na-Gael and he told her that he was very busy and feeling uncomfortable in the heat of Washington from where he was writing the letter: 'I envy you in the coolness of Granard and the quietude of your peaceful home knowing nothing of the cares and worries attendant in such work as mine. I enjoy the memories of my very delightful trip to see you and pray that you may be ever happy'. He was disappointed that she was not replying to his letters and cards and he wondered why.[13]

Patrick McCartan was changing his mind about supporting Éamon de Valera and Harry since the Chicago Republican Convention debacle. Unknown to Harry he had written a letter to Joe

McGarrity suggesting a meeting of true Republicans in America to finish the internal feuding. He did not want to have De Valera and Harry present at the conference because 'they come to a conference not knowing what they want. Have an unconscious contempt or seem to have for opinions of others'. He also thought that Harry, De Valera and O'Mara 'left a big organisation – Sinn Féin – in Ireland' but what was wanted in America 'was a policy which they would get the present organisations to adopt and make their own'.[14]

Harry met the full executive of Clan-na-Gael in New York on 15 August. As Judge Cohalan was not a member of the executive he was not at this meeting, but John Devoy was. Éamon de Valera was not present as he was not a member of the IRB, but Harry was accepted 'as a duly authorised Envoy of the IRB, fully empowered to act for it'.[15]

The problem of Clan-na-Gael opposing the policy of Éamon de Valera, Príomh-Aire (Chief Minister) of Dáil Éireann, was discussed for ten hours. Harry insisted that there must be at least one basis to any agreement and that was 'that on all questions regarding the policies and wishes of the Irish Republic, the wishes of the president should be respected and followed: that where differences arose the final decision on such matters should rest with the president to whom they were to pledge the support of the organisation'. He said he could not budge one inch from that position and if they, as American citizens, could not see their way to give the help which Ireland wanted the De Valeraites would get other people to help them.[16] The majority of the Clan-na-Gael executive did not agree with him but eventually an agreement was hammered out that had the unanimous approval of those present. Before this conference it was estimated that only 30% of Clan-na-Gael were prepared to follow the policies of De Valera.

Harry suspected that Judge Cohalan, who was not there but who was an ordinary member of the clan, might oppose this deal.[17] The Clan-na-Gael executive issued a statement on 21 August explaining to its members that 'some differences had arisen between the officers of the organisation and the representatives of the home organisation over matters of public policy in America'. A meeting of the executive had been held and 'at that meeting all differences were adjusted'.[18]

De Valera was not too grateful to Harry for arranging a visit to America for Sinéad and he had mixed feelings about the proposed visit – he longed to see his wife and family again but he thought the timing was disastrous. Dev was a workaholic, seldom relaxing and stopping only for food, sleep and religious services. He was so taken up with the conflict with Devoy and Cohalan, and Dáil Éireann business in the USA, that he found it impossible to take even a one day break. When Harry wrote to Kitty some time later he said that 'Mrs de Valera is here now and has made a fine impression on every one, the "Chief" is a new man as a result and we are all very happy to have her here'.[19]

Dev was planning to get the Friends of Irish Freedom under his control as Harry had done with Clan-na-Gael. Early in August he wrote to the new National President of the Friends of Irish Freedom, Bishop Gallagher, asking 'that a convention, preferably a race convention, for many reasons should be held before the end of the fall'. But the Cohalan dominated Friends of Irish Freedom stalled for some time before doing anything.

Cork Lord Mayor, Terence MacSwiney, went on hunger strike with ten other men in mid-August and his hunger strike had a deep effect on all members of the Irish mission. They knew when MacSwiney said something, he meant it and his fast was grabbing the headlines in America and getting more notice than any single incident in the War of Independence.[20]

The Friends of Irish Freedom replied a month later and agreed to hold a national council meeting in New York on 17 September – but not a race convention. De Valera planned to use this meeting to amend the constitution of the Friends of Irish Freedom – to curb the power of Judge Cohalan as Harry had done at the Clan-na-Gael meeting. Motions had been submitted to the meeting on proposed changes to the constitution but the chairman, on a point of order, overruled De Valera and would not let him speak. About one o'clock in the morning, after he had been criticised by various members, Dev staged a walk-out and was accompanied by a great many of his followers.[21]

What Harrry feared most about his 15 August agreement with Clan-na-Gael happened – Judge Cohalan worked against it. Harry had tried to circumvent this by having a committee of three visit the judge and advise him of the settlement, but Cohalan told the delegation that Boland had inveigled them into a position where Clan-na-Gael was only an auxiliary of the Supreme Council of the IRB in Dublin. Harry described what happened after that:

> John Devoy came back from that meeting and published in the columns of the *Gaelic American* an article by (CH) Breherton, an English propagandist, reproduced from the *Philadelphia Public Ledger*, with a photograph of Mick Collins in full uniform, and insinuating that Mick was elected and President de Valera deposed.[22]

'Michael Collins speaks for Ireland', the article said. But Collins protested to Devoy: 'Every member of the Irish cabinet is in full accord with President de Valera's policy. When he speaks to America, he speaks for us all'.[23] Harry now knew that the 15 August agreement was in shreds. The *Gaelic American*, through the pen of John Devoy, was again attacking De Valera and Harry made one final attempt to redeem the situation. He spoke to the judge for an hour and pulled no punches – telling him that the executive of Clan-na-Gael had made the agreement and that no one outside the executive, even a judge, had the authority to wreck it. 'We have made the agreement, you are not a member of the executive, you hold no responsible position and as an ordinary member you should obey orders'. But Judge Cohalan did not listen and continued to whip up support on the clan executive for his own viewpoint.[24] Harry saw that he had only one alternative – but waited to see if anything else would develop.

Harry was extremely happy when a cable first arrived from Kitty and then a long letter. She had been on a holiday and Harry wrote back asking her did she ever think about the 'member' (himself) as she meandered in a boat along the Shannon, through South Roscommon. He said that the same 'member' was very miserable and lonely when he had not heard from her. He told her that, 'Seán Nunan and I are on the look out for digs, we are sick of hotel life and hope to have a little home of our own very soon where we can chat and smoke of an evening'. Then he spoke about Terence MacSwiney's hunger strike: 'We are all anxiously waiting the outcome of Mayor MacSwiney's protest, and have been doing our utmost to procure American sympathy and action'.[25]

The efforts of De Valera, Mellows, Boland and their other co-workers in getting support for MacSwiney's struggle led Irish-American women to form a picket line at the British consulate in New York. Later these women went to the waterfront and called out the dockers to support MacSwiney. The unplanned dock strike spread to Boston and the Pacific coast,[26] with dockers refusing to handle British cargoes. Dudley Field Malone, a well known lawyer and a candidate for governor of New York State, standing for the Farmer-Labour Party, supported them.[27]

Harry wrote again to Kitty and told her that he was on his way to Norfolk, Virginia on a steamer and sailing down Chesapeake Bay: 'It is fine and early in the morning and I want to let you know that I am thinking of you and longing to meet you again':

> Just fancy how time flies, here I am thousands of miles away from you. Yet it seems but a few days ago since last I saw you and I am wondering when I shall see you again. Dear Kitty, I wish I could see my way clear for the home trip, yet I dare not even guess at it, so I needs must carry on the work as best I can until I am permitted to return.[28]

The Friends of Irish Freedom held another meeting of the national council on 14 October. This time De Valera was not present but Rossa Downing, who supported him, proposed a motion saying 'that the entire question of the revision of the constitution be referred to a committee of ten, five to be selected by the National President, Bishop Gallagher, and five suggested by President de Valera'. Amid jeers it was rejected by 72 votes to 12.[29] President de Valera realised that his influence over the Friends of Irish Freedom was minimal, and his only course now was to push forward a plan to found a new organisation which could do the same work as the Friends of Irish Freedom in as efficient, if not better, manner.

Harry discovered that Judge Cohalan had won the support of five members, a majority, of the Clan-na-Gael executive in his opposition to the agreement of the 15 August. He wrote to Dev on 14 October:

> I suppose that you will have read Mr Devoy's latest article by the time this reaches you. Personally, I have made up my mind finally and forever to cut the connection that their organisation has had with ours in Ireland ... After six months of temporising ... I do not feel further disposed to treat with these men again.[30]

Harry, on 18 October, acting in the name of the Supreme Council, disaffiliated Clan-na-Gael from the IRB. Under the heading of 'Lord High Executioner Boland Swings His Axe on Clan-na-Gael', the *Gaelic American* printed the statement Harry released to the press:

We have tried in vain to secure the co-operation which we believe the rank and file of the Clan-na-Gael wishes to give us, but we have found that the clan executive itself is powerless against the veto of Justice Cohalan ... Until it is clear, therefore, that the organisation is free to co-operate with us, speaking with full authority in the name of the Supreme Council of the Irish Republican Brotherhood, I hereby announce that the Clan-na-Gael organisation is no longer affiliated with the Brotherhood.[31]

John Devoy ignored Harry's efforts to expel him calling it 'the tail wagging the dog' as Devoy's clan held on to the majority of the executive and a majority of the members.[32] In the *Gaelic American*, Devoy, as editor, wrote that the action itself 'was an act of gross discourtesy. It was taken without a conference with the general body'.[33] He also complained about Harry's publication of the expulsion statement in the press saying 'that it was a violation of the obligation of secrecy that has governed the relation between the two organisations (Clan-na-Gael and the Supreme Council of the IRB) for the past fifty years.[34] Patrick McCartan, although he agreed with Harry's action, disagreed with the manner in which he had published his disaffiliation order. He had heard Harry was about to publish this order 'and thinking it unwise to inform the American public of a schism even in our secret organisation, I tried to stop him, but he published it'.[35] Luke Dillon explained that 'the lists of the membership of the Clan-na-Gael were refused to Harry Boland. His only source of making known to the men of Clan-na-Gael, the action he took was by giving publicity to it in the newspapers'.[36] John Devoy claimed that Harry did not have the authority to disaffiliate Clan-na-Gael from the Supreme Council of the IRB,[37] but Patrick McCartan, P. S. O'Hegarty and Denis McCullough (members of the IRB), contradicted that argument:

Harry Boland's severance of the connection between the Home Organisation and the wing of the Clan-na-Gael which supported John Devoy and Judge Cohalan was based on the fact that that wing, led by Devoy and Cohalan obstructed the work of President de Valera and the Dáil Éireann official mission to America. This severance was concurred in and sanctioned by the Supreme Council of the IRB here (Ireland) and Mr McGarrity was asked to reorganise that wing of the organisation which accepted the policy of the home organisation and worked in harmony with the president and the Dáil official mission.[38]

Harry said:

I issued that statement (of severance), not on my own responsibility; I issued it on the orders of the Irish Republican Brotherhood. At any rate, I think that the people are satisfied that so far as we were concerned we did not take precipitate action. We waited, under the vilest abuse, for eighteen months, and I was the one who thought all along that peace could be accomplished.[39]

Joe McGarrity, the chairman of Clan-na-Gael who remained loyal to De Valera, declared the places of the Secretary, John Devoy and four other executive members vacant because they were 'more faithful to Cohalan than to the Irish Republic'. He appointed Luke Dillon to act as Secretary until such time as they could call a conference or convention, and Hugh Montague retained his position as Treasurer. Devoy said 'it was the first time in history a minority had expelled the majority'. He continued to act as Secretary of the severed clan, holding on to a majority of members, and he expelled McGarrity and Montague.

It was inevitable that when Harry disaffiliated Clan-na-Gael from the IRB organisation that Éamon de Valera would have to bring about fundamental changes in the Friends of Irish Freedom because Clan-na-Gael and the Friends were inextricably related. Harry, as a member of the Supreme Council of the IRB, had acted independently in his move against Clan-na-Gael but there was an understanding between him and De Valera in what they were both doing.[40]

On 9 November, De Valera sent telegrams to many prominent Irish American citizens in all parts of the USA asking them to come to a conference on organising a campaign to secure recognition for the Irish Republic and to assist Irish people now suffering so cruelly in Ireland. A week later this conference came together in the Raleigh Hotel, Washington.[41] De Valera opened the conference:

You are friends (of Ireland) and you read the dispatches as they appear in the press daily of the burnings and destruction of homes – of the murders of men, of women and of children ... You must feel, as I do, that now or never Ireland's friends must act ... Now if you do propose a new organisation, it will be worse than useless unless some provision be made so that any line of action taken with a view to Ireland's interest ... may not cross that of Ireland's own direct representatives.[42]

The new association was called The American Association for the Recognition of the Irish Republic, and it became known as the AARIR. It was very successful and the vast majority of the members of the Friends of Irish Freedom joined it. Diarmuid Lynch, who had stayed on as Secretary of the Friends, now believed his hard work was damaged and blighted.[43] Great numbers of Irish Americans who had not joined the older organisations joined the AARIR. Patrick McCartan said, 'Had the Association been started earlier it might have done much to justify its title. It fulfilled De Valera's need to form an organisation to supersede Cohalan's'.[44]

In the *Gaelic American* Devoy wrote that 'De Valera had proceeded to do as Boland did in his attempt to destroy the Clan-na-Gael, and assumed that he knew better than the elected leaders of the Irish people in America, the feelings and wishes of the rank and file'.[45]

Warren Harding, the Republican Party candidate, was elected president of the United States. Frank P. Walsh said that Senator Harding had written to him during the presidential election campaign expressing 'a very sympathetic feeling for the movement to bring about the independence of Ireland and the establishment of Irish nationality that is the national aspiration of any liberty loving people'.[46] Governor Cox, the Democratic nominee, had also said he would aid Ireland's cause 'through the bar of public opinion of the world, through the agency of the League of Nations'.[47] Irish-Americans now hoped President Harding would remember his words.

Harry had not written to Kitty since the end of September and he realised that keeping a romance alive when he was in America and Kitty was in Ireland was not an easy matter. Unknown to Harry, Kitty had suffered a traumatic experience in Granard. An RIC Inspector, Kelleher, who just arrived in Granard, was said by locals to have stated that he came to Longford 'to spill blood'. At this time Kevin Barry, the eighteen year old UCD medical student reared in Rathvilly, Co. Carlow, was under sentence of death in Mountjoy Jail for his part in an ambush on British troops in Old Church Street, Dublin. Terence MacSwiney had died on hunger strike a week earlier and there was tension in the air. The Longford Brigade IRA, under the command of Seán MacEoin, decided to kill RIC Inspector Kelleher and GHQ ratified their decision. Kelleher lodged in the Kiernan Hotel and was frequently seen having a drink there at night. Two IRA Volunteers went into the bar, found Kelleher drinking at the counter and shot him dead. Kevin Barry was hanged in Mountjoy Jail a few hours later, as the British had previously arranged. As a reprisal for killing Kelleher, lorries of British soldiers drove into Granard and ravaged the town. One of the buildings burned down was the Kiernan Hotel. Kitty was arrested and held for three days. Harry was thousands of miles away when Kitty needed comfort.

Éamon de Valera realised that prospects for the recognition of the Irish Republic by the US administration were slim. He decided to try to have the Irish Republic recognised by Russia. He asked Patrick McCartan to see the Russian representatives in America – Harry Boland's old friends, Martens and Nuorteva. Dr McCartan asked the two Russians if their government would conclude a treaty with the Republic of Ireland and they asked if his government would not make peace with England on a basis of less than complete independence. De Valera then asked McCartan to go to Russia.[48] Before he went to Russia the Irish mission, through Harry, advanced a further sum of $20,000 to Ludwig Martens on condition that arrangements were made so that its equivalent might be made available later for the accredited representative of the Irish Republican government at Moscow. De Valera signed an authorisation for Harry to hand over the money to Ludwig Martens.[49] He signed the receipt in his capacity as representative in the United States of the Russian Socialist Federal Soviet Republic.[50] McCartan left New York on 29 December, 1920 for Moscow.[51]

President de Valera was deeply upset by atrocities occurring in Ireland. Led by McGarrity, the members of the Irish mission held meetings to protest about each outrage and Cohalan's followers also protested. An American commission to investigate the British atrocities in Ireland was set up. Harry helped to have witnesses brought from Ireland to describe such occurrences as the burning of Balbriggan, and Cork, the Thurles atrocities and the sacking of Mallow. Ex-members of the RIC made startling revelations concerning the manner in which superior officers incited British soldiers in Ireland to loot, burn and shoot to kill. Reporters for the American media recorded the accounts and gave them full coverage in their papers.[52]

At the end of November Éamon de Valera thought seriously about returning to Ireland because Arthur Griffith, acting President of Dáil Éireann, and Professor Eoin MacNeill, Minister for Industries, were arrested on 26 November. Michael Collins became acting President of Dáil Éireann and this surprised Dev as he had expected Arthur Griffith to nominate Cathal Brugha. There were other factors which influenced Éamon de Valera to leave America

132

at this time – martial law was being imposed over many counties and the British were executing prisoners.[53] Stories were reaching America that peace moves were being made by Lloyd George and De Valera, as Príomh-Aire of the Dáil, would be needed if negotiations were to start.

Dev spent his last two days making preparations to return to Ireland. The Bond Drive had reached the $3,000,000 dollar mark and Harry was one of five trustees appointed by De Valera to oversee the use and disposal of these funds.[54] The Chief also informed Harry that he was making him the representative of Dáil Éireann in America until a permanent appointment was made by the cabinet in Dublin. Dev gave his farewell message to the American people to Harry but it was not to be published until he had disembarked in Ireland.[55] Joe McGarrity and Diarmuid Fawsitt said goodbye to De Valera and Harry went to see him off aboard the *SS Celtic*. He arrived in Ireland on 23 December.

Harry spent a miserable Christmas Day alone in the Wolcat Hotel. On 31 December he released De Valera's farewell message to the American media:

> And farewell the many dear friends I have made and the tens of thousands who, for the reason that I was the representative of a noble nation ... gave me honours they denied to princes – you will not need to be assured that Ireland will not forget and that Ireland will not be ungrateful.[56]

A Joyous Day

Mary MacSwiney, sister of Terence, arrived in New York in December and testified to the American Commission on British Atrocities in Ireland. She spoke of the struggle at home and painted a picture of the poor circumstances in which many Irish people were living due to the devastation caused by the armed struggle against England. Mary was looking for an enthusiastic young person, preferably a female, to help her in her work when she met Catherine Flanagan. Catherine accompanied her across America.[1] Mary was speaking at big meetings around Pittsburgh and she wrote frequent reports to Harry on how fruitful, or sometimes unproductive, her speeches and conversations were with Americans in general. She was a very serious woman when she mounted a platform to speak but was relaxed when writing to Harry:

> I have been trying to write sensibly but Catherine Flanagan and Miss Madden, are discussing the respective merits of yourself, Liam Mellows and the various other attractive specimens of our race that they have met. The results are disastrous to my letters. This makes the third time that Catherine is in a beseeching tone – urges me to send you her love – in fact threatens dire things to me if I don't – so here it is X X X X.[2]

The atmosphere was easier amongst the members of the Irish mission since De Valera left – Dev was hard on himself and on others who worked with him. Though Dev had his own quiet sense of humour, Harry was less inhibited in his display of good cheer with those around him.

There had been no letters between Harry and Kitty for three months. She met Mick Collins in Dublin and he asked her if she had heard from Harry but Kitty said, 'Cruel Harry that never writes'.[3]

When Dev left America he asked Harry to get the American Committee for the Relief of Ireland going and to ask prominent Irish Americans to head the committee.[4] Harry had less help as Liam Mellows also went home, but he got it going quickly and Captain Maloney launched the committee following a dinner in the Commodore Hotel. Californian oil magnate, Edward L. Doheny was its leading member – he was a nephew of Michael Doheny, one of the Young Ireland leaders of 1848. The two cardinals, O'Connell of

Boston and Gibbons of Baltimore, also became members of the committee. Bishop Gallagher of Detroit, president of the Friends of Irish Freedom, J. J. Pulleyn, president of the Emigrants Industrial Bank, many directors of other banks as well as chairmen of shipping boards played prominent parts in the movement.[5] The American Relief Committee enjoyed great success and amongst those who contributed generously were Count John McCormack, the Irish tenor, and Babe Ruth the famous American baseball player. President Warren Harding and Herbert Hoover telegraphed support for the committee.[6]

In a letter to Harry on 1 January 1921, Dev said that he was establishing the Irish White Cross to distribute the proceeds from the American Committee for Relief and he wanted Harry to help in setting up an American branch. Dev hoped that the Irish White Cross would be recognised by Geneva. He thought the British government might object to money being collected in America for the relief of distress because they might say that the money was being used to buy arms for the IRA. The country was producing enough food but so many were out of work that they had no money to buy food and he thought the best way to distribute the funds was for the American branch of the Irish White Cross to come over to Ireland.[7] By reducing hunger and hardship Dev knew the money would indirectly help Dáil Éireann to keep up their resistance to British rule. The American White Cross collected $5,000,000.

Dev also asked Harry to work on 'the pushing ahead of the new organisation' – the American Association for the Recognition of the Irish Republic.[8] Harry delegated much of the organisational work of the AARIR to James O'Mara and he realised that when Jim took on a task he became so immersed in it that he tolerated no interference. James began to spend more of his time in Chicago where he met liberal Americans prepared to offer their services to forward the Irish cause of freedom. O'Mara felt it would be beneficial to widen the movement for Irish recognition beyond Irish-Americans and he founded the Benjamin Franklin Bureau in Chicago. (Franklin, one of the authors of the American Declaration of Independence, had travelled in Ireland before the outbreak of the American War of Independence and had found that 'Our [America's] part is warmly taken by the Irish in general, there being in many points a similarity in our cause'.) The members of the bureau wrote hundreds of letters to the State Department in Washington protesting against British tyranny in Ireland. O'Mara felt that recognition could only be obtained if American public opinion was strong enough to force enough USA senators and congressmen to push it through Congress and the Senate – Irish-American citizens alone would not be powerful enough to do this.

Harry spent some time in Chicago and it was there he played his last game of hurling. He was thirty-four years of age but he still turned out for the local club and displayed his natural instinctive skills in wielding the camán. They have never forgotten in Chicago that Harry played hurling there and today there is a hurling club, 'Harry Boland's', wearing green and gold as their colours.[10] He wrote to Dev in mid-January, 1921, and he told him that Mary Mac-Swiney was widening the network of contacts, like O'Mara in Chicago, by insisting that non Irish Americans were invited to her meetings. Harry felt that many prominent women, involved in the suffrage movement, would be won over by Mary and would take up recognition work.[11] She was happy with the results of her drive for the AARIR and she wrote to James O'Mara from Fort Wayne, Indiana:

> Do you realise that we are reaping the reward of the president's (De Valera's) work for the last year and a half, combined with the sentiment aroused by Terry's death, and I must say that I find the latter much stronger and deeper than I had expected? ... We must get these people to act while the enthusiasm is fresh, and the new administration will listen to them. Already they are planning a storm of telegrams for Harding on the 4 March which, while congratulating him on his entry to office, will ask that his first act should be the recognition of the Irish Republic.[12]

Harry was getting impatient and wanted to return home during January of 1921. He was at Madison Square Garden when he was called on to speak at the end of a meeting. 'I let my heart run away with my head' and he got a severe mauling from the press for a few days. His friends told him that he just expressed what was in all their hearts, but feeling down-hearted he wrote a long letter to De Valera:

> I hope you will appoint a representative at your earliest convenience and would respectfully suggest the name of Art O'Brien, whom I understand is no longer able to carry on his work in London, and in my opinion he would be ideal for the position here.[13]

Dev reprimanded him over his Madison Square Garden address and advised on how to avoid a repetition:

> Your only hope when you have to speak is to prepare your speech carefully and give your summary to the press ... You must never allow the enthusiasm of an American audience to swing you off into thinking you are addressing our own people in Ireland. In any case it isn't the audience in front of you, you are addressing, but the whole American people through the press.[14]

Harry told Dev, in early February, that he had changed his mind about leaving America to go home. The mission in America was now going well and James O'Mara had agreed to remain on the job in the USA 'as long as Harry was there' so he 'did not think it desirable that he should end his work there'.[15]

On 27 January 1921, Michael Collins sent a memo to America that eventually reached Joe McGarrity. Enclosed with the memo was an article on the newly invented Thompson submachine gun that described it 'as a machine gun in the form of a pistol' and said it was soon to come on the market in America. Collins finished his memo with the comment, 'I'd like to know what it costs'.[16] Kathleen O'Connell, who had handled Dev's secretarial work, returned to Ireland at this time and brought dispatches with her from Harry to Michael about the cost and availability of Thompson machine guns.[17]

Harry went to the first conference of the Re-organised Clan-na-Gael in New York City on 20 March, 1921. He made a long speech in which he covered all his activities since he came to America in 1919 and he described to the delegates how the guerrilla warfare against British forces was progressing back home:

> Our people are steady, they have the offensive and are on the offensive still. ... the army of occupation is in the position of having to live in barracks and fly through the country in heavily armoured cars.

He unfolded his new scheme of action for the re-organised clan:

> We know that there are thousands of the men only willing and anxious to go over and help our people in the fight in Ireland. If this organisation would have close co-operation with us, we would simply ask that your executive be empowered to work in the closest harmony, taking Ireland as your headquarters, and you as a brigade, a base of supplies; that the orders would be obeyed implicitly by your officers who in turn would be

obeyed by you; that you will be prepared to support them financially; and that in each district the young men should have military discipline and military drill. We feel sure that if you can give your support you can now become an auxiliary of the Irish Republican Army ... I can guarantee that any man who is prepared to go and who has the necessary training will be given the opportunity to take his place in the firing line.

When he had mentioned this plan before the Clan-na-Gael split, Judge Cohalan said 'you know, Mr Boland, that there is such a thing in America as the Espionage Act and that we are American citizens and of course could not do anything against American law'. Harry had more to say about the idea he was advocating:

We have planned to keep the fight going for three years, and in our own quiet way we have England on the run. We lack a few military leaders which I am sure this organisation can supply. You can now know that you are in an organisation in close touch with the Irish Republican Army.[18]

Joseph McGarrity, leader of the Re-organised Clan-na-Gael, recommended a card index system which amongst other details would require each member to say whether he was ready to answer a call for military service. He also proposed that men who had been in the American Forces of the First World War be formed into units or camps and made available to give their advice and service if needed.[19] Following Harry's address the conference agreed to set up a secret military committee composed of men with active service experience to work with the executive.[20]

When the convention was over Joe McGarrity worked on supplying the IRA in Ireland with some of the Thompson machine guns. He bought some of the guns and through his new Clan-na-Gael organisation recruited two former US army officers, both of them Irish-born, to return to Ireland to train the IRA in the use of the weapons. Ex-Lieutenant Patrick Cronin who had fought on the Mexican border and in France against the Germans in the First World War and ex-Major James Dineen, a commander in the same European war, brought at least two Thompson sub-machine guns to Ireland and others were smuggled in later.[21]

It was to Harry's tailoring shop in Middle Abbey Street that the American officers reported to show the guns to IRA leaders. Kathleen Boland got in touch with Joe O'Reilly and he called Diarmuid O'Hegarty, Gearóid O'Sullivan and Liam Mellows to handle the guns and meet the Americans one Saturday afternoon.[22]

Since Liam had returned to Ireland he had become Director of Purchases in charge of importing arms and ammunition. These machine guns were used in Ireland to attack British troops in late June – in an attack on a troop train bringing a detachment of Gordon Highlanders to the Curragh. A report sent to the State Department in Washington from the American consul in London said:

> The Irish Republican Army has secured in some manner some Thompson guns from the United States ... It appears from what is published in Irish newspapers that at least on two occasions, Thompson guns have been landed in Ireland from the United States but I can obtain no information as to how or when this was done.[23]

Joe McGarrity, making use of all his American connections, purchased a large quantity of arms and ammunition, about 490 Thompsons, drum and box magazines, and a big supply of .45 calibre ammunition. Harry had received a letter from Éamon de Valera a week before warning him 'that British consuls at important ports in the USA had been directed to furnish direct reports of suspicious cargoes'.[24] But still Joe and Harry made arrangements with the captain of a coal-boat named the *Eastside* to smuggle the arms from New York to Ireland. US agents seized the boat while it was docked in Hoboken near the Hudson River and this was a big loss to Clan-na-Gael and to Harry's plans.[25]

De Valera faced criticism in Dáil Éireann in March over the high expenditure of the Irish Mission in the USA. Michael Collins, Minister for Finance, hinted that expenditure in America might not be covered by the amount of money collected. President de Valera had to defend the level of expenditure of the Irish mission in Dáil Éireann:

> In America they had three million square miles to cover and it was only now being organised ... After all the expenses of the first Loan were paid, he calculated they would have $4,000,000 dollars left.[26]

Harry and James O'Mara were planning a big convention of the AARIR in Chicago on 18 April when Dev wrote to Harry telling him that they would have to cut down considerably on their American establishment. The maximum outlay allowed for the maintenance of the diplomatic and political systems during the following year must not exceed $100,000. He said that many of the activities now being carried out by the American mission should be handed over to the AARIR and suggested a levy for each member of the organisation. He wanted all offices, including the Benjamin Franklin Bureau in Chicago, the flagship of James O'Mara, closed by 1 June. All surplus workers would be transferred home to Ireland.

Five thousand delegates representing the forty-eight states of America turned up for this first convention of the AARIR. They showed great enthusiasm and when Harry spoke about the proposed levy in his speech the convention pledged itself to raise $1,000,000 for Ireland. Although differences arose between some delegates as to the best way to proceed to gain recognition of the Irish Republic an acceptable agreement was reached. Harry and James O'Mara were pleased that good officers had been elected although Harry had to involve himself 'in many little intrigues' to get the right men elected. Edward L. Doheny was re-elected President and the other officers were men and women who could be trusted to work in close co-operation with members of the Irish mission.[27]

James O'Mara wrote an angry letter to De Valera on 25 April:

> A cable from you was read at the great Convention of the American Association for Recognition of the Irish Republic asking for a guarantee of a million dollars yearly. It was translated into action by levy of five dollars a member of every member of the Association – which practically includes every active person of our race. Neither Mr Boland or (*sic*) myself was consulted on the matter. There are nearly three million dollars lying idle here to the credit of the American trustees at the disposal of your government ... to use your own words when we last discussed the matter: "crops will not grow on trampled ground". I would advise you to promptly send someone to this country who has your confidence if such a person exists, and having done so don't constantly interfere with his work.[28]

De Valera wrote a conciliatory memo to Harry on the 29 April but it was mid May before he received the letter. Dev referred to the future role he had in mind for Harry:

> At times the pressure of business and correspondence is very great. I wish you were here, Harry. I badly want an assistant, not tied to any particular department, but free to deal with those one hundred and one odd jobs that are daily turning up and needing personal attention, but which I cannot really attend to myself. When you have cleaned up over there and put them on a permanent basis report here.[29]

This was not the type of assignment that Harry had wished for – he preferred to have a part in the fighting line. He had written to De Valera on 28 April saying: 'I again repeat that if my personal wishes were consulted, I would be home to take my place alongside the men who are bearing the brunt of the battle'.[30]

On 30 April James O'Mara tendered his official resignation to Éamon de Valera stating, 'I tender my resignation as the most emphatic protest that I can make against what must be the utter disruption and destruction of organised American aid'. He also placed his resignation as Sinn Féin TD for South Kilkenny in the hands of Canon Doyle, President of Sinn Féin for South Kilkenny.[31]

In a letter to Harry on 13 May Dev said he now believed that 'except in a crisis in which America's own interests were involved and when it might be convenient to hit England through us, is there any chance of securing recognition?' He advised Harry to concentrate on the provision of funds to help them to carry on the fight and do reconstructive work at home.[32] Dev told him 'you will have yourself to remain on, I fear, despite the fact that your are badly needed in other directions'.

On 25 May, 1921, James O'Mara's resignation as a trustee of Dáil Funds was accepted by the Cabinet of Dáil Éireann. Stephen O'Mara, a brother of his, and Mayor of Limerick, was appointed as representative and agent for the trustees.[33] James went to Toronto and spent some time travelling in Canada before going home to Ireland six weeks later.[34]

John Devoy, in the *Gaelic American* alleged that Harry was using money contributed by Irish-Americans as Bond Money in an attempt to smash The Friends of Irish Freedom movement. He first denounced him for spending too much money on the Chicago AARIR Convention which he described as only 'a mass meeting composed of "delegates" gathered from all over the country whose expenses were paid by lavish expenditure of the Irish Republic Bond Money and had no right to speak for the American Irish'.[35] Then he upbraided Harry for spending $10,000 in Pittsburgh in an attempt to compete with a meeting organised by Bishop Gallagher on behalf of the Friends to plead for recognition [a meeting of the AARIR had clashed with meeting of the Friends of Irish Freedom]. Bold massive headlines in the *Gaelic American* newspaper proclaimed:

The 'Lord High Executioner' of the Clan-na-Gael who has failed to disrupt it, expends $10,000 dollars of the Irish Republic Bond Money contributed by the Clan and the Friends of Irish Freedom in a futile attempt to spoil an Assemblage at which Bishop Gallagher pleaded for Recognition – Brass bands, Special Trains, Big Advertisements in the Daily Papers, Fireworks, Flash Light Pictures and other devices of the Cheap Politician.[36]

In April, 1921 Kitty received a letter from Harry which was short and guarded because he had not heard from her and he did not know where he stood. Kitty replied by return and explained that she had written a letter to him early in October and she wondered if he had ever received it – he did not. But now she was delighted to get Harry's letter and she felt happy that he had not forgotten her. She said she feared she was being neglected for another Kathleen – Ireland:

> I'm greatly afraid that the other Kathleen comes first in yr (your) affections – I'm only an after thought! Anyway yr (your) first love seems to be holding her own very well and I'm braving it very well too!!

Kitty described her feelings:

> You will be amused to hear yr (your) other pal whose photograph you sent me with yr (your) own slept in the same house as I was in, one night but we never met. Neither of us were interested! I'm afraid if it had been Harry, things would be somewhat different. – Some Night! Goodbye to the good old days when we made things hum at the Greville Arms.

She joked about taking a trip out to see Harry in the USA but then had second thoughts. Still she would seriously like to see Harry again and she remembered him often in her thoughts:

> I'd love to see you again, what luck that we should be so far apart (+ life so short!). What of all those fascinating women over the herring pond – have you not fallen a victim? Anyway I am delighted that you haven't forgotten those happy days we spent together because I haven't. It will soon be a year now ... Harry I never forget you + often say a little prayer for you + long for happy time (sic) to meet you again. Do you remember the lake? It will soon be time to go out here again now + I know I'll be often wishing you were near me.

She finished by saying:

> Now be a good sport and write to poor Kitty soon again ... When writing

say if there is any chance of us meeting soon again. Could you not come
even on a short holiday?

Wishing Harry goodbye, she said, 'this is not a love letter, because
you didn't write one. So you will have to be content with no
kisses!!'[37]

The 'Partition Election' was held in Ireland on 24 May, 1921. The
Government of Ireland Act 1920 which set up the partition of
Ireland committed the British government to stage elections to the
two parliaments provided under the act, the parliament of Northern
Ireland and the parliament of Southern Ireland. Dáil Éireann, the
Republican government, set up in accordance with the 1918 general election mandate, decided to recognise these elections so that
the will of the people in regard to self-determination would be
demonstrated. Dáil Éireann recognised the elections but not the
partition of Ireland. Nomination for the elections was fixed for 13
May and the proportional representation method of voting would
be used for the first time in an Irish general election.

When nomination day arrived only Sinn Féin candidates
were proposed for 124 of the 128 seats in the twenty-six counties.
Four Unionists were similarly unopposed for the Trinity College
constituency. All 128 candidates were returned without a contest.

Harry, although in America, was chosen as a Sinn Féin candidate for the constituency of Mayo South–Roscommon South.
Only four candidates were nominated in all for this four seat constituency and they were all returned unopposed. Representing the
constituency with him were three other Sinn Féiners, Thomas
Maguire, Daniel O'Rourke and William Sears.[38]

Familiar names were gone in other constituencies – James
O'Mara had resigned his seat before nomination day in South
Kilkenny and was not re-nominated by Sinn Féin. Diarmuid
Lynch had resigned as TD for South-East Cork ten months previ-
ously and was not considered. This time several Sinn Féin women
deputies were elected including Mary MacSwiney, Kathleen Clarke,
Countess Markievicz, Margaret Pearse, mother of Pádraig and
Willie, Katherine O'Callaghan and Dr Ada English.

The story was much different in Northern Ireland where in
the partitioned six counties every seat was contested. Unionists returned 40 representatives and had a majority in the north-east cor-

ner. Sinn Féin had six of their candidates elected while Nationalists took another six seats. The overall result in the whole country was 130 seats for Sinn Féin, 44 for Unionists and 6 for northern Nationalists – this showed nearly a three-quarters majority against partition.

Harry heard that Joseph Scott, of Los Angeles, a member of AARIR, had canvassed the western states for President Harding and he was a personal friend of the president. Harry wanted him to come to Washington so that he could present a case for Ireland's independence to President Harding. 'If Scott were here he could go up to the White House and see the president without appointment and could also be received at any time by the members of the cabinet'. Scott did come to Washington and waited for his opportunity to make an approach to President Harding.[39]

Since May moves had been afoot in London and in Dublin to attempt to find a solution to the Irish problem. In mid-May Lloyd George admitted that they had failed 'to restore order', that they wouldn't succeed in doing so for some months but they would get there in the end.[40] Churchill said, in the same debate, that it was of great public importance to get a respite in Ireland. The British were getting a bad reputation and the problems in Ireland were poisoning their relations with the United States. They could continue to go on but they should do everything to get a settlement.[41] De Valera, Harry Boland and the other members of the Irish mission in the USA were having an impact. In an interview for the *New York Herald* in May, De Valera expressed a willingness to open conversations with Lloyd George.[42] Around the same time, through the mediation of Art O'Brien, Ireland's representative in London, De Valera spoke to General Smuts who later had lunch with the king. Smuts pressed him to use the occasion of his speech at the opening of the Belfast parliament to make a grand gesture of reconciliation to the people of southern Ireland. General Smuts, at the king's request, wrote a letter to Lloyd George stating that 'the present situation in Ireland tended to poison both their empire relations and their foreign relations'.[43] The king made his speech to the Northern Ireland parliament and said:

> I speak with a full heart when I pray that my coming to Ireland today may prove to be the first step towards an end of strife amongst her people ...[44]

His initiative went further when he urged the British cabinet to use the opportunity to open talks with Sinn Féin. Lloyd George wrote to De Valera inviting him to a conference in London. After an exchange of letters between the two leaders, a truce was arranged and armed hostilities were suspended. De Valera then agreed to meet Lloyd George in London.[45]

The American consul in London reporting to the State Department in Washington at this time stated:

> I am informed by one who should know that Lloyd George ... uneasy as to the power of the Irish in Australia, South Africa and the United States ... decided that efforts must be made by him to obtain a settlement of this centuries-long problem.[46]

Harry wrote in his diary when the Truce was declared, 'Joyous day in Ireland ... Is it finish (end) – methinks not'.

Joe Scott, whom Harry had brought from Los Angeles, had a meeting with President Harding, seeking his good offices in the matter of the peace. Harding said that he had already had three interviews with Geddes, the British ambassador, and that he had urged him to impress on the British government the importance of settling the Irish question.[47]

Harry put the organisation headquarters in Washington at Stephen O'Mara's disposal when he arrived in Washington in order to help him raise the new loan targeted for $20 million. Éamon de Valera wrote to Harry on 4 August and said that if Harry could be in two places at once he would have him in Ireland but in case negotiations should break down it would be vital that Harry should be in America. He said that Patrick McCartan was home from Russia but that his views on that country were now diametrically opposite to what they had been before he left.

The first meeting of the Second Dáil was fixed for 16 August. All the elected representatives, including Boland, received a summons to this assembly. All the envoys abroad, who were elected in the 1921 general election, were recalled. This time crossing the Atlantic was different for Harry, as the British government had given him a passport, and he travelled in luxury – no more stoking in the sweltering furnace room. He sailed for Ireland on the *Olympic* on 13 August accompanied by Mary MacSwiney. He left with the good wishes of all – except John Devoy and Judge Cohalan.

John Devoy wrote a scurrilous editorial in the *Gaelic American:*

> The true friends of Ireland in America who have had experience of Mr Boland will wish him luck in the Old Land and pray that he may never return to America. He has done nothing but mischief here ... It was an unfortunate thing for Ireland that he was sent here, and though his actions in America probably had nothing to do with his recall, it is a great relief to be rid of him, even for a brief spell.[48]

GAIRLOCH AND KITTY KIERNAN

When President de Valera opened the first session of the Second Dáil on 16 August, he welcomed home the representatives from abroad. Harry Boland was not in the Dáil to hear De Valera as he was still about half ways between America and Ireland. Dev greeted the envoys as 'apostles of liberty'. Though they hadn't succeeded in getting the Irish Republic officially recognised abroad, he said that 'in the hearts of the people of the countries' which they had traversed 'the Republic was recognised'.[1]

The Department of Foreign Affairs had received reports from all the representatives and the following day they submitted the reports to Dáil Éireann. Harry said that Senator La Follette had introduced new senate resolutions on recognition and they had now been referred to the committee of Foreign Affairs and many American political friends of the Irish mission were agreed that this time there was more hope of recognition. One loyal supporter of Ireland's cause, Congressman Billy Mason, of Mason Bill fame, died of a heart attack in his apartment in a Washington Hotel in June. Before his death he had been instrumental in getting Illinois state legislature to pass a resolution urging President Harding to recognise the Irish Republic. Harry's report confirmed other state legislatures who had passed similar motions – New Jersey, Montana, Minnesota, Pennsylvania, and Wisconsin.[2]

The report received from Patrick McCartan, the representative in Russia said 'that the Russian Foreign Office had got the impression that Ireland would compromise and that this effected their readiness to recognise'.[3]

Harry was in Dáil Éireann on 25 August when President de Valera proposed that a Grand Committee of deputies be formed in case war was resumed and the whole body of Dáil Éireann could not meet for four or five months. This smaller committee could come together in times of emergency (they could keep a check on the cabinet's work) and could temporarily halt any measure which they did not favour. After further discussion, De Valera's proposal was adopted with a few changes to his original idea. The committee would be elected from present Dáil deputies on a provincial basis, of the 31 members to be elected seven were to come from

Connacht.[4] Harry was third in his province in order of votes and he was selected.[5]

Harry had spent the previous evening with De Valera and they discussed American affairs and the lack of progress in negotiations with the British.[6] Dev said that the British government were not going to agree to an Irish Republic.[7] He discussed his ideas for External Association with Harry and drew a large circle on paper representing the British commonwealth. Inside this circle he drew five smaller circles representing the five self-governing countries within the commonwealth. Then he drew a circle representing Ireland and put it outside the large circle containing the five small circles but touching the borders of the large circle. This explained the whole idea that Ireland could be associated with the commonwealth but not a member of it. Dev thought this was what they should go for in the negotiations. He had put the idea before the cabinet on 27 July and they approved it[8] – External Association became the target to aim for in negotiating with the British. De Valera, through this compromise, felt he would unify all sides – the Ireland he had in mind in his External Association idea would be an undivided 32 county state. Dev told Harry that he might have to return to America again when the talks got underway.[9]

Harry realised that things were not the same as when he was last home in 1920. He found a feeling of distrust where formerly there was comradeship. Michael Collins had written to him before he left America and he had warned him about the change in the leadership circle of the revolutionary movement:

> I think it right that you should be warned of the changes here. There's something about which I don't like, and I have the impression that the whole thing is pressing on me. I find myself looking at friends as if they were enemies – looking at them twice just to make sure that they really are friends after all. I mention no names. After all it may be a wrong impression that's got into me. Frankly, though, I don't care for things as they are now.[10]

Harry knew that De Valera and Collins had their differences over certain aspects of the Bond Drive in America but those were not serious matters and Harry was a unifying element between both.

Robert Barton, a member of the Dáil Éireann cabinet, who had been in prison for the previous 15 months, also found a different atmosphere when he returned. There was an obvious rift between

Brugha and Stack on one side, and Collins and Griffith on the other. Dick Mulcahy, who was Chief-of-Staff, was at loggerheads with his superior – Cathal Brugha, the Minister of Defence. Collins was supporting Mulcahy; Stack was supporting Brugha. Brugha distrusted Griffith because he was not a Republican. De Valera played the role of peace-maker and Robert Barton supported him. Barton had been a friend of Collins but he now felt that because he tried to take what he thought was an impartial stance in the quarrel, both sides regarded him with distrust. Barton thought that Collins also resented Dev for not siding with him.[11]

Michael Collins had been down in Granard and he asked Kitty to come to the horse show with him:

> When I was speaking to you I had a kind of idea that the Horse Show was coming off this week, but it's next week, and that's a very long time to wait to see you. I must continue that talk with you. At the moment I don't know if I'll be able to go down for the coming weekend but I'll try ... When do you come up yourself? I mean what day, and what time? Am really anxious to see you.[12]

Kitty wrote to Michael and in Collins' letter of 21 August, the day Harry arrived in Dublin at 6am, he thanked her for her nice note and said that Harry had arrived back – 'Will that entice you to come to town to give you that chance to which he is entitled? Do you remember what I said to you about this?' Harry was with him as he was writing this letter and he excused himself for not writing a longer note: 'I am laughing too much at Harry who yarns about things across the Atlantic'.[13] Michael wrote very frequently to Kitty that week, three times before Harry went to see her in Granard on the first Sunday after he arrived home. He went there with Michael, Seán MacEoin and Emmet Dalton[14] and he stayed there that Sunday night and the following day. There was a sing song, a drink and a laugh and a walk in the countryside just like the good old days of May, 1920 but the situation was changing by the day. Collins and Boland travelling the country together, were writing now to the same girlfriend, both expressing their love for her. Kitty was writing more letters to Michael. Harry was pressing his case – De Valera had told him that he might have to return to America soon and he thought that he had only a short time left to win Kitty's heart.

On 26 August Harry proposed that the Dáil approve Michael

Collins' appointment as *Aire Airgid* (Minister of Finance). When the question of the appointment of plenipotentiaries came up for discussion for the first time three main points emerged from the debate. De Valera said 'that he was perfectly willing to leave it to the cabinet on the undertaking that (in) any negotiation that took place there would be no suggestion that there would be any compromise on the principle of the status of Ireland'.[15] He wanted the plenipotentiaries to be nominated by the cabinet and ratified by Dáil Éireann. He also advised strongly 'that the negotiating plenipotentiaries sent over should be given a free hand other than the terms already laid down'.[16] De Valera also intimated for the first time that 'he did not propose on tactical grounds to be one of the plenipotentiaries himself'.[17]

Early the following week Harry and Michael Collins went to see Dev and they discussed the plenipotentiaries issue. When Michael wrote to Kitty the next day he said that he had to talk very high politics from 10.30 until 2.30 and that he stayed up most of the night advocating a case for Harry to be included in amongst the negotiating team.[18] Harry stayed with Dev in Glenvar that night and the next day he prepared his report on the activities of the re-organised Clan-na-Gael in America for a meeting of the Supreme Council of the IRB on 1 September. Kathleen O'Connell, Dev's private secretary typed the report for Harry. At this meeting the IRB, chaired by Michael Collins, also discussed the question of 'peace with honour or war' but no decision was reached.

Harry wrote to Kitty on 1 September and told her that 'the Chief' had informed him that he would have to return to America at a later date but that he would be in Dublin pending the start of the Peace Conference:

> I will tell you of my love and the great hopes thats (*sic*) in me that you and I may go hand in hand through life ... You are the only girl in the world ... (I) feel that I could laugh with you in your gladness ... Goodbye Sweetheart ... Ever yrs (*sic*) with love.[19]

The following Sunday Michael Collins went to Armagh with Harry and Seán Milroy and they had an escort of cars and Thompsons.[20] Collins was the Sinn Féin TD for Armagh and he addressed a huge gathering of all his Armagh constituents, both Nationalists and Unionists. He asked the Unionists to come in with the south and share in the government of their country. Harry then went to his own constituency of South Mayo-South Roscommon with his sister, Kathleen, and Frank P. Walsh who had helped both Harry and De Valera in America.[21] Harry and Michael wrote letters to Kitty about their visit to Armagh. They both knew that Kitty was going on a holiday to Donegal and they wished her a good rest up there. Harry finished his letter with a more imaginative last paragraph, 'If you see a wee bit of white heather, you might pluck it for me and send it for luck ...'[22]

Robert Barton delivered a reply to Éamon de Valera from the British cabinet about further negotiations. Harry and Michael went out that evening to Glenvar to see Dev and consider Lloyd George's reply. The tone of his letter was rigid and uncompromising and the last paragraph amounted to an ultimatum:

> You will agree that this correspondence has lasted long enough. His Majesty's government must therefore ask for a definite reply as to whether you are prepared to enter a conference to ascertain how the association of Ireland with the community of nations known as the British Empire can best be reconciled with Irish national aspirations. If, as we hope, your answer is in the affirmative, I suggest that the conference should meet at Inverness on the 20th instant.[23]

Collins had got a letter from Dr Fogarty, Catholic Bishop of Killaloe, a trustee of the Dáil Funds, which sounded a note of warning to the Irish leaders:

> I am very uneasy about the shape things are taking these days in the papers ... A war of devastation without the goodwill of the people behind it would be a ruinous disaster ... Apart from partition, which may be remedied in whole or in part, the people feel that there is in the proposals something very substantial to negotiate and work upon.

Michael Collins sent this letter to De Valera with a note telling Dev that he had intimated to the bishop that 'they were not without regard for their responsibilities'.[24] The bishop's message was reflecting public opinion at the time – they were becoming impatient and wanted action. A 'butter and margarine argument' appeared in the evening papers.[25] They decided that Dev would consult the cabinet of Dáil Éireann and draft another letter to be sent to Lloyd George who was holidaying in Gairloch, Scotland. Harry and Joe McGrath, a Dublin Sinn Féin TD, would travel to Gairloch and present the letter to him.

President de Valera had a long cabinet meeting on Friday and the cabinet reluctantly decided that they would respect Dev's wishes that he would not take part in the proposed conference with Lloyd George and the British representatives. Leaving out De Valera and subject to the approval of Dáil Éireann, five plenipotentiaries were appointed: Arthur Griffith, Michael Collins, Éamonn Duggan, Robert Barton and George Gavan Duffy.[26] At a meeting of the cabinet the following day, the members decided that Harry should accompany the delegation secretariat.[27] They then discussed their reply to the British and on Sunday Dev wrote the letter that Harry and McGrath were to bring to Gairloch.[28]

That Sunday, Harry and Collins relaxed in Croke Park. Kilkenny were playing Dublin in the Leinster Hurling Final and Michael was scheduled to throw the ball in. The *Freeman's Journal* reported that 'a multitude' was present. Both of them went to meet the players at the Hill 16 end of the stadium before they came out on the pitch. Kilkennyman, Alderman James Nowlan, introduced the players to Collins and Boland. Mick Collins told them, 'You are not only upholding a great game, but you are also upholding one of the most ancient and cherished traditions in Ireland'.[29] Harry was delighted when Dublin won.

The following morning, 12 September, Harry and Joe left Dublin by boat to deliver De Valera's letter to Lloyd George. They went via Manchester. Dev's plan was that Harry and Joe would deliver the letter to Lloyd George the following day (Tuesday) and they were not to discuss the contents with him. Dáil Éireann would assemble on Wednesday in the Mansion House to ratify the letter. The president would announce the names of the plenipotentiaries, approved by the Dáil, whom he planned to send to the conference with Lloyd George. He would then publish the letter along with the names of the plenipotentiaries.[30] That would make the conference with Lloyd George a *fait accompli.*

Harry and Joe arrived in Gairloch, having driven sixty miles in one of those Ford Model T open cars without heating of any kind. Lloyd George appeared from the back of the house. Boland noticed his lively quick step and his big mop of flowing white hair.

'You are from Ireland,' he said, '... Well! Well! Two Celts like myself, warm yourselves at the fire. Have you got news for me?'

Joe McGrath gave him De Valera's letter. He read it through. He read back some of it again. He came to the second paragraph.

He sat down at the table as he read this paragraph aloud to himself:

> In this final note we deem it our duty to reaffirm that our position is and can only be as we have defined it throughout this correspondence. Our nation has formally declared its independence and recognised itself as a sovereign state. It is only as the representatives of that state and as its chosen guardians that we have any authority or powers to act on behalf of our people.[31]

Lloyd George ran his right hand through his soft white hair and grimaced. 'He can't mean this', he repeated as he rose from his chair at the back of the table and began to pace across the room with one hand in his hair and the other on his hip.

'He knows we can't negotiate with him if he insists that Ireland is a sovereign state. We can't negotiate if he repudiates all allegiance to the crown and all membership of the British commonwealth.'

Harry kept looking at him. He remembered the Chief's instructions that they were to keep their mouths shut and not interpret the contents of the letter.

'You must alter the second paragraph. It will not do.'

Joe explained their instructions. Their job was just to deliver the letter. Lloyd George sat down again and spoke slowly this time.

'A wonderful opportunity missed. I could have given De Valera a Gaelic system of education, his own army and police force, his own flag and anthem. I asked him to use any phrase but "a sovereign nation". That's the one thing he can't have.'

He got up and paced the floor again.

'That's the end of it. My power is at an end? Could you get him to alter the letter?'

Joe cut in and said, 'The Dáil is to meet to sanction it.'

'Worse again, couldn't be worse! You must stop him. Telephone him. I'll ignore the letter as if I had not received it at all. My cabinet colleagues will not negotiate at all on those terms. They will insist on calling the negotiations off altogether. Will you take the letter back with you now?'

Joe and Harry looked at each other. Joe refused.

'You want to discuss it. Very well. I'll go out of the room. Ring the bell when you have decided what to do.'

Joe and Harry decided it would be better to phone Dublin and report what Lloyd George said. They rang a bell and the Prime Minister returned. He told them the nearest telephone was in Inverness – 80 miles away.

They arrived at Inverness after midnight and got through by phone to the Mansion House. The message they sent to De Valera was that Lloyd George objected to paragraph two of the letter and that he strongly exhorted that the meeting of Dáil Éireann for the next day should not be held and the letter should not be published. Joe spoke to Desmond Fitzgerald who said that he would pass on the message to De Valera.

Harry and Joe drove back to Holyhead.

The following morning De Valera was handed the message. He threw the note on the table.

'I told them,' said De Valera, 'that they were not to discuss the contents of the letter with him.'

De Valera went on with the Dáil Éireann meeting and carried out his programme as planned. Harry reached Kingstown that night and he went with Robert Brennan to see De Valera. The Chief was in bed when he called.

'We didn't discuss the contents of the letter with Lloyd George,' said Harry. 'But he gave us a lecture himself'.

'I know,' said Dev, 'he told you about all he was going to give us and only for him the British army would be making a desert of Ireland. He said the same thing to me.'

'He's some actor,' said Harry.

'No harm done, Harry,' said Dev.[32]

President de Valera proposed in Dáil Éireann that the plenipotentiaries be ratified. After some discussion the members of the Dáil passed a motion ratifying the five names put forward by the cabinet. Dev then proposed Erskine Childers, Harry Boland and Kevin O'Higgins as secretaries to the delegation. Cork deputy J. J. Walsh, said that he thought that one of the secretaries should have a knowledge of Irish and he urged the appointment of Piaras Béaslaí, a fluent Irish speaker who represented the Kerry-Limerick West constituency. Kevin O'Higgins agreed with J. J. Walsh and withdrew his own nomination, claiming that it would be a matter of considerable inconvenience to him if he had to go. Pádraig Ó Máille, an Irish speaker from Co. Galway, then proposed that

Erskine Childers and Harry be nominated. Piaras Béaslaí said it was not necessary to have the secretaries ratified by the Dáil. He suggested that their appointment be left to the Ministry's decision.[33]

At their meeting on 3 October, the Dáil cabinet decided to appoint Erskine Childers and Fionán Lynch, an Irish speaking deputy from the Kerry-Limerick West constituency, as secretaries to the Peace Conference.[34] Subsequently John Chartres was added to the list.[35]

It was a mistake that Harry was not used in the negotiating team – he understood Collins better than any other Dáil deputy and was loyal to Dev. He was particularly suited to be a courier between London and Dublin, since De Valera did not go with the negotiating team. He was always able to bring Michael Collins and De Valera together.

Dev wanted Harry to return to America and Harry wrote to ask him not to request him to return to America. He felt that there was a strong possibility that the Truce would break down and that war would resume and if this happened he wanted to be with the fighting men in the line of fire. If war came he would never forgive himself for being so far away.

As Harry waited for Dev's reply he wrote to Kitty. Besides saying that he was feeling lonely and that he was always thinking of her, he mentioned for the first time that he knew he had a formidable opponent in his bid for her hand. 'Let me say good night, sweet love, and I am certain I will win you against the formidable opponent with which (sic) I am faced'.[36]

Dev's reply came on 20 September:

> Notwithstanding your protestation, it is absolutely necessary that you return to the United States. I see the force of all you have put forward, but you will understand that it cannot be a question of personal likes in this case. You know you cannot be replaced in the United States just now, whilst we have men enough for the fighting line.
>
> There is a further consideration I am loath to mention: It is unwise to have all our eggs in one basket in the phase about to open. The worst may happen – we must have reserves outside the country, and you have been so closely in touch all through, you'll be well fit to head another rally and carry on.[37]

Three days later Harry received a letter from the Under Secretary for Foreign Affairs directing him to return to America and to resume his position as representative of the Republic in Washington. He enclosed Harry's credentials and £100 to cover the expenses of his journey. He told Harry that his salary as representative was increased to $10,000 as from the 30 September.[38]

During his last fortnight in Ireland Harry relaxed. He went to Navan Races with Joe McGrath, Austin Stack and Jim Clarke and they adjourned to the Gresham Hotel afterwards where they met Michael Collins. On the last Sunday in September Harry went to Croke Park to see a benefit hurling match between Dublin and Leix. The proceeds from the match were to help a Dublin Brigade IRA commandant who was badly wounded in the Custom House attack. Dublin won and Michael Collins presented the medals. Harry felt lonely leaving Croke Park that day because he knew he would be going to America in a week's time and he did not know how long he would be away.

In his last week in Ireland Harry wrote four letters to Kitty begging her to marry him:

> Is it not peculiar that Mick Collins and me (sic) should both long to marry you. I am wondering how it is that he and I have been thrown so much together and now we are in competition for the hand and love of a lady.[39]

He also told her:

> I cannot imagine life without you and promise to love and adore you always as I do now and have done since I saw you first in Granard ... I am coming on Monday to hear from your own sweet lips the answer to my pleading that you will be my wife and I know you will answer 'Yes'. You and I then for America for just a little while – home again to a free Ireland where we shall live one grand long life of love and joy.[40]

He went down to Granard three days later and stayed overnight but did not get the answer he hoped for. He wrote to Kitty at 4am on the day of his departure from Dublin to Cork to catch the boat to America. He had returned from Vaughan's Hotel where 'all that (sic) is best in our movement' had given him a rousing send-off party. Collins had been there and Harry told Kitty that he had spoken directly to Michael at the function about their love affair with her:

> I told Michael how matters stood between us and he, I fear, was most upset ... I told him as well as I could that you and I are engaged and further that if he (M) had not entered into yr (your) life that I wd (would)

now have you as my very own wife. Of course he was upset and assured me that it did not follow if you did not marry me that you would marry him.[41]

Harry was going to fight for his Kitty's hand:

I, no less than any other man cannot soar to such heights of altruism as to say that I wd (would) willingly give you up to another, I have a firm and final resolve to make you my wife and until you have decided otherwise I will try my 'damnedest' to convince you that you and I are destined to tread life's path together.[42]

Harry considered Kitty's feelings and became more sensible about the love affair later in the letter:

I can quite see that you are rent and torn with conflicting emotions and wonder what is best for you to do as between me and M. Let me offer you an advice! On tomorrow morning (Sunday) after yr (your) prayers go for a nice walk by the cool roadside and go alone, forget all the romance of having two suitors such as M and I, ask yourself honestly and fearlessly which of the two wd (would) you be happier with and which of us you love and feel you could be happy with, having made up your mind go right ahead and decide to be a one man woman and may I be the lucky man.[43]

Harry began his long goodbye:

Kitty, a leanbh, write to me and say that you will come to me as soon as possible so that we may join together in what must be perfect bliss and joy ... Mick will, I have no doubt, press forward his suit as best he can. I only ask that you will do whatsoever you think and feel is best for you to so do.[44]

After five hours' sleep Mick got up to see Harry off at Kingsbridge. Harry wrote to Kitty from Cork and told her 'I need not say to you how much I love him, and I know he has a warm spot in his heart for me, and I feel sure in no matter what manner our triangle may work out, he and I shall be always friends'.[45]

In Cork Harry was delighted to hear from Mary MacSwiney that De Valera and Lloyd George had agreed on a formula for a Peace Conference. Having heard this news Harry wrote to Kitty from Cork:

You will know by now that we have agreed to the conference, but what may come of it I cannot say. We will know very soon if it is to be Peace or War. If peace, I will be home in about six months. If war, I shall be in America until Dáil Éireann replaces me, and I would just love to have you come to America where we will spend our honeymoon in perfect bliss![46]

On Sunday, 2 October, shortly before he went aboard the *Celtic* at 11.30am he wrote another letter to Kitty:

I want to say Slán leat to my own Kitty, and I wish you a very happy and pleasant time in Dublin next week. Write to me often and I shall be happy ... Say a wee prayer now and then for your wandering Lover.[47]

HOME TO VOTE ANTI-TREATY

Harry left Queenstown for New York. According to the *Irish Independent*:

> Accompanied by the Lord Mayor of Cork and Mr Barry Egan, Mr H. Boland TD, the Irish Ambassador to America, reached Cobh on Saturday night en route to America ... Objects of interest were two blue Irish terriers indigenous to County Kerry which Mr Boland was carrying out to the States as presents for friends.[1]

In an interview with the *Cork Examiner* Harry said he was returning to America to help float a $20,000,000 loan. Stephen O'Mara, Mayor of Limerick, was in America and the money would be raised under his direction. He said he wanted to explain to the American people that even though the Irish Republican Army commanders had signed a truce with the British army commanders thousands of Irish soldiers were still in jail and there could be no peace until these prisoners-of-war were released. Referring to the coming Washington Disarmament Conference he felt that the English representatives could not face the American people until they had first made peace with Ireland.[2] Harry was sent to America for another reason – Dev wanted to prepare the Irish-Americans for a probable External Association settlement for an undivided Ireland.[3] Harry's instructions were to break this news in America by degrees as the negotiations progressed.

Sailing with Harry on the *Celtic* was Dr Phelan – a native of Johnstown, Co. Kilkenny – Bishop of Sale, Melbourne, Australia. He had met Michael Collins a fortnight before and it was arranged that he would use his visit to America to boost the Irish cause and address some public meetings there.[4] He was glad Harry was a fellow passenger and he used the opportunity to acquaint himself with the negotiating strategy in Ireland. While the *Celtic* was on the high seas, the delegation of plenipotentiaries left Dublin for London. Bishop Phelan wondered why President de Valera had not headed the delegation. Harry supported Dev's action:[5] 'De Valera is the president of the Republic. If he went to the conference he could accept nothing less than a Republic, and he knows that a Republic will not be granted'.[6] The majority of the members of

159

Dáil Éireann agreed that De Valera should not go.[7] Barton said, 'If De Valera remained in Ireland we could always break off negotiations ... and still have De Valera in the background ... If he remained in Dublin the scene of negotiations must return there before the final rupture'.[8]

Bishop Phelan asked Harry about the powers of the plenipotentiaries. Harry told him that a meeting had been held the week before in which the powers of the plenipotentiaries were defined – what they might accept from the British government and what they were bound to refuse.[9] He was referring to a unanimous decision of the cabinet at their meeting of 7 October, when the president's outline draft for a Treaty of External Association was approved as the basis of an acceptable settlement.[10] The delegates were also told: 'It is also understood that the complete text of the draft treaty about to be signed will be similarly submitted to Dublin and reply awaited'.[11]

Harry told the bishop that if he should speak about Ireland in America that the best lines he could follow would be to assure the American people that they could place their utmost confidence in the Irish representatives, then in London. They would wring the last ounce from the British government.[12]

Though Harry did not realise it he was being watched and investigated by the office of the Secretary of State in Washington. A telegram arrived ahead of him from the American Consul in Queenstown saying that 'Harry Boland, representative Irish Republic, sailed Queenstown to New York, 2 October, to assist raising $20,000,000 for Dáil Éireann'.[13] A letter was sent from the State Department to the Commissioner of Immigration, Ellis Island enquiring if Harry Boland had entered the country legally. Inspector Traubner reported that Harry Boland was in possession of a British passport and there was no irregularity.[14]

When he arrived in New York City Harry was delighted to find a cablegram from Kitty waiting for him. He wrote back soon afterwards saying that he was still hoping that she would come out and join him in America and that they would go on their honeymoon to California. He told her that he would be in Chicago later in the month but he would not go to California until she arrived to marry him.[15] Harry wrote six letters to Kitty in October asking her to join him in America. In mid-October he wanted to know how Kitty felt about him: 'I am hopeful that your letter will tell me that you are very happy and have bought the Ring and further that you intend to wear it'. He tried to make her a little jealous: 'Mrs O'Mara's sister is with her as a companion and we are sure to have a good time together. Watch me when you arrive and note what a wonderful dancer I have become ... I hope Helen (Kitty's sister who had just married) will send me a wee piece of wedding cake so that I may sleep on it and dream of my own sweet girl; You! I'll never be happy again until I claim you for my very own. You – most elusive of all the "Restless Sex".'[16]

Two days later he used a different strategy as he described New York in great detail:

> Writing of New York reminds me of you, it is a city with a wonderful charm all its own, a city of strong appeal to youth, full of joy and vivacity ... I know you will love it and I can see you now either strolling on Broadway doing the shows or treading the Plutocratic (*sic*) Fifth Avenue in open-eyed amazement ... but most of all I want to see you here for my own selfish sake.[17]

He went on to tell her that he was joining an athletic club and he hoped to get into great form again: 'A few weeks training will make me slim and fit, I will not rest until I can do the hundred yards in ten and a half and the mile easy'. He finished by saying: 'If any one told me that I should ever be so madly in love with anybody as I am with you, I would have laughed and said impossible! ... I won't cross the Rocky Mountains until you cross them with me en route to California!!!'[18]

Harry was disappointed he was not getting any reply from Kitty: 'I have had letters from Mick (Collins) and Emmet (Dalton) from London; with all their troubles they had time to write to me – and you have not even posted a wee note, God forgive you!!!' He wanted Kitty to send on a photograph of herself to him, 'Don't forget the wee photo. I want to carry it in my watch'.[19]

At home in Ireland Michael Collins had resumed his romance with Kitty as soon as Harry left for America. Michael was busy at the Peace Negotiations in London but still he was writing love letters to Kitty almost every day. From the second week of October, Kitty was writing to Michael every day and sometimes twice a day. She wrote to him and spoke about Harry:

> I know how you feel about the Harry business, that is why I mention it so early in this note. It is wise what you say about H. (Harry) etc. I haven't

written yet. I don't know exactly what to say. I wish you were here, it would be so much easier to discuss it. It was obvious without my saying a word to him ... I told H. (Harry) I didn't love him, and he was prepared to risk it with the idea that I might grow to love him, and I think I told you all the other little things before.[20]

Soon after that Kitty explained her relationship with Harry to Michael:

I realise it's a foolish idea for a young girl to get into her head, but I can't help it and I do know that everything depends on the man once a girl gets married ... that's why I even entertained the idea that I could ever possibly marry H. (Harry), and he knows this too. I may be wrong but I think he is capable of deeper affection (for me) than most men, but he also knows that I don't love him – it's no effort for him to be a great lover and of course (he gets) no thanks.[21]

At the end of October Kitty wrote to Michael saying: 'My hand is getting cold. I can't write, but I want you to know that I love you. I love you oh so much ... I'll not fall out with you again, even if you want to'.[22]

In October Harry was talking about External Association for a 32 County united Ireland:

On the outcome of the London conference depends the future of Ireland ... Final peace between the two nations can come with Ireland's independence, and with that only ... The six counties (Antrim, Armagh, Down, Derry, Tyrone and Fermanagh) which have been partitioned from Ireland by British Act of Parliament are not an historical entity ... Two of the six counties are Republican in majority, viz, Tyrone and Fermanagh ... The six-county area is the burial place of national saints and the high kings and great warriors of Ireland.[23]

In a report sent to Éamon de Valera, dated 18 October, Harry said:

I fear that the British propagandists have succeeded in convincing the mass of Americans that England's offer to Ireland embraced full Dominion government. Therefore, I endeavoured to offset this propaganda by analysing the proposals and quoted the Bulletins with good effect.[24]

In a letter to Kitty at the end of October he said, 'I have to prepare all my speeches carefully now so that I may not prejudice the peace talks'.[25]

John Devoy and the Friends of Irish Freedom did not agree with the policy of External Association:

The inspiration for External Association came from De Valera ... On 16 August in Dáil Éireann he said 'we are no republican doctrinaires ... We (John Devoy and The Friends of Irish Freedom) are opposed to external as well as internal association of Ireland with the British empire'.[26]

Harry wrote to the Secretary of State in Washington saying he would be happy to present his credentials as Envoy of the Republic of Ireland, but the Secretary never met him as the American government did not recognise the Irish Republic.[27]

He was sharing an apartment with Stephen O'Mara and his wife in Washington. Stephen had done a lot of preliminary work on the Bond Drive and he planned to launch it in Washington DC and in the State of Illinois on 13 November. Harry was exploring every avenue in the Senate, with the help of Senator La Follette, trying to get Ireland's friends to consider what action would be best to strengthen the hands of the delegates in London. They thought it might take the form of a resolution but Harry warned that this should be carefully worded so as not to embarrass the London conference.

Kitty did not reply to the six letters he wrote in October. On the 30 October having addressed a meeting in Cleveland, he scribbled a quick note to her, 'I write to say I am thinking of you with love – thirty days today I sailed from Ireland – and not even a line or a postcard from you. God forgive you'.[28] Writing to Collins in November Kitty said 'if only H (Harry) and his friends – would stop storming Heaven with his prayers, I wouldn't be getting unhappy and such mixed and peculiar feelings'.[29] Kitty got Harry's short letter, chiding her for not replying to his letters, about the middle of November and she wrote to Michael on 15 November, saying she 'must really write Harry soon, got this yesterday. Poor Harry, he's getting used to me at last, and seems quite happy now TG'.[30] En route to Boston on 19 November Harry wrote a sharp and short letter to her: 'Why don't you write to me? Even if you have nothing to say, you can at least write and tell me to go to Hell!!!' That letter provoked Kitty into decisive action. She first wrote to Michael assuring him of her total love: 'Now I feel that it rests with me as well as you, and if you don't ever take advantage of my love when you know for certain that it's there (No Harry), and only for you, I believe all will be well, and we shall be a happy pair'.[31]

The Bond Drive was in full swing in Illinois and Washington DC. Harry wrote to De Valera telling him that the Illinois organisation had a membership of 96,000 and a scheme of organisation comparable to the Sinn Féin organisation in the general election of 1918. Stephen suggested that it would be a good thing to entertain a group of influential politicians in their Washington apartment around the time of the Disarmament Conference. Harry was not in favour of this but friends in Washington convinced him that it was very necessary.[32]

American Volunteers went to Ireland during the Truce as Daniel Sheehy an IRA man on the run in America related in his letter to Boland in December:

> I had been on the run for over 12 months before I got out here as a stoker. But I am ready at any time called upon to go back. I know it is my duty as a soldier of the IRA. What I want you to do, Harry, is to put my name down in the next batch of fellows going home after Xmas. I do not mind what part I am sent to. I am ready for action.[33]

Seán McMahon, the IRA quartermaster-general, acknowledged that the number of machine-guns on hand increased during the truce from six to fifty-one – almost all of these had been smuggled in from America.[34] The British army knew that the IRA had increased its armaments.

John Devoy addressed a meeting of the Friends of Irish Freedom in Baltimore and condemned the offer Lloyd George had made to De Valera in July. He denounced the partition of Ireland because the six county area contained two counties, portion of two others and the second largest city in the Province of Ulster, Derry, where the majority of the people did not want to be separated from the rest of Ireland. He said that it looked to him that if Britain offered real Dominion Home Rule to all of Ireland, the Irish people would accept it as a temporary settlement. He believed that the only real solution of the Irish question was total separation from England.[35]

American newspapers gave coverage to the Anglo-Irish negotiations in London as they progressed. On the last day of November they reported that De Valera said in Ennis, Co. Clare, 'we have gone as far as we can go, consistent with those principles for peace. We cannot and will not go any further'.[36] The Sinn Féin peace delegation returned to Dublin on 3 December with the draft of new Irish proposals.[37] After a meeting between the Sinn Féin plenipotentiaries and the Dáil Éireann cabinet the delegates returned to London. Prospects of the possible collapse of the Irish peace negotiations came on 4 December with Sinn Féin's rejection of the latest British plan and the Unionists' announced intention of ending the talks on the following Tuesday unless something definite developed before then.[38] The same day Éamon de Valera delivered a short address in Galway saying 'Freedom was never won without sacrifice: the country must be as prepared now to face sacrifices as it has been in the past'.[39]

Harry stepped off the train in Washington and as he walked towards the front exit the headlines in the newspapers of Tuesday, 6 December were staring him in the face – 'Irish Accept New Terms'. The report went on to say that at 2.15am a British cabinet minister came out of the conference and declared, 'An agreement has in fact been reached. The full terms will be given you for publication in Wednesday morning's papers'.[40] The difference between the two time zones of London and Washington made it possible for the American news editors to get the newsflash printed for the newspaper editions of that Tuesday. No details of the agreement made were given. Harry thought from the headline that the negotiators had followed their cabinet instructions that the very minimum they would accept was External Association, and that they had succeeded in getting that measure of freedom from the British government. Rashly, Harry issued a statement to the newspapers which appeared on Wednesday:

> A treaty of peace has been signed and an agreement reached between the representatives of the Irish nation and representatives of the British empire – an agreement that restores Ireland to the comity of nations ... We feel sure that the agreement reached between Britain and Ireland will be received in America with great joy.[41]

Comment in the American newspapers of Wednesday was guarded and general in tone because the terms of the agreement had not been studied. The observations by Judge Daniel Cohalan, spokesman for the Friends of Irish Freedom, were cautious because of his legal background, 'I desire to wait until all the details have been made known'.[42] The confusion in America was reflected in the comment of an active leader of the AARIR about the agreement, 'Any treaty entered into between Ireland and Great Britain and signed by Éamon de Valera, Michael Collins, Arthur Griffith and Robert Barton will vitalise in its operation the principle of government by the governed'.[43] The *New York World* stated, 'On what conditions exactly the new Irish state will be in association with the British empire has not been made clear'.[44]

On Wednesday night, having had an opportunity to study the full text of the articles of agreement, as published in the daily papers, Harry was asked to comment on the Bond issue and said that 'the Irish Republican Bond Certificates will be exchanged for 5% bonds as soon as the government of the Irish Free State is organised and operating. No change will be made as a result of the agreement entered into between the British government and the Irish plenipotentiaries'. He took advantage of the opportunity, to give an account of the whole Bond Drive in the United States since he arrived in America. 'In the first issue of Irish bonds a total of $5,400,000 was subscribed ... in the second issue, opened three weeks ago, subscriptions totalled $390,000'.[45] Americans had subscribed a total of almost $6 million apart from what they had subscribed to the American Committee for Relief in Ireland.

In Thursday's papers a statement appeared from Judge Cohalan, who, having read the text of the Irish settlement, termed it the greatest diplomatic triumph of Lloyd George's career. 'Lloyd George,' he said, 'has braced up the tottering British empire for the moment by attaching to it an apparently satisfied Ireland'. Diarmuid Lynch denounced the London agreement: 'With an Ireland swearing allegiance to a foreign king, the use of the term Irish Free State is an insult to the dead who died fighting for an independent Irish Republic'.[46] Harry issued a statement, published in Friday's newspapers, sharply criticising Judge Cohalan and Diarmuid Lynch:

> The statements of Justice Cohalan and Mr Lynch, national secretary, Friends of Irish Freedom against the Anglo-Irish peace pact would come from them with better grace had they stood by the existing Irish Republic in its hour of trial ...[47]

On Thursday night Harry and Stephen O'Mara attended a meeting in Washington where invitations had been sent out to wealthy Americans inviting them to subscribe to the Bond Drive. A good crowd turned up but they cancelled the Bond Drive on account of the London agreement and 'they turned the meeting into a meeting of rejoicings. Senators were present and they sang hallelujahs'. Harry made a speech in which he spoke against the Treaty and the following morning his address was reported in the *Manchester Guardian* as their representative in America was among the invited guests. Harry's speech opposing the settlement 'was on record five hours before President de Valera came out against the Treaty'.[48] He opposed the Treaty 'because it denied the recognition and the sovereignty of the Irish nation'. He was also against 'swearing allegiance to his Majesty King George V'.[49]

In Dublin that Thursday, Éamon de Valera said that he could not recommend the acceptance of this treaty either to Dáil Éireann or the country. The American papers published his statement the following morning:

> The terms of this agreement are in violent conflict with the wishes of the majority of this nation as expressed freely in successive elections during the past three years. I feel it my duty to inform you immediately that I cannot recommend the acceptance of this treaty either to the Dáil Éireann or to the country. In this attitude I am supported by the Ministers for Home Affairs and Defence ... A public session of Dáil Éireann is being summoned for Wednesday next at 11 o'clock ... There is a definite constitutional way for resolving all political differences, let us not depart from it.[50]

Arthur Griffith's statement was published in the American papers on the same day as De Valera's:

> I have signed the treaty between Ireland and Great Britain. I believe this treaty will lay the foundations of peace and friendship between the two nations. What I have signed I shall stand by, in the belief that the end of the conflict of centuries is at hand.[51]

The treaty caused division in America as well as in Ireland. Harry's mind was made up and he wrote in his diary on Friday, 'Hunting all upset until De Valera speaks against Pact. Happy again'.[52] The following day he issued a statement to the American press, 'The appeal of President de Valera to the Irish people to maintain a calm front at this crisis can be extended to all friends of Ireland in this country. The decision rests squarely on the men who are representatives of the Irish people'.[53]

Joe McGarrity in Philadelphia was confused like everyone

else. His paper, the *Irish Press* welcomed the agreement first, stating that 'Ireland's sovereign independence is acknowledged'. But in his next issue he condemned England for dividing the Irish by their offer and said that De Valera's rejection was 'sufficient evidence that the minimum standards of Ireland have not been secured'.[54]

On the Sunday Harry attended his last meeting of the re-organised clan. He was satisfied that the predominant feeling of the meeting was anti-Treaty but they decided to send a delegate [Joe McGarrity] to Ireland 'to make an investigation and bring back a report'.[55]

American senators and congressmen praised the Irish settlement as a happy ending to a political question that had long agitated the American people. American administration leaders expressed their gratification that the cause of a threatened embarrassment to the armaments conference had been removed.[56] Some conservative wealthy groups of Irish-Americans were quick to claim the peace terms as a testimonial to both the Irish plenipotentiaries and Lloyd George in the face of many discouragements.[57] Oil magnate Edward L. Doheny, National President of the AARIR, supported the Treaty: 'The accomplishment of the Irish Free State is what I have hoped for'.[58] But Fr Francis Duffy, former chaplain of the Fighting 69th Irish-American Regiment, discussing the situation before the League for Political Education, said that the partition of Ireland would create trouble for the next hundred years.[59]

The American press was overwhelmingly in support of the Treaty. An editorial in *The New York Times* said, 'De Valera is too much of a dreamer and a doctrinaire ... Had he gone to London as a delegate in place of Griffith and Collins he would have broken up the whole conference'.[60] The *Kentucky Irish American*, always sympathetic to Irish views, announced that 'throughout the world there is rejoicing that a treaty has been signed by the Sinn Féin and British cabinet which grants freedom to Ireland and raises her to the status of a Free State'.[61] There was a light-hearted touch in one comment of *The New York Tribune*, 'perhaps it may turn out that the Shan Van Vocht never really was the poor old woman, but that she was all the time the Dark Rosaleen gloriously young, with gleaming jewels in her raven hair'.[62] Harry felt that the bulk of the American people and almost all the American press supported the Treaty but the men and women who did all the work and organising, with some notable exceptions like Edward L. Doheny, were anti-Treaty in outlook.[63]

Harry received a letter from Kitty saying she wanted to take a full and deliberate survey of her own heart and mind before she decided on her future life. She said she had been keeping calm and cool and giving careful consideration to Harry's passionate proposal and that was the reason she had not written. Harry replied immediately saying that she was perfectly right to do so though he still felt that she should have written a note to him. He assured her that he was 'agreeable to wait three months or just as long as you wish'. He said he was prepared to hear the worst from her and now felt like a man 'reprieved'. He still loved her and he wished she could measure the love 'there's in my heart for you'. He replied to Kitty's letter by return of post because 'it may be I will be in Ireland as soon as this letter, for the great Crisis has come, and we must face it like men'. He hoped to vote on the Treaty but if the text of the Treaty as published in America was correct he would vote for its rejection. He hoped to see her for Christmas and he sent his love and kisses.[64]

In Dáil Éireann on 19 December Arthur Griffith moved the following motion, 'that Dáil Éireann approves of the Treaty between Great Britain and Ireland, signed in London on 6 December, 1921'.[65] Harry received a cable calling him home. He thought that he would not arrive in Ireland before the end of the big debate on Arthur Griffith's motion, so he sent the following cable to Dáil Éireann:

> As I cannot reach Dublin in time to take part in the Treaty discussions, I must insist on my right to vote. Having no official information, I am compelled to take my decision on the text as published here. I desire to record my vote against the Treaty and pray that Dáil will reject the instrument.[66]

He decided to go home as soon as he could get his affairs in order. Harry and Stephen O'Mara met the national directorate of the AARIR the following Saturday and Edward L. Doheny chaired the meeting. A few days later the national executive of the AARIR, knowing that Harry was leaving for Ireland adopted a resolution that 'the national executive committee tendered its heartfelt appreciation to Harry Boland ... for his splendid executive ability and tireless energy that have been of incalculable value to the cause of Irish freedom'. The first person to sign the resolution was the president of the AARIR, Edward L. Doheny.[67]

Harry went to a meeting of the re-organised clan executive on 21 December. He had $60,000 dollars for the Irish Republican Brotherhood. The IRB in Ireland decided in favour of the Treaty and so it was decided to lodge the money in the Merchants Bank, Washington in the names of H. J. Boland, Luke Dillon and Joe McGarrity. It would be handed over to the IRB when the executive of the re-organised Clan-na-Gael and Harry were satisfied that the money would be used by the IRB for the realisation of an Irish Republic.[68]

Máire Ní Bhraonain wrote to Harry from New York City, 'I see by this morning's paper you are to sail for home next Saturday ... I am glad you took the Chief's side ... The Ulster part of the treaty, I could never agree to ... I'd like to see you return to us even for a time.'[69]

Harry went to dinner on Christmas Day to the Carmelites in New York.[70] When he was packing for home he made sure to bring the Russian jewels with him and he sailed from New York aboard the American *Panhandia State* steamer with Liam Pedlar, Seán Nunan and Frank Dempsey. They celebrated the New Year of 1922 at sea.[71] He was going home to vote against the Treaty.

LIKE FATHER – LIKE SON

Seán O'Donovan, a Cork-born veterinary surgeon, met Harry at Queenstown. Seán had spent two periods in Wormwood Scrubs during the War of Independence and was engaged to Harry's sister, Kathleen.[1] As they travelled to Dublin by train Seán brought Harry up to date with the recent developments. At Kingsbridge Station Kathleen met her brother and he headed straight for Dáil Éireann – the vote on the Treaty was pending at any time and he did not want to miss it.

The debate on Arthur Griffith's motion 'That Dáil Éireann approves of the Treaty between Great Britain and Ireland signed in London on 6 December, 1921'[2] had gone on until 22 December when it adjourned until 3 January, 1922. The public session of Dáil Éireann was in progress when Harry arrived at about 4pm on 5 January and he was heartily applauded as he entered the chamber. He was there only for a half-hour when the session adjourned, but he did not like what he saw and felt and heard. He listened as the speaker read out a letter in Irish from Frank Drohan of the Waterford–Tipperary East constituency announcing that he regretted he felt compelled to resign from the Dáil as his heart and mind would not allow him to vote for the agreement and his local comhairle ceanntair Sinn Féin (Sinn Féin district council) demanded he support the settlement.[3] Many of the anti-Treaty deputies in the Dáil did not like the Christmas adjournment as they felt it gave influential public figures, who supported the Treaty in local communities, almost two weeks to put pressure on wavering anti-Treaty TDs to re-consider their decisions 'not to plunge the country into war'.

That evening Harry, Seán Nunan and Liam Pedlar went to see Éamon de Valera in Kenilworth Square where he was staying while the Dáil sessions were in progress. Seán and Liam went away early, but Harry remained until 11pm[4] and they discussed many aspects of the Articles of Agreement. Piaras Béaslaí said, 'Mr de Valera had become an object of hero-worship with Boland, and he determined to follow him through thick and thin'.[5]

Harry spoke at a private session of Dáil Éireann on Friday morning. He had heard that the Chief-of-Staff of the IRA, General Richard Mulcahy said in the Dáil that 'we have not been able to drive the enemy from anything but from a fairly good-sized police barracks' and he wanted to question that assertion. He started his speech by rubbing his chin and remarking that 'being a kind of stranger here' which elicited a good laugh in these tense hours and then he added:

> I would like to know if it is true that the Irish Republican Army that brought the British government to discuss terms of peace is not strong enough to take a good sized police barrack, because I know something at any rate about the difference in equipment that the army had when I left here last October and what it has today.[6]

Richard Mulcahy interrupted to say that he wanted to leave the room for a moment to get one of the references to deal with Harry's enquiry. Some minutes later Cathal Brugha asked Harry to repeat the question and he then dealt with the matter, in private, as the details might give information to the enemy.[7]

When the Dáil adjourned, Harry went to meet Michael Collins in the Gresham Hotel intending to hand over the Russian jewels. Harry gave the jewels to Michael who put them in his pocket and he also gave him a receipt from Ludwig Martens of the Russian Socialist Federal Soviet Republic for the second loan of $20,000.[8] Collins gave Harry a receipt dated 6 January. Harry said he heard that Michael had announced in the Dáil that he was engaged to Kitty. Michael told Harry 'that he (Harry) had little chance in that quarter now'. Collins spoke to him about the Treaty and he tried to get Harry to change his mind about voting against it. Michael told him that the agreement was the best they could get and that it was not a final settlement of the question between England and Ireland. He did not succeed in changing Harry's anti-Treaty stance and a quarrel developed between them.[9] In the course of the row, Collins took the jewels out of his pocket and threw them at Harry, saying, 'take these back, they are blood-stained'. Harry picked them up and left, but he also had the receipt for the jewels that Michael had given him.[10] Collins wrote to Kitty that day and said, 'Saw H. last night. He was friendly, of course, and very nice. I'm afraid though he was not so nice today, but not about you – I mean on the subject of you. I'm afraid he wasn't fair in his home coming in what he said about our side today. He's working like the very devil against us, but God is good'.[11]

When the public session of the Dáil opened later that evening the members were surprised when President de Valera said that he was coming before them to resign and he would ask for his ministers' resignations because he could not carry on while a certain section of the cabinet 'stands for one fundamental policy, and another section of the cabinet stands for a fundamentally opposite policy'. There was total silence as the president spoke about the events of the week preceding the signing of the treaty. On Saturday, the 3 December, the plenipotentiaries having come back from London presented the cabinet with a document 'which represented the proposals of the British government at that stage'. The document involved 'allegiance to the crown'. De Valera rejected those proposals and 'Cathal Brugha, Minister for Defence, pointed out that it meant definitely there would be a split in the country if such a document was signed'. The chairman of the delegation, Arthur Griffith, gave a guarantee that 'such a document would not be signed until it was submitted to this Dáil'. De Valera then said he was shocked and surprised when he read in the newspapers that the Treaty had been signed without any final consultation with him:

> So certain was I of that promise being fulfilled to the letter that when I heard an agreement had been reached I said, 'We have won'. And when I saw in the newspapers that the agreement that was reached was one absolutely incompatible with our position – a subverting of the state as it stands – I knew a step which was practically irrevocable had been taken.[12]

Harry knew when the plenipotentiaries had returned to London some alterations were made in the proposals but they were not fundamental in the cases of the oath of allegiance and partition clauses. All the Irish delegates agreed to sign the Articles of Agreement when Lloyd George declared that the signature of every member of the delegation was necessary or war would follow immediately. The bill had not been submitted, without signature, to the Dáil as promised. Arthur Griffith was questioned about this by three of the anti-Treaty group, Seán Etchingham, TD, representing Co. Wexford, Cathal Brugha and Éamon de Valera. He said:

> On that Saturday after I came back I was at the cabinet meeting, and I told them I would not break on the crown ... when I was going away the president asked me to try and get the thing back to Dáil Éireann. I tried, and I tried all I could, to get the matter kept back for a week. I could not succeed. I was faced with the responsibility of signing or not signing. The re-

sponsibility was placed on me and I signed. I protest against the misrepresentation that I was a man who pledged his word to something.[13]

Harry wondered why the delegation did not do as Joe McGrath and he had done in Gairloch when they travelled 80 miles to Inverness to phone to De Valera when they had met a complication. Even though De Valera was in Limerick on the very day that the Treaty was signed, the IRA were sufficiently well organised to get in touch with him from Dublin within a short space of time if a phone call had been made.

Michael Collins, countering De Valera's move to resign, put forward another way of getting a united cabinet and suggested that those members of the government who were opposed to the Treaty, with the president at their head, should ask for the resignations of those ministers who supported the Treaty, and have the house vote on that. Collins said he thought Dev's plan of having a vote taken on the personality of De Valera rather than on the motion on the agenda of approving the Treaty was 'a red herring'. Collins added as a parting shot 'We will have no Tammany Hall methods here. Whether you are for the Treaty or whether you are against it, fight without Tammany Hall methods'.[14] (Tammany Hall political methods were identified with a New York City corrupt system of politics in the 1800s.)

Harry spoke in favour of debating De Valera's resignation and then launched into his first attack on Collins:

> I presume the remarks of the Hon. Member for Cork were intended for me. I am sorry that he has seen fit to make such a suggestion. I will say this: that I don't know anything about Tammany Hall except this, that if he had a little training in Tammany Hall, and reserved some of his bullying for Lloyd George we would not be in the position we are in today ... We sent those plenipotentiaries to negotiate a treaty; we sent them from Dáil Éireann. They returned with a document, not to Dáil Éireann but to the southern parliament.[15]

Harry said that the Treaty denied even the existence of Dáil Éireann.

Éamon de Valera spoke in support of Harry. 'Mr Boland came back from America, and then there is talk of Tammany Hall; but I make up my mind for myself, now and always. Mr Boland didn't know anything about it until I myself told him this morning'.[16] Dev was visibly upset by insinuations of trickery and then he conceded that if they decided to have a vote on the Treaty within forty-eight hours he would be satisfied to withdraw his resignation proposal. Arthur Griffith agreed with this and Dev withdrew his threat to resign.[17]

When Harry went home to Marino Crescent that evening he was in a blazing temper after his row with Michael Collins. He gave the jewels to his mother and she hid them in a box in a hole in the back of the chimney recess behind the kitchen range.[18]

When the members of Dáil Éireann came together at 11.20am on Saturday 7 January the atmosphere was highly charged. Harry was the first speaker to rise and his slight nasal twang was distinctly trans-Atlantic.[19] In his first sentence he said he was against this Treaty and he objected to it 'because in my opinion, it denies a recognition of the Irish nation'[20] ... 'I am asked to surrender the title of Irishman and accept the title of West Briton' because he was being forced 'to swear an oath of allegiance to be faithful to His Majesty, King George V'. He was speaking from his heart:

> We were the heirs of a great tradition, and the tradition was that Ireland had never surrendered, that Ireland had never been beaten, and that Ireland can never be beaten. And because of that great spiritual thing we young men went out to follow our fathers ... Many deputies in this House know that my father himself had to fly from this country and suffer ... because he believed in a Republic. His son was privileged to stand on public platforms and to ask the Irish people to subscribe to the Republic – and they did. We stand, therefore, where our fathers stood before us.[21]

He argued strongly against what he regarded as the injustice of partition. He was willing to compromise somewhat on the issue of an Irish Republic for national unity but with the Treaty he was neither getting one nor the other. He regretted that old comrades were now divided and had the fondest memories of old times but he understood they were divided on fundamental principles and he thought that Lloyd George was bluffing with his threat of immediate war. 'If we reject that Treaty England will not make war on us,' he pleaded, 'if she does we will be able to defend ourselves as we have always done'.[22]

The morning passed as other speakers declared for or against the treaty. There was a long lunch and then the last speakers rose and they were all brief. At around 5pm the speaker called on Cathal Brugha to wind up the debate on behalf of the anti-Treaty side. For over an hour Cathal spoke, sometimes in Irish, then switching unconsciously into English and then back to Irish. He emphasised that 'if I were to accept this Treaty... I would be breaking the national tradition that has been handed down to us through the centuries'.[23] Arthur Griffith spoke for as long as Cathal Brugha but in a quieter tone and finished his submission by describing the benefits of the Articles of Agreement. 'The Irish people get for the first time in seven centuries, a chance to live their own lives in their own country and take their place amongst the nations of Europe'.[24]

A large crowd began to gather outside University College. In the chamber a clamour of excitement announced the calling of the roll and De Valera answered 'Ní toil' (Against) followed soon afterwards by Griffith's response of 'Is toil' (For). Harry's turn came and in a firm clear audible unmistakable voice he replied 'Ní toil'. The scrutineer counted the votes and the speaker, Eoin MacNeill, stood up and announced the result. 'The result of the poll is sixty-four for approval and fifty-seven against. That is a majority of seven in favour of approval of the Treaty'.

Michael Collins showed no animosity towards De Valera. 'The president knows how I tried to do my best for him. Well, he has exactly the same position in my heart now as he always had'.[25]

President de Valera rose slowly to say the last word. 'It has been four years of magnificent discipline in our nation. The world is – is looking at us – now ... '[26] His lips twitched.

He sat down and buried his face in his hands.

The Ship has a New Captain

Dev met the anti-Treaty members of the Dáil at the Mansion House the day after the Treaty was ratified to discuss what action they should now take as they were a minority in Dáil Éireann and strongly opposed to the Treaty or putting it into operation. They formed a new political party called Cumann na Poblachta (The Republican Party). Harry, always a good organiser, played a prominent part in getting it off the ground. They formed sub-committees in charge of organisation, publicity, elections and parliamentary procedure. They also discussed plans for the next day's sitting of the Dáil.[1]

Cathal Brugha returned with De Valera to Kenilworth Square where he joined him for lunch with Mary MacSwiney, Harry, Liam Mellows and Austin Stack. Erskine Childers called and spent some time talking with them.[2] At the outset of Dáil Éireann's public session the next day, Éamon de Valera resigned because he had lost the vote 'that was tending to subvert the Republic which I was elected to my present position to defend and maintain'. Michael Collins said that no one in that gathering or in Ireland wanted to be put in the position of opposing President de Valera and he thought that the practical step was to form a committee, if necessary from both sides, for some kind of public safety. But he said that on their side they would put their own committee together to get on with the work of 'taking Ireland over from the English'. De Valera did not agree as he said that Dáil Éireann must choose its executive according to its constitution and go ahead from there. Peter Hughes who represented the Louth-Meath constituency said that since President de Valera had signified his intention of not having anything further to do with the government the obvious thing to do was to appoint somebody else.[3]

Then came the surprise of the day when anti-Treaty Deputy Kathleen Clarke, proposed Éamon de Valera for re-election as president of the Irish Republic.[4] Arthur Griffith thought that the whole affair was a 'political manoeuvre to wreck the Treaty'. Harry joined in the debate supporting De Valera and indicated that he was going to oppose the pro-Treaty party, tooth and nail, in a constitutional fashion.[5]

There was a straight vote on the proposition that De Valera be re-elected president of the Irish Republic. When his name was read out Dev abstained. Robert Barton, who voted for the Treaty, switched over to the anti-Treaty side and supported De Valera and so did Peter Paul Galligan representing Cavan. Tom O'Donnell of Sligo-Mayo East and Liam de Róiste of Cork City did not vote. The scene during the taking of this vote was tenser than on the issue of the Treaty – no one could say definitely who was going to win until the last vote was cast and counted The result this time was very close – 58 votes were recorded for the re-election of President de Valera and 60 votes against, a majority of two against De Valera.[6] (Laurence Ginnell, anti-Treaty, was in the Argentine and missed the vote. Another anti-Treaty supporter Frank Drohan had resigned before the vote on the Treaty was taken.) Before the house adjourned Harry asked would the new Provisional Government honour the pledges given in the Republic's name when its representatives had raised money in America and at home. Michael Collins assured him then that he would do his best to see that every pledge was honoured.[7]

Next day's Dáil session began when Michael Collins proposed a motion that Arthur Griffith be appointed president of Dáil Éireann. 'He did this,' he said, 'because the Irish nation was at that moment a ship without a captain'.[8] The time was approaching for a division when De Valera rose and announced that he, at any rate, was not going to be a party to the election of someone who was bound by the Treaty conditions to undermine the Irish Republic. He left the room followed by all his party TDs including Harry Boland. As they left there was a sharp exchange of taunts between Michael Collins and those who were leaving.[9] When the roll was called for deputies to register their votes 61 deputies were still in the chamber. They voted to elect Arthur Griffith to be the new president of Dáil Éireann.[10]

De Valera and his 56 anti-Treaty deputies, including Harry, only absented themselves from the Dáil for less than three hours, including the lunch time break.[11] They were back in their seats by five o'clock to resume the debate in a political and constitutional manner on the future of Ireland. Kathleen O'Connell wrote in her diary that 'Dev was awfully depressed and sad. He did not go home tonight. He met Divisional Commandants of the IRA at Mansion House. Lynch broke down. President very sad'.[12]

Harry knew that Michael Collins had said publicly in Dáil Éireann that he (Collins) was engaged to Kitty Kiernan.[13] Harry decided that the best thing for him to do in the circumstances was to write to Kitty and congratulate her on her engagement. His letter was short, 'Kitty, I want to congratulate you. M told me of your engagement, and I wish you long life and happiness'.[14] Kitty replied to Harry within a few days and when Harry wrote to her thanking her for her letter he told her that he had intended to go down to talk things over with her but when he went to the train he found that Michael Collins had gone to Granard a few hours before him so he went home.[15] He referred to a remark by Kitty about the quality of the other people who were on his side in opposition to the Treaty:

> The only comment I make on your letter is that you are most unfair in your suggestion that my attitude on the 'Peace' is to be condemned because men on my side may not be all you or I wd (would) desire!!! You know from my American letters that I had made up my mind without the aid of outside influence and I hope you will respect my views in this matter.

He said he would like to meet Kitty so that she would be easy in her mind and he finished by wishing her all joy and happiness.[16]

Harry attended a meeting of the Ard Comhairle of Sinn Féin at which a new standing committee was elected. A majority of pro-Treaty members were elected but the two co-secretaries were Harry and Austin Stack (anti-Treaty). The Ard Comhairle decided to summon an extraordinary Ard-Fheis to interpret the constitution of the organisation with special reference to the situation created by the Articles of Agreement for a Treaty between Great Britain and Ireland and its approval by Dáil Éireann. This Ard-Fheis also had to decide the policy of the organisation for the forthcoming elections.[17] Much of the work for organising this national convention of Sinn Féin was left in the hands of the two secretaries, Boland and Stack.

Kathleen, Harry's sister, was sorry that the Boland family were becoming estranged from Michael Collins: 'I must say that although Mick made no personal appeal to me as a man, he was a trojan worker and kept everyone up to the mark'. Kathleen said that Michael was very disappointed that Harry did not go with him on the Treaty and he came to her mother to get her to persuade Harry to come over to his side: 'Could you persuade Harry, Mrs Boland, to come with us. He'll have two jobs.'

Catherine replied with tears in her eyes, 'Ah Mick! We never had much money but we had patriotism and Harry couldn't sell it. It was born with him'.[18]

After the ratification of the Treaty the next step according to its provisions was the setting up of the Provisional Government. One of the conditions of the Treaty was that a meeting of members elected to the southern parliament in the general election of 1921 must be summoned to constitute a provisional government. The British government would transfer the powers and machinery necessary to that government prior to the establishment of the Free State – the British government would deal only with the Provisional Government and not with Dáil Éireann. The British government committee under Winston Churchill pushed for the setting up of the Provisional Government and they wanted the Irish representatives to come to London to discuss the removal of British troops, an amnesty for prisoners, and the submission of the Articles of Agreement to the British House of Commons for their ratification.[19]

Arthur Griffith moved quickly – as chairman of the Irish delegation of plenipotentiaries he issued a summons to all the elected representatives for the twenty-six counties to attend a meeting to give formal approval for the setting up of a Provisional Government. This new government group would oversee the British withdrawal and prepare for the foundation of the Irish Free State.[20] The southern parliament he was calling together was only for candidates elected in the 26 counties at the 1921 general election and so it recognised partition for the first time. Seán O'Mahony, a native of Thomastown, Co. Kilkenny, was not invited to attend because he was the Sinn Féin representative for Fermanagh-Tyrone – and if he had presented himself he would have been excluded. The four unionist members for Trinity College attended.

Éamon de Valera was summoned to attend as well as his 56 anti-Treaty deputies. Harry refused to go and his answer was the same as De Valera's, 'we don't recognise any such parliament'. He felt he could not go because this provisional government's function was to put into operation a Treaty which he and his fellow Republicans despised. A correspondent from the *Irish Times* said that De Valera by his absence 'has committed public suicide'.[21]

This meeting first ratified the 'Treaty between Great Britain and Ireland – Articles of Agreement'. Then it approved of a provisional government of eight pro-Treaty deputies who were virtual governors of Ireland until the Irish Free State came into existence. Arthur Griffith was not included in the Provisional Government as he was already president of Dáil Éireann.The general body of the southern parliament of Ireland never met again and left the transitional work to the eight ministers. Michael Collins was elected as chairman of the Provisional Government at its first cabinet meeting on 16 January.[22]

Besides founding a new Republican Party, Cumann na Poblachta, De Valera, seeing that he lacked support in the Irish newspapers during the Treaty debates, established a newspaper, *Republic of Ireland*. Erskine Childers was the editor and Liam Mellows was on the editorial board, and when the first issue appeared on 2 January Dev was very pleased. Harry gave Dev a loan of £500 to start the newspaper.[23] A week later at a meeting of Cumann na Poblachta, Harry and Seán T. O'Kelly were appointed as co-secretaries.[24]

Harry was one of the four representatives from the anti-Treaty side at the Irish Race Convention in Paris. Gavan Duffy, now Minister for Foreign Affairs, selected the representatives for this convention. He wrote to De Valera inviting him to nominate four delegates from his party while the pro-Treaty group would also send four representatives.[25] Harry sent a short letter to Kitty telling her that he was off to Paris but when he returned he would make his promised visit to her in Granard to renew old 'friendships'. In his last line he wrote, 'Tell Larry I will be delighted to join him in a hunt and, for your own information, I don't care if I never return from the hunt'.[26]

In Paris Harry met delegates from America, the Argentine Republic and Australia. He went to a lecture and he took a special note of a quotation from John Keats: 'Men may vote for falsehood, but they only die for truth'.[27] He found the Republican stance on the Treaty received support at the conference, De Valera was elected as president of the executive council and Robert Brennan, an anti-Treaty supporter, was proposed as secretary but Eoin MacNeill wanted joint secretaries. MacNeill returned home and said Seán T. O'Kelly, the Irish representative in Paris, and Art O'Brien, the Irish envoy in London had used the occasion to propagate anti-Treaty views instead of remaining neutral.[28]

Sinn Féin issued a report in mid-January saying that 'in the political situation of the moment and considering the aims of the organisation as set forth in the constitution, there were sharp differences of opinion as to what should be the future policy of the organisation'. Sinn Féin was split right down the middle because of the Treaty. Each comhairle ceantair (district council) met to elect representatives to the Ard-Fheis on 7 February. De Valera was still president of the movement and there were thousands of Sinn Féin clubs throughout the country. 'Tatler' writing in the *Nationalist and Leinster Leader* said:

> I am one of those who remember the Parnell split – young as I was – its chaos, its bitterness, its deplorable effect on Irish politics. Ireland is standing at the beginning of a split compared with which, if it is allowed to develop, the Parnell split will have been but child's play ... I would call particularly on the leaders to act more practically. Personalities have been indulged in; even mud – to use a common expression – has been thrown.[29]

Republicans were encouraged with the support they were getting from the Sinn Féin clubs. Cumainn were appointing delegates following a vote on the Treaty and sending them to the Ard-Fheis as anti-Treaty or pro-Treaty representatives according to the majority vote of the club. At least half of these delegates were against the Treaty and possibly a little over 50% of them were in favour of De Valera.[30] As the situation began to unfold a circular was issued from the offices of the *Republic of Ireland* newspaper saying:

> The help of every Sinn Féin Cumann and Comhairle Ceanntair should be secured for the Republic as far as possible. Where the Republicans form the majority in Cumann and Comhairle Ceantair they should select delegates to the Ard-Fheis who can be relied upon to support the existing Republic by every possible means. If the majority of any cumann or Comahirle Ceantair should prove to be on the side which seeks to subvert the Republic the name of the Republican members of those bodies should be noted and meetings held and the names of such members forwarded at once to Messrs. Seán T. O'Kelly and H. Boland ...[31]

Four days later George Gavan Duffy, Minister for Foreign Affairs, issued a memorandum to the foreign representatives containing guidelines for the future conduct of their affairs both private and public. One section of this report stated:

> As national unity is now broken by the emergence of two political parties

in the Republican state, members of the diplomatic service will be under the obligation of reflecting faithfully the policy of the government, whatever their personal opinion on party politics. It will be their duty to refrain from propaganda either for or against the Treaty.[32]

Harry was still the Irish representative in America and these instructions applied to him as they did to Seán T. O'Kelly who was the Irish representative in Paris.

On 28 January Harry received a formal letter of complaint from Gavan Duffy. He referred to the circular about the Ard-Fheis:

You will see that your name is cited in it as if you were one of the persons responsible. In view of the character of the circular and of the fact that you are a diplomatic representative of the government, I shall be very glad to receive your disclaimer of responsibility in the matter.[33]

Harry was in trouble.

BOLAND LOSES OUT

Two days later Harry replied to Gavan Duffy saying the content of the circular was to his mind 'compatible with my position as representative of the Government of the Republic and I shall be very glad to know what portion of the circular determined you to seek a disclaimer from me'.[1] He signed the letter as the 'Representative of the Republic to USA'. Gavan Duffy told Harry that he was publicly identifying himself with active party propaganda against the present government and that it was impossible for him to retain his position as a diplomatic representative of Dáil Éireann. However in view of his long service to the government of the Republic he was prepared to be lenient with him and suggested 'that you should in the circumstances send in your resignation rather than compel this department to take action'.[2] Gavan Duffy sent two more letters to Harry before he got a reply. Harry then said that all his activities in Ireland and abroad had been directed towards the upholding of the Republic and its government and he refused to resign on an 'unsupported allegation which evidently originated in the minds of a minister and cabinet suffering the agonies of guilty consciences'.[3] One week later he spoke with Gavan Duffy and after that received a short and sharp letter from the minister telling him that 'this letter terminates your appointment under the diplomatic service of the government' and that it was regretful 'that you did not see your way to sending in your resignation'.[4]

When Eoin MacNeill returned from the Irish Race Convention in Paris he said, at a cabinet meeting of the Dáil ministry on 3 February, he thought that Seán T O'Kelly should be replaced as Irish representative because he was doing everything in his power to work against the government. O'Kelly was suspended pending a report on the situation in Paris. Then a question about Boland's and O'Kelly's circular concerning the Sinn Féin Ard-Fheis arose and Seán T. was dismissed from his post as Irish representative in Paris.[5]

Madame Markievicz and Mary MacSwiney questioned Gavan Duffy about these dismissals in Dáil Éireann on 1 March. He said that civil servants or diplomatic servants of the government could not take part in party politics and that he was enforcing this universal rule in Ireland as other governments did everywhere else. Mary MacSwiney countered by stating that these servants 'had devoted their lives to the establishment and maintenance of the Republic' and this aspiration was 'a matter of life and death to the nationhood of their country'.[6] Then the Dáil moved on to the next business on the agenda.

When Harry was dismissed Joe McGarrity was on his visit from the re-organised Clan-na-Gael in an effort to heal the rift in Ireland, not only on a national level but inside the IRB. To Harry his dismissal also meant the loss of his salary of $10,000. In a letter to Stephen O'Mara he wrote, 'I had an interview with Mr Gavan Duffy today and received a letter from him. So I am no longer "a Wandering Statesman".'[7] The rest of the family were angry and his mother said that he had told her and his brother Gerry that when he was in America 'he did not take his salary as he thought the higher salary would bankrupt the Dáil'.[8]

The responsibility of drawing up a constitution for the twenty-six counties fell on the Provisional Government and especially on Michael Collins. A constitutional committee was set up at a meeting of the cabinet held in the Mansion House on 17 January and seven experts from legal and other fields were brought together. They first met as a group on 24 January. Collins instructed the committee to try to draft a constitution that would be acceptable to Republicans and should therefore bring peace. He even hoped that the Irish constitution would not include the oath of allegiance,[9] but Lloyd George insisted that the draft Irish constitution be shown to the British cabinet before its publication by the Provisional Government.

Over 3,000 delegates from all parts of Ireland met in the Mansion House for the Sinn Féin Ard-Fheis. Éamon de Valera proposed his resolution advocating adherence to the spirit and letter of the Sinn Féin constitution, declaring the aim of the organisation should continue to be international recognition for Ireland as an independent Republic. Arthur Griffith appealed to the opponents of the Treaty not to obstruct those who saw a chance of salvation for the nation in the Treaty. Michael Collins urged unity.[10] Dev received more applause and it was felt that if a vote were taken, his motion to keep to the spirit and letter of the Sinn Féin constitution would prevail. The delegates had come to vote either for De Valera or Griffith – as instructed by those they represented in Sinn Féin cumainn and they were waiting impatiently for the opportunity to do so.[11] When Fr P. Gaynor spoke the whole attitude changed. He suggested that De Valera and Griffith and their friends should try to come to an agreement to carry on and co-operate without an election and in an assembly in which they could all sit without offending any of their principles.[12] 'A plague on both your houses', was his theme and his appeal for unity impressed the gathering.

Dick Mulcahy proposed an adjournment to let the leaders confer. Éamon de Valera and Austin Stack on behalf of the Republicans met with Arthur Griffith and Michael Collins representing the Free State Party. They decided to adjourn the Ard-Fheis for three months. Dáil Éireann was to meet regularly and was to continue operating as it did before. Arthur Griffith and his cabinet were to remain in charge notwithstanding any vote in the Dáil, even if it went against the pro-Treaty party. The new Irish Free State constitution would be ready before parliamentary elections were held and could be put before the people.[13] The agreement met with almost unanimous approval. A split in Sinn Féin was averted but many Republicans thought De Valera should have gone ahead with the vote. Kathleen O'Connell was disappointed no vote was taken because she thought that the vast majority of those present were Republicans. 'What a pity a division wasn't taken. Delays are dangerous,' she wrote.[14] Most of the anti-Treaty group were happy to postpone the parliamentary election as many of them, including Harry, shared De Valera's view that they needed more time to strengthen their anti-Treaty organisation.

After the Ard-Fheis agreement Arthur Griffith and Éamonn Duggan were summoned by Churchill to London to explain themselves and they succeeded in satisfying Churchill. He reported to the House of Commons that the Irish leaders had reassured him: 'The constitution will be submitted to the Irish people by and with the authority of the Provisional Government and not by and with the authority of Dáil Éireann'.[15]

The anti-Treaty side had started on a programme of political meetings all round the country in an effort to increase their support. A huge anti-Treaty political demonstration took place in Sackville Street, Dublin with three platforms erected. De Valera was the chief speaker and Harry was one of the fifteen speakers. De Valera opened his speech by declaring that the meeting had been called as it had been said that 90% of the people were in favour of the Articles of Agreement signed in London and he was asking the people to come out to show that this was not true.[16]

Stephen O'Mara invited Harry to speak in Limerick. Stephen said that the Republican Party must have a definite policy and he suggested they should not compromise with the Free State – they must remain purely Republican. They should announce that they rejoice that the long struggle for Irish freedom was forcing the enemy to evacuate from the south of Ireland rather than let the advocates of the Treaty get credit for achieving this.[17] Harry made it clear that he was against a Treaty which contained an oath of allegiance and partition:

> In 1918 I believed in the Republic of Ireland and I believe in it now. If it was right and proper in 1918 that an English King should not be acknowledged in Ireland it was right and proper today. They were not going to exchange that flag (the flag of the Republic) for an alleged Free State for three-fourths of their country.[18]

The pro-Treaty party responded by holding large public meetings themselves. Michael Collins and Arthur Griffith addressed many meetings at the weekends and they held a huge demonstration in favour of the Treaty in College Green, Dublin early in March. Arthur Griffith said that the anti-Treaty side had no alternative except the gambler's choice. On the other hand 'the Treaty had been concluded which recognised the nationhood of Ireland for the first time in the history of the two countries'.[19]

Besides work of a political nature, Harry helped other causes. Always in sympathy with Labour, he promised John Moore to give his support to a new Irish Union of Woodworkers which had been established in Dublin at the end of 1921.[20] He promised Hanna Sheehy Skeffington and K. K. Connery of the Irish Women's Franchise League to support a measure to extend the franchise to women under thirty on the same terms as granted to men if the proposal came before the Dáil.[21]

The Supreme Council of the IRB had issued a statement to its members supporting 'the present peace Treaty between Ireland and Great Britain should be ratified'.[22] This directive helped to create a majority in Dáil Éireann for the Treaty. Harry who had been president of the Supreme Council disagreed with the executive over this ruling. He still kept attending meetings of the Supreme Council but he was thinking of severing his connection with the organisation – he hoped that the IRB would change its policy. When he now found that the Army Council of the IRA was going to hold 'Ireland for the Republic' and had not sufficient funds, he wired Luke Dillon to send him the $60,000 lodged in the bank in Washington and he handed it over to the Army Council of the IRA.[23] He received a receipt for this money and sent that on to Luke in America.

The agreement made at the Sinn Féin Ard-Fheis meant that there was relative peace on the political front, but difficulties were beginning to appear on the army side as the Irish Republican Army was deeply divided and unlike the IRB, the majority of IRA members were against the Treaty.

Oscar Traynor, commanding officer of the Dublin Brigade IRA and the officer under whom Harry fought in 1916, explained how the ordinary members of the IRA felt about the division in their ranks:

> We, the volunteers, could now see clearly the division which was taking place among our most trusted leaders. I actually saw men shed tears of rage when the subject was being discussed.[24]

All the major barracks in Ireland were transferred into Irish hands – beginning with Beggar's Bush, Dublin and followed by Clonmel, Carlow, Kilkenny, Maryborough, Templemore, Tipperary and Wexford.[25] Local forces of the IRA, operating in a disciplined manner, paraded through the main streets of most of these cities and towns on their way to the barracks, often accompanied by bands playing Irish martial airs.

DRIFTING TOWARDS CIVIL WAR

In some towns pro-Treaty garrisons took over, in other parts anti-Treaty forces occupied the barracks. The British also supplied arms, ammunition and equipment to the Irish Provisional Government. Churchill said in the House of Commons on 12 April that over 4000 rifles, 2200 revolvers, six machine guns and appropriate quantities of ammunition had been transferred to the Provisional Government.[1]

Richard Mulcahy said in Dáil Éireann that 'if any assurance is required the army will remain the Army of the Irish Republic'.[2] Cormac Mac Cárthaigh said in an article in *Agus* that 'one of the first things that Michael Collins did was to recruit an army ... Some of the recruits had full uniforms, others half uniforms, and some had no uniforms at all but there was no scarcity of guns, or ammunition'.[3] Some members of the IRA and some Irish political prisoners coming out of jails and internment camps joined the force and went to Beggar's Bush barracks for training. Gearóid Ua hUallacháin, an active member of Dublin Brigade described the way things were:

> Men like Joe Cullen moved into Beggar's Bush Barracks with the Republican forces and these took the Treaty side when the split came. Everything was against those who opposed the Treaty ... One would talk to a man who was wildly Republican one night, and the next day he would have gone over to the other side. They got big officers' money and only the strongest men could hold out.[4]

Senior IRA officers opposed to the Treaty asked the Minister for Defence, Richard Mulcahy, to call a convention of the army to reaffirm its allegiance to the Irish Republic, and to maintain it as the army of the Irish Republic under an executive to be appointed by the convention.[5] They wanted the convention to represent both shades of opinion on the Treaty. Each IRA company would elect one delegate or more according to the number of members in each company and these delegates would attend a brigade convention that would send on 5% of the total number of delegates to attend a national convention to debate and decide matters of importance to the army. Richard Mulcahy reported to the cabinet of Dáil Éireann that he had received this request from certain members of the

HQ staff and certain divisional commandants. He intended to reply that this proposal was entirely outside the constitutional powers of the Dáil cabinet. The cabinet approved his decision.[6] He did not throw out the proposal altogether and said he was making arrangements to meet the signatories of the letter to discuss the matter.[7] He called a conference of the whole army, including pro-Treaty and anti-Treaty elements and there were arguments against the holding of the convention, that Dáil Éireann was the elected government of the Republic and until the people decided otherwise the army must remain under its control.[8] It was eventually decided that an army convention would be held on Sunday, 26 March.[9]

Harry attended a meeting of Company F, Second Battalion, Dublin Brigade – the company he fought with in 1916 – and he was elected as a delegate to the brigade convention. He was one of those named to represent the Dublin Brigade at the national convention.[10]

The commandant of Mid-Limerick Brigade, Liam Forde, rejected the authority of GHQ. British forces were at that time evacuating Limerick City. The pro-Treaty military leaders ordered Commandant Michael Brennan from the Clare area into Limerick City to take over barracks. There was a split inside the Mid-Limerick Brigade and the quartermaster, Captain Hurley, organised the pro-Treaty side to take over posts in the city. Anti-Treaty elements from as far away as Kilkenny, Tipperary and Cork converged, by order, on Limerick to reinforce the anti-Treaty troops under Forde. They occupied hotels and a wing of the mental hospital. They arrested Captain Hurley and the situation became explosive.

De Valera wrote to Richard Mulcahy, Minister for Defence, warning him of the serious situation which had developed:

> From information to hand I am convinced that a very serious situation is developing in Limerick. If taken in hand at once it maybe possible to settle it without bloodshed but if let go it may well be the beginning of a civil war ...[11]

Mulcahy's secretary answered De Valera's letter saying that the Minister for Defence accompanied by the adjutant general had left for Limerick.[12] They did not settle the matter nor did Stephen O'Mara, Mayor of Limerick, who tried to get the sides to come to some agreement. But O'Mara persisted and went to Dublin where he spoke to Arthur Griffith. Griffith said the anti-Treaty forces would have to withdraw because they were 'in mutiny' and challenging the authority of Dáil Éireann. When Stephen persevered, Griffith said he should see Mulcahy[13] who met him in Beggar's Bush Barracks in Dublin. Liam Lynch and Oscar Traynor were called in. Seamus Robinson, Tom Barry and Harry also took part in the discussions.[14] Richard Mulcahy and Michael Collins were present when an agreement was reached. They authorised Liam Lynch and Oscar Traynor to go to Limerick and mediate[15] – and the problem was solved amicably.[16] Liam Lynch was happy 'to see about 700 armed troops on each side who were about to engage in mortal combat eventually leave Limerick as comrades'.[17] What shocked him was that Arthur Griffith 'tried hard to press the issue in a manner which would have resulted in fearful slaughter in the streets of Limerick'.[18] Richard Mulcahy keeping notes on the army convention issue wrote:

> In the meantime there occurred the Limerick episode, 3–11 March, indicative of the thoughts and undisciplined tendencies that were developing in the army as a result of the political influences working upon it. Specially discussing on 15 March at the Dáil cabinet the implications of the Limerick episode and the convention which had been called, the Minister for Defence had to admit to the cabinet that he could not guarantee that if this convention was held a military government would not be set up.[19]

The cabinet used the Limerick crisis to justify banning the national army convention. But the brigade army conventions had been held and it was clear from these results that there would be a considerable anti-Treaty majority.[20] Florence O'Donoghue estimated that taking the total army strength into account, it did not appear to be an exaggeration to say that anti-Treaty delegates would have represented 80% of the army strength.[21] Arthur Griffith, issued the order on 16 March banning the convention:

> It is quite evident to the unanimous Dáil cabinet that at an army convention contemplated for 26 March, it was proposed to endeavour to remove the Army from under the control of the government elected by the people, which is Dáil Éireann. Such a purpose is illegal and you are hereby instructed that the holding of the convention is forbidden.[22]

It was also decided that, 'as long as officers of the army remain loyal and obey orders the Provisional Government would continue its financial support, but that in the event of disloyalty or disobedience to orders such support would be withdrawn'.[23]

Despite the ban, the anti-Treaty officers met and decided to go ahead with the convention on the original date. They summoned all the delegates who had been elected at the brigade conventions irrespective of what views they held on the Treaty. On the instructions of Richard Mulcahy, Minister for Defence, the Chief-of-Staff of the IRA, Eoin O'Duffy issued an order to the adjutant general and to each divisional and brigade commandant and O/C of each barracks in Ireland stating:

> All officers and men who attend the convention on Sunday next, the 26 instant, automatically sever their connection with the IRA. You are simply to regard them as suspended and report on each case separately to GHQ.[24]

The convention assembled in the Mansion House, Dublin on Sunday, 26 March. According to Florence O'Donoghue, who took notes while the roll-call was being taken, a large majority of the total strength of the IRA was present.[25] Eoin O'Duffy denied that this estimate was accurate, particularly in divisions outside Munster. Oscar Traynor, the commanding officer of the Dublin Brigade, said that '200 army officers representing fifty brigades elected an army executive to control the forces they represented'.[26] There were now two armies in the country, the army of the Provisional Government – the Free State Army – and the forces controlled by the executive – the anti-Treaty Army. The Provisional Government, as threatened, suspended all those who became members of the anti-Treaty army and cut off all financial support.

Harry did not take a prominent part at the convention, but his brother, Gerry, C/O of a South Dublin Battalion, remembered the IRA being split into three factions, not two. One faction was under Collins – Free State army (pro-Treaty), the second faction was under Liam Lynch – anti-Treaty Forces, and a third group, of extreme anti-Treatyites, under the leadership of Rory O'Connor and Liam Mellows. 'The majority group was under Liam Lynch'. Gerry Boland praised Dick Mulcahy for his great efforts to secure unity in the army at this time. He said that Mulcahy had obtained agreement with the Lynch sector but Rory O'Connor and Liam Mellows on one side and Arthur Griffith on the other prevented a settlement. Gerry said that at the final army convention, Cathal Brugha had not been allowed to talk. Even Liam Mellows was not a welcome speaker because he was a TD. 'We don't want any politicians', was the cry.[27]

The army convention brought many young IRA officers from all parts of the country to Dublin. There were many IRA officers who would not take an oath of allegiance to a British king or queen. Their grandfathers and fathers had been out in previous risings and though, after defeat, they were a small minority, they had held on to the 'Fenian Faith'. Some of these young men had come from areas 'where the king or queen's writ never ran'. Ned Aylward, leader of an active flying column in West Kilkenny, was a member of Dáil Éireann and had voted against the Treaty. He was walking back to his lodgings with Dinny Lacey, the Tipperary flying column leader, and they were discussing the oath of allegiance in the Treaty. 'I could not live in an Ireland with an oath of allegiance ... I must either leave Ireland or fight against it', Lacey said.[28]

Harry continued to attend meetings of the IRB Supreme Council and Michael Collins and some of the top officers in the Free State army were on the council.[29] A conference which comprised Supreme Council members together with the division and county centres of the whole organisation was called. They tried to convince the anti-Treatyites that the Republic would be better served by accepting the Treaty but they failed. According to Florence O'Donoghue if a vote had been taken it would have shown a small majority against the Treaty.[30] Instead of taking a vote they turned instead to try to unify the organisation and the country again. Piaras Béaslaí said Harry 'maintained the friendliest of relations with Collins, and other supporters of the Treaty, and made a special point of cultivating their company'.[31]

Donal O'Callaghan, Lord Mayor of Cork, wrote to Harry on 8 March telling him that he had met Mr Castellini in Cobh, one of the best friends that members of the Irish mission ever had in the USA. He was shocked at the prospect of two rival delegations, one pro-Treaty and the other anti-Treaty going to the USA to seek support for their respective sides. 'The results will be deplorable' and he would not take part 'in a divided and probably acrimonious campaign'. Donal suggested to Harry that the pro-Treaty and anti-Treaty interests should come to an agreement to avoid a platform campaign in America. He asked Harry to present Mr Castillini's views to De Valera.[32] Harry replied two days later saying that it was true to say that the division at home would have its reaction in America 'but as the split is inevitable that it was up to us to se-cure whatever support we can from our friends in America'.[33] Liam Pedlar, in New York, wrote to Harry and said that even Joe Mc-Garrity was not (to say the least) pleased as he felt he should not introduce one side or the other until he had been able to give his official report of his trip to Ireland to a convention of the re-or-ganised Clan-na-Gael.[34] The two rival delegations from Ireland to America arrived in New York on the same boat and in the spring of 1922 they were about as welcome there as 'an outbreak of small-pox'.[35]

Luke Dillon, on behalf of the Executive of the re-organised Clan-na-Gael in America, wrote to Harry asking him to return the $60,000 which Harry handed over to the army council of the IRA. Harry wrote back saying that 'I thought the very best thing I could do with it was to place it at the disposal of the army – that body that is determined to preserve the Republic'. Harry also said that he was optimistic that a planned IRB convention for the following week would change things 'and throw all its strength behind the army'.[36] This did not happen and left Harry with the problem of the $60,000 still unresolved. Harry also wrote to Joe McGarrity and ex-plained why he handed the money to the IRA: 'Since you left this country the army has taken a decisive step towards maintaining the Republic and I have not the slightest hesitation in placing the money at their disposal'.[37] Harry waited some time and then he wrote to Liam Lynch on 30 May. He reminded Lynch of the monies which he had placed at the disposal of the IRA Army Council:

> Were it not that I had your approval in the matter and that you were a colleague of mine on the S.C. (Supreme Council) I would have hesitated longer ere I handed the money over to the IRA. Happily the situation is now clarified and I want to secure a return of the money so that it can be lodged in the names of Commandants McKelvey, Liam Lynch and Harry Boland pending a convention of the organisation, after which we shall hand it over to the new S.C. (Supreme Council).[38]

Harry was very anxious 'that my action in regard to the monies shall not be twisted by knaves to make a trap for fools'.[39]

Even though Kitty and Michael had become engaged Harry continued to visit Kitty and her family as a friend. Harry used the skills of his old trade as a tailor to make himself a pair of jodhpurs[40] and went down to Granard to take part in the hunt with Larry. In a letter to Kitty he first spoke of the hunt and then he asked her to excuse him if, in the course of defending his anti-Treaty stance, he may have offended her during 'the many bombardments'. Then he built hope for the future. 'No one would be more happy than I, if old comrades were re-united, maybe this week may see an effort to procure harmony!'[41] When he was saying goodbye on his last visit, he whispered in her ear and said 'Don't worry, Kitty, Michael will be all right'. As he went away smiling he looked back and laughed and with that slow drawl of his he said, 'Arah, I know how to make you happy'.[42]

This confrontation between the Free State forces and the anti-Treaty forces revealed itself in many places when the British moved out of a barracks and there were two forces claiming it. There was a serious fight for possession of an army barracks at Tullow, Co. Carlow. The barracks was first occupied by the Free State army. At 3.30am a force of between 60 and 70 anti-Treatyites armed with rifles and shotguns attacked the barracks. The fight lasted about an hour and a half and one member of the garrison was wounded – three of the attacking party were seriously wounded. The attackers afterwards withdrew.[43]

Disorder spread in the country chiefly because financial support was cut away from the anti-Treaty forces. They were in possession of military barracks but found it impossible to either give their soldiers any money or buy food to feed them. The ordinary rank and file craved cigarettes and in many cases they robbed banks and used the money to run the barracks. There were two banks robbed in the west of Ireland during one week-end in which an Irish Republican army officer lost his life and five men were arrested. In one of the raids they got away with an estimated £2,000.[44] Incidents like these lost sympathy for the anti-Treatyites amongst the ordinary people. Cars were often taken without permission and in many cases from well-off business people and this made the prosperous antagonistic to the anti-Treaty side. An editorial in the *Irish Times* declared 'the two Irish armies ought to act as one army in protecting life and property and both ought to be subject to the most rigid discipline'.[45]

Harry thought that members of Dáil Éireann should tackle the army question and the lack of funds for the anti-Treaty force. Debts had been incurred before the split and they were still held responsible, by the local community, for policing the areas under their control. Harry asked Liam Lynch, Chief-of-Staff, for details of the money owed and for an estimate of the cost of maintenance of barracks at present occupied by the anti-Treatyites.[46] But as 'it had been decided by the executive that matters relating to the army (anti-Treaty) should be raised by army officers who are also members of Dáil Éireann',[47] Harry and Éamon de Valera, though anti-Treaty, had little control over the anti-Treaty military forces and were kept at arm's length by them.

Batt O'Connor, a pro-Treaty supporter and a friend of Michael Collins wrote to Harry saying that the situation was hopeless:

> Civil war is only a step away and I hope the Provisional Government will resign sooner than see the country come to that. In fact, I am surprised Mick does not step down and take a holiday and give De Valera a chance to see what better terms he will be able to get.[48]

Both parties were holding political meetings all over the country. Harry addressed Republican meetings at Miltown and Glenamaddy in North Galway. He said that they were asked to accept the Treaty because it meant freedom to achieve full freedom. The Republican attitude was that they wanted to maintain what they had already won. They insisted that in any election the register of the electorate must be brought up to date to give a vote to the young men and women who had done most of the fighting in the War of Independence. As regards Northern Ireland 'he would give Ulster and, perhaps, Munster too, a form of government of their own within the Irish Parliament'.[49]

At a meeting in Maryborough, Co. Leix, he spoke of the dilemma that the Treaty had caused:

> If the Irish people ratified the Treaty no body of Irishmen dare to go out and assert the Republic again. Why? Because there were cases of brothers, one brother in the Four Courts and another brother in command of the Free State troops to see that the Republic is disestablished.[50]

At many of the pro-Treaty meetings disorder broke out. Michael Collins had great difficulty in addressing the crowd in Castlebar because of interruptions. A pro-Treaty meeting to be addressed by President Griffith in Sligo was proclaimed by General Pilkington who was in charge of anti-Treaty forces in the area. Despite this ban Arthur Griffith travelled to Sligo to assert the right of free speech.[51] When Michael Collins went to Tralee he found that all the roads leading to the town had been blocked, railway lines torn up and telephone communications severed. He later addressed a meeting of 4,000 people.[52] In Dungarvan, Co. Waterford the lorry which Collins had mounted to use as a platform was driven away by young men with all the speakers still aboard.[53] In a letter Collins wrote to Joe McGarrity he described the way the pro-Treaty meetings were disrupted and wrecked:

> The opposition policy is making it almost impossible for us to hold useful meetings. The crowds assemble all right, but twenty, or thirty, or forty interrupters succeed in most places in preventing the speakers from being heard. That apparently is the official policy, accompanied by blocked road and torn up railways to prevent the excursion trains from bringing the people to our meetings ... I greatly fear that the civil war that they have been threatening is now close at hand.[54]

Ireland went a big step closer to civil war when the Republican army council, of the anti-Treaty forces, decided that a military headquarters was required in the capital city of Ireland and the Dublin Brigade IRA was ordered to occupy the Four Courts and establish the headquarters there. On 13 April they took over the huge building on the quays, barricaded the windows with sacks filled with clay and fortified other parts of the building. They were planning a long stay.

There'll be no Civil War

Limerick had shown everyone the stark possibility of civil war. Worse trouble broke out in Kilkenny at the end of April when anti-Treaty troops in the city took over Kilkenny Prison and stored a quantity of whiskey taken from the bonded stores in the city. They said the whiskey had been seized because of the economic boycott of goods from Belfast[1] and put it in the prison for safe-keeping.[2] This was disputed afterwards by pro-Treaty troops. Commandant J. T. Prout, who controlled the city, threatened that unless the goods were returned and the prison evacuated he would take the building by force. The anti-Treaty forces, a minority in the city, left the jail and returned the goods.[3]

Later, however, Ned Aylward, Callan, and Seamus Robinson from Tipperary ordered the anti-Treaty forces in Kilkenny to mobilise[4] and asked armed anti-Treatyites from Callan, Mooncoin, Paulstown and other parts of Kilkenny, Waterford and Tipperary to reinforce them and occupy buildings in the city. They seized about a dozen places, including the Round Tower of St Canice's Cathedral, the City Hall and Kilkenny Castle.[5] The castle was the residence of the Marquis of Ormonde and was built on the site of an older castle erected by Strongbow in 1172. It was the first time it was invaded and Lord and Lady Ossory refused to move to a place of safety. They were treated in a considerate and courteous manner by their anti-Treaty visitors.[6]

A force of 200 troops arrived from Beggar's Bush by train and an armoured car came from Dublin in record time manned by Tom Ennis, Joe Leonard, Tom Flood and David Moran.[7] A three days' siege of Kilkenny followed, shooting broke out all over the city. Shops closed and people stayed indoors. Gradually each building was taken by the Free State troops who were far better armed and equipped with machine guns and ammunition. The armoured car menaced the anti-Treaty forces in the centre of the city and Kilkenny Castle was the last garrison to surrender.[8]

Meanwhile word reached Clonmel of the fight in Kilkenny between Free State troops and anti-Treaty forces. A 100 men under Dinny Lacey left Clonmel barracks to reinforce the Republicans. When they reached Cuffesgrange, five miles from Kilkenny, they found Free State troops, from Beggar's Bush, under Joe Leonard blocking their way. Shooting began but did not last long because a group of prominent IRA officers, Dan Breen and Seán Moylan from the anti-Treaty side and Gearóid O'Sullivan and Brigadier Breslin from the pro-Treaty army, arrived to make peace. The Tipperary anti-Treaty forces withdrew back beyond Callan.[9] Peace was restored in Kilkenny City and 120 anti-Treaty prisoners were released. There was one civilian casualty, a young girl, Margaret Loughman had her knee shattered with a ricochet bullet.[10]

When Commandant Seán O'Hegarty, O/C of the Cork City Brigade of the Irish Republican Army addressed Dáil Éireann on 3 May 1922 he warned the assembly of pro-Treaty and anti-Treaty deputies of an imminent civil war. 'To my mind,' he said, 'it means not alone that you do not maintain the Republic but that you break forever any idea of it, that you break the country utterly ...'[11] Seán was speaking on behalf of a number of officers who had been amongst the most prominent fighters during the War of Independence and who were now on opposite sides.

Harry was present and he nodded in approval of every word that Seán said. He had been trying to get people to listen to him over the past six weeks. In a letter to Michael Collins, dated 25 March, 1922, Richard Mulcahy said:

> After seeing you and Mr Griffith on Wednesday last, Harry Boland again came to me, urging the fact that agreement of some kind of peace between the two parties could be arranged as far as his party was concerned ... It appeared to be something like a suggestion that a certain percentage of seats be allotted to them. He mentioned 20%.[12]

Because of O'Hegarty's address, Dáil Éireann set up a Peace Committee of ten TDs to actively engage in seeking peace. Harry welcomed this committee but he asked that in the event of the panel agreeing, would the leaders on each side honour the agreement. He suggested that each side nominate six men to explore every avenue.[13] He was still on good terms with Michael Collins:

> If the army can get together men who, as the Minister of Finance (Michael Collins) said, may understand each other – which is equally true of the army executive – and settle the army question, there will be very little difficulty in dealing with the politicians, so-called.[14]

But Arthur Griffith did not support Harry's proposal: 'As to the point of Mr Boland about honouring any agreement, that is a matter, of course, for the Dáil. This committee reports to the Dáil and the Dáil decides'.[15] Griffith also suggested that each side select five members rather than six. Harry was one of the five nominees on the anti-Treaty side. The other members were Ald. Mrs Tom Clarke (Dublin), Patrick Ruttledge (North and West Mayo), Seán Moylan (South West Cork) and Liam Mellows (Co. Galway). Representing the pro-Treaty side were Seán Hales (Cork South-West), Pádraic Ó Máille (Co. Galway), Joe McGuinness (Longford-Westmeath), Seamus O'Dwyer (Co. Dublin) and Major-General Seán MacEoin (Longford-Westmeath).[16]

There are entries in the diary of Harry Boland for this period which show how the Peace Committee progressed. They agreed on an army truce while their talks went on. On Friday, 5 May Harry noted that the committee came together for three hours and that various proposals were made but no agreement was reached.[17] Seán Moylan, IRA commandant from South-West Cork, an anti-Treaty member, had his car parked outside on the road while this meeting was going on. Seán Moyler of Cork was driving both Moylan and Liam Mellows to and from the meeting. Moylan, a tall man, once an apprentice carpenter, came out.

'How did ye get on at the meetin',' enquired Moyler.

'There'll be no f— Civil War if I can help it,' answered Moylan.

Moyler was surprised as he himself was not thinking about civil war at all.[18] Harry Boland's diary gives short details of meetings held on Saturday, 6 May and on the following Monday but the entry for Tuesday, 9 May reads 'Peace Committee – P. Ultimatum – Break down'.[19]

Boland and Seán MacEoin were conciliators and in a letter to Joe McGarrity Harry said, 'as you know I was the liaison or medium acting between our party and Collins'.[20] The pro-Treaty proposal stated that 'the Treaty, having been approved by the majority of Dáil Éireann would in the circumstances, be accepted by a majority of people'. The anti-Treaty group would not accept these words as they stood and demanded their omission. – they could not agree to a settlement that in their opinion committed the people to the acceptance of the Treaty. In the end, as a result of much argument and compromise on both sides, it was agreed to 'leave undiscussed, for the time being, those clauses which had caused the break'.

When the Dáil met on Wednesday 11 May, the speaker had reports signed by Kathleen Clarke, as chairman of the anti-Treaty group and Seamus O'Dwyer for the pro-Treaty side. The pro-Treaty side recommended that there be an agreed election and that a coalition government be formed after the election. The anti-Treaty report proposed that the present personnel of Dáil Éireann constitute the next Dáil and that it be accepted and understood that no issue was being determined by the election – the acceptance or rejection of the Treaty should not be an issue in an agreed election. Harry put forward his own draft, the second clause of which defined his idea of an 'agreed election'. He recommended that 'Dáil Éireann should decree that the planned elections declared by England be not contested but that the present personnel constitute the Third Dáil'.[21] The anti-Treatyites were also hoping to have a representative from their side appointed as Minister for Defence in a coalition government.

The big difference centred on how many candidates each side should nominate to a coalition panel of pro-Treaty and anti-Treaty candidates to be presented for election. They failed to agree on an acceptable proportion after protracted talks and the reports concluded by informing the Dáil that the conference had finally broken down.

Harry called into the Sinn Féin office and he threw his revolver on the mantelpiece.

'It's war,' he said. 'And I'm not going to fire on Mick. So I can't fire on any of Mick's men.'

Robert Brennan who was watching him said that Harry meant it at the time.[22]

According to Frank Aiken:

Harry Boland was on a committee which broke down. I got Harry and the others to agree to come to a meeting. Mick and Cathal were there. Their hair rose like two terriers. Michael Collins said that if there was to be an agreed election and coalition cabinet, he would hold out for a secure majority for the Treaty side. I asked him to be content if he had the same representation as he had. They all agreed if there was to be an agreed election that the same representation could be retained.[23]

Tempers were short in the Dáil. Dr McCartan complained about the lack of progress of the Peace Committee:

We are going forward to Civil War as far as I can see. We are going to shoot each other for a few members on one side or other in the Dáil. Every man should be prepared to face that issue that they were going to kill each other.[24]

Liam Mellows, anti-Treaty deputy, replied: 'We are anxious to evade the Treaty and get rid of it'.[25]

Harry, who was trying so hard for unity and peace, was disappointed. If the peace talks were going to break down over each side demanding a certain number of candidates on the Sinn Féin panel, he volunteered that 'I here and now offer myself as the first one to resign'.[26]

Cathal Brugha made an ominous remark during the debate:

> I for one would prefer to die by an English bullet or an Orange bullet rather than by a bullet fired by one of the men with whom we have been fighting together during the last six years, on and off. I am never going to fire a bullet at any of these men and I hope that I am not going to die by a bullet from any of them.[27]

De Valera wound up this debate:

> Our attitude in a coalitional co-operation would be definitely that we would not be committed to the policy of the majority, because the Treaty is not our policy, because we cannot act with it, we cannot agree with it as a policy but that which is Ireland's we would use for Ireland's interests.[28]

Collins and De Valera were absent from the Dáil for seven hours on 18 May 1922 and there were rumours that they were talking. Seán Moyler of Cork was a telephone operator in the Civic Hall, which had been taken over by the Provisional Government and he heard Collins speaking to a female on the phone (Kitty Kiernan):

'I spent two hours with De Valera last evening,' he said.

'You must have been thoroughly bored.'

'On the contrary,' replied Collins, 'they were about the two happiest hours I have spent for many months'.[29]

President Arthur Griffith, unaware that Collins and De Valera were talking together, proposed a motion in Dáil Éireann on 19 May which called for elections to be held in twenty-eight constituencies in southern Ireland on the 16 June. Referring to the anti-Treaty members, of whom Boland was one, he stated:

They have refused everything; and they have refused everything with the

insolent threat to us of civil war. No one wishes to see civil war. It is an
abhorrent thing. But the government of a country that would be held up,
having gone to the last limit – the last extreme – by a threat of civil war
from any small body of men representing not two per cent. of the people
... would be condemned forever as a government of poltroons.[30]

Griffith, while right in his assumption that the majority of the people of southern Ireland were in favour of the Treaty, was wrong in
saying the anti-Treaty side had only the support of 2% of the people in the twenty-six counties. Kevin O'Higgins seconded the election motion of Arthur Griffith: 'Personally, I am glad that no such
oil-and-water and wolf-and-lamb coalition was agreed upon'.[31]

'It would not be very good for you,' Harry retorted.[32]

Richard Mulcahy, on the pro-Treaty side of the house, inter-
vened to say that they should go back and find out on what particular point in their discussions of the previous day did De Valera
and Collins disagree. This cooled the atmosphere when all deputies
became aware that the two leaders were meeting. Patrick O'Keeffe,
West Cork pro-Treaty deputy, proposed that the house adjourn
until eight o'clock that night to allow Collins and Dev report on
their talks. Michael Collins explained that De Valera and he were
having pleasant conversations which did not result in anything
and he recommended that instead of the house adjourning for a
few hours that it rise until three o'clock the following day, Saturday.

That Friday night Collins had dinner with John Chartres, one
of the secretaries at the Treaty negotiations in London. The following morning (Saturday) Chartres got in touch with Seán T.
O'Kelly urgently. Seán asked his wife to phone her sister, Richard
Mulcahy's wife, to tell her that Seán T. wanted to talk to her husband. They met about nine o'clock that morning. O'Kelly outlined
to him briefly his plan for a pact. Mulcahy in principle accepted
the pact and he said he would bring Collins to meet O'Kelly immediately. Collins arrived shortly afterwards and said he would
accept the plan if Seán T. could secure The Longfellow's (Dev) acceptance. Seán T. got in touch with Dev who left a morning meeting of anti-Treaty deputies to meet Collins at the Mansion House.
Later O'Kelly asked Harry to accompany him to the Mansion House
and they both met Richard Mulcahy. A messenger was sent into
the room, where Collins and De Valera were in discussion, asking

if they had made any progress with their report but they replied 'we have made no progress whatever'. Seán T. suggested to Mulcahy that they both go in and take part in the meeting and O'Kelly asked Harry to come with him. When Mulcahy, Boland and O'Kelly joined De Valera and Collins, O'Kelly said, 'This is a new meeting. I am chairman ... Since you cannot agree on the first line, let us start at the last line and work backwards'. After much recrimination and outbursts of anger and resentment, they all agreed to a Pact which Collins and De Valera signed after four hours of argument. Both sides had resolved to nominate a coalition Sinn Féin panel of pro-Treaty and anti-Treaty candidates in the same proportion as in the Second Dáil. They also made provision for Labour, Farmer and Independent candidates to stand in the general election. They agreed that after the election a coalition government would be headed by a president elected by the majority of Dáil deputies. The Minister for Defence would represent the Free State army and would be acceptable to the anti-Treaty forces as well. Of nine other ministers five would be from the majority party and four from the minority. After discussion and some criticism De Valera got the sanction of his party for the Pact. The problem then was to get approval from the pro-Treaty Party. Seán T. was sitting in the Dáil chamber when Harry went in and said, 'Mick wants to see you outside'.

Collins said Griffith was very vexed and refused to accept the Pact. O'Kelly said, 'You are the boss, if you really want it you can get it accepted'.

Collins went back to the meeting but soon sent Harry for O'Kelly again. This time Collins said that Griffith and a number of his principal backers were totally against the Pact and he asked O'Kelly to talk to Griffith. O'Kelly and Griffith were old friends and they went into a vacant office and had a long talk. Eventually Griffith agreed to drop his opposition to the Pact.[33]

The deputies went back into the Dáil chambers at 4.35pm that Saturday evening, 20 May 1922. Michael and Harry were talking in the lobby. They both had worked hard for peace and they now believed that significant progress had been made. At 4.40pm Arthur Griffith and his cabinet marched into the chamber. As he passed in, Michael Collins placed a document on the speaker's desk that gave the terms of his latest consultations with De Valera.

When the Dáil heard that a Pact had been agreed, the members cheered[34] and the agreement was approved by Dáil Éireann.[35] The deputies, smiling and cheerful, quickly passed out into the street in better spirits than had been seen for a long time.[36] The country breathed a sigh of relief. Seán Etchingham, the anti-Treaty Sinn Féin TD for Co. Wexford said, 'there's an atmosphere of peace and goodwill amongst the men who were a few days ago bitterly opposed and I have great hopes now that Ireland is and will be united again'.[37]

An Phoblacht the anti-Treaty newspaper of the period welcomed the agreement. 'If it leads, as we trust it will, to the unification of the army, it thereby averts the terrible final decision of civil war ...'[38] But *Young Ireland,* Griffith's newspaper, struck a note of caution: 'Let there be no muddled thought about its implications. It does not involve either the abandonment of the Treaty or the suspension of its advocacy'.[39]

Harry wrote to Joe McGarrity on 30 May 1922:

I delayed writing to you until I had something to report you which would give you pleasure. You will have read of the 'Collins-De Valera Pact' and all I can say is this – that I worked very hard to secure unity and am quite happy with the present situation.[40]

He ended this letter with note of uncertainty:

The whole game is now in the hands of Mr Collins. We shall see how he will act. I, for one would like to think that he will direct all his actions towards the Republic. I cannot say that I doubt him; yet I am uneasy as to his intentions.[41]

BOLAND'S PEACE PACT ON THE ROCKS

Harry received widespread congratulations from all over America because of the Pact agreement. Liam Pedlar wrote from New York: 'I feel happier since I heard it than I have been for months ... wait till John [Devoy] gets after you in next week's *Gaelic American* – now you go and upset all his theories by making peace. Mo náire ort (Shame on you)'.[1] James K. McGuire wrote from Washington: 'I was glad to see that your own name was frequently mentioned in the press dispatches, as having been responsible for the pact and that it was largely along the lines of your ideas and resolution'.[2]

All interested people could contest the election.[3] A comparison between the way this pact election functioned in Harry's own constituency of Mayo South-Roscommon South and how it fared in the Co. Wexford constituency explains the mechanism of the Pact election. In the 1921 general election, the Mayo South-Roscommon South constituency had returned four Sinn Féin deputies, Harry, Thomas Maguire, William Sears and Dan O'Rourke. When division came on the Treaty issue, Harry and Thomas Maguire voted anti-Treaty and William Sears and Dan O'Rourke voted pro-Treaty. When the Pact Election was called these four candidates were nominated by Sinn Féin and they were put forward on the national panel but Boland and Maguire were defined as CR meaning Coalition Republican candidates and O'Rourke and Sears as CT which meant Coalition Treaty candidates. As no Labour or Farmers' candidates were nominated they were returned unopposed. If this pattern were repeated in all the other constituencies the Third Dáil would have the same anti-Treaty and pro-Treaty representation as before the election, but this did not happen in every constituency. In Co. Wexford four Sinn Féin deputies were elected in the 1921 general election. Two were from the northern part of the county, Seamus Doyle and Seán Etchingham. The other two were from the southern part – James Ryan and Ald. Richard Corish. When they voted on the Treaty, only Ald. R. Corish, voted for it.[4] The Pact Agreement now required Co. Wexford Sinn Féin to put up the same four candidates who voted on the Treaty.

Before the Collins–De Valera Pact, the Labour Party in Wexford held a nominating conference and Ald. R. Corish and Denis O'Callaghan, Enniscorthy were chosen by 60 delegates as Labour's two candidates for the expected general election. Ald. R. Corish would not agree to be nominated as a Sinn Féin Coalition Treaty candidate and he said he voted for the Treaty but 'I am not a member of any political party now but the Irish Labour Party and I am fully alive to the anxiety of the Labour Party to maintain its independent position'.[5] He explained that 'the national assembly would scrap the old laws of England, under which we are living for so long and hence it was absolutely necessary that the Labour Party should be in that assembly'.[6]

On Monday 29 May a meeting of the Co. Wexford Republican executive in Enniscorthy selected the three sitting anti-Treaty members as election candidates on the Sinn Féin coalition panel – Etchingham, Ryan and Seamus Doyle. The delegates were asked to work with their old comrades, leaving aside all consideration of party interests, and keeping only in mind the welfare of the nation.[7] J. J. O'Byrne, member of Wexford county council, was picked at a pro-Treaty convention in Wexford town to replace Ald. R. Corish.[8] A convention of the Wexford Farmers' Association selected two candidates, Michael Doyle, president of the Wexford Farmers' Association and W. H. Johnson, Monamolin, Co. Wexford.[9] There were four Sinn Féin coalition candidates, two Labour candidates, two Farmer candidates – eight candidates in all for four Dáil seats.

There were seven other constituencies like Mayo South-Roscommon South where there were no contests held: Clare; Donegal; Kerry-Limerick; Leitrim-Roscommon; Limerick City-Limerick East; Mayo North and West. Trinity College was also uncontested where four Unionists stood for four seats. In constituencies where there were elections because other interested groups put forward candidates the fact that Sinn Féin recommended a national panel of candidates prevented the Treaty becoming a controversial topic at election meetings. In the great majority of cases, both anti-Treaty and pro-Treaty candidates stood side by side on the same platform under the Sinn Féin banner.

Winston Churchill held a cabinet sub-committee meeting in Westminster before the Pact Election and complained bitterly about how Michael Collins was conducting his political affairs. He said that the Four Courts and other buildings in Dublin were occupied and Michael Collins was making no effort to prevent this. His defence was that 'he was not going to make martyrs of the De Valeraites'. There had been a proposal for an 'agreed election according to which the Free Staters would have eighty seats and De Valera's people forty seats. But

> Boland (De Valera's secretary) put forward a different proposal. He asked for 'an agreed election' on the basis of the existing representation. The Provisional Government refused this and Arthur Griffith made a terrific speech against it on Friday. On Saturday night came the announcement that Boland's scheme – almost exactly had been swallowed by Collins.[10]

General Macready who was present at the meeting said that 'Boland was the true architect of the pact'. Chamberlain then read the reference to Boland's share in the agreement as set out in a memorandum of Mr Curtis'.[11]

Churchill summoned Arthur Griffith, Éamon Duggan, Kevin O'Higgins and Hugh Kennedy, law officer to the Irish Provisional Government, to see him in London. He explained that the first difficulty confronting the British government was the character of the election. He warned that if that election were not valid in all respects, then the parliament resulting from the election would not be capable of making laws 'in the manner of the Free State'.

'There is no difficulty in the Sinn Féin party holding an election themselves – but such a process had no validity,' he said. 'It will be a convention like an Ard- Fheis.'

'It would be an assemblage of members gathered by electoral law to be a Provisional Parliament,' Hugh Kennedy replied.

'We could not recognise it,' retorted Churchill.

Churchill probed further.

'Take a case where an anti-Treaty candidate puts up, e.g., North Tipperary, will there be any other candidate other than the Sinn Féin candidate in that district'.

'There will be non-panel candidates.'.

'But as a matter of fact, as between the Sinn Féin party, there will be no issue of Treaty and anti-Treaty,' enquired Churchill.

'The Labour Party will contest seventeen or eighteen seats. These will compel the Farmers' Union to run candidates in opposition. By 6 June there will be a great many Independents in the field. We shall have Treaty and anti-Treaty, Agriculture and Labour,'

Kevin O'Higgins replied.

Griffith came out in support: 'At the worst we will go back with a ten or eighteen majority instead of four. Not all the panel candidates will go back.'

'If the opinion here is that the election is being a farce, our parliament will not recognise it,' warned Churchill.

'Most of the people wished to avoid the conflict. Two-thirds of the people believe that we have got out of the difficulty by means of this Pact,' answered O'Higgins.

Churchill turned his attention to the part of the Pact that applied after the election. According to the agreement the executive would be formed which would consist of a president, the Minister of Defence (representing the army), and nine other ministers – five from the pro-Treaty Party and four from the anti-Treaty Party – each party to choose its own nominees.

'After the election you propose to form a coalition government with four Republican ministers,' said Churchill. 'The Treaty will be broken if these ministers do not make a declaration of acceptance of the Treaty.'

'The cabinet will sign and we will have these four as extern ministers,' answered Griffith.

'I believe that will be held to be a breach of the Treaty,' retorted Churchill.

'Does it matter if De Valera is in charge of education,' replied Kevin O'Higgins.

'Boland, De Valera's secretary, got the core of his proposals adopted,' said Churchill who knew more than the delegation expected. 'I am certain if ministers of your parliament do not sign, it will be proved technically to be a breach of the Treaty and if the Treaty lapses, I do not like to contemplate the situation.'

Griffith had the last word: 'We have a small number of Bolsheviks and a vast number of men returned from the Great War who have lost the normal attitude to human life and property. We want to divorce them from fighting. This pact was concluded as a way of doing that.'[12]

The subject was left to be discussed at a bigger conference a few days later. The Pact Election was in the balance as far as the British government was concerned.

Back in Ireland the Collins-De Valera Pact was unanimously ratified by the Sinn Féin Ard-Fheis. Éamon de Valera, still President of Sinn Féin, addressed the gathering.

> The two sections of the organisation has agreed to send out a common panel and we ask the organisation to back these panel candidates against all others irrespective of the views they hold on the Treaty.[13]

Michael Collins seconded the motion and stated:

> If, as has been said, the agreement imperils the Treaty, we have to face that situation in this manner; that we have made an agreement which will bring stable conditions to the country which is more valuable than any other agreement.[14]

Collins seemed to be putting the Pact Agreement before the terms of the Treaty for the sake of stable conditions in Ireland.

At a meeting of the Provisional Government it was pointed out that 'already as a result of the agreement the election registers for certain areas, which had been seized by raiders have been returned to the proper authorities, with the result that the elections could now be held'. But the Provisional Government made it quite clear also that they were determined 'to stand by the Treaty'.[15]

All the legal work on the drafting of the Irish constitution was over on 25 May. The constitution being presented to the British was radical in nature and, if adopted, would allow De Valera to again get fully involved in Dáil Éireann.[16] There was no clause in it that required elected representatives of the Irish people to take an oath of allegiance to a British monarch. It also contained an article which allowed for a number, not exceeding eight, of external ministers to the Dáil. This would allow representatives of the anti-Treaty side to enter a coalition government, something already arranged in the Collins–De Valera Pact.

On Saturday, 27 May, the British met an Irish delegation, which included Collins and discussed the proposed Free State constitution. The British Prime Minister was angry and said 'that the draft constitution was substantially a setting up of an independent Republic in Ireland and that it was a complete going back on the provisions of the Treaty'. He then said that he had told Collins he took a grave view and Collins retorted that 'the interpretation of the Treaty rested not so much with them as with the legal team'. Churchill said the British government thought that it was not worth while taking any steps to facilitate the elections. Arthur Griffith, Michael Collins and W. T. Cosgrave put up a spirited opposition and Lloyd George said the British government would allow the election to proceed as they did not want to put the Irish ministers in a position of having it said that his majesty's government 'was interfering with a dominion on a point of date of an election'. They agreed to this on the understanding and definite assurance of Griffith and Collins that 'they proposed that the constitution should be brought within the Treaty where there was a difference between the two'. Arthur Griffith agreed and Michael Collins said that he would send for the other Irish legal advisers.[17]

At a British cabinet meeting three days later Churchill said that 'the distance between the constitution (presented by the Irish delegation) and the Treaty was almost as great as when the Prime Minister began his negotiations with De Valera'. He feared that 'if the four Republican ministers did not take the oath, it was possible there might be resort to some subterfuge'.[18]

The next day the British sent Tom Jones to see Arthur Griffith and Michael Collins to tell them how grave the situation was. Jones reported that Collins was in an irreconcilable mood and consistently reverted to the position in Belfast and Ulster. He even referred to going back to fight with his comrades, Mulcahy and MacEoin, since the British seemed bent on war. Jones proposed a further conference on the following day. Griffith readily accepted but Collins after considerable reluctance said he would attend if asked.[19]

The following day Griffith and Collins had an interview with Lloyd George. Collins said that 'they were not prepared to have the English common law forced upon them'. He said that 'the British were paying the specials who murdered Catholics; it had not been so in Canada'. The Prime Minister reported that Collins was obstreperous all during the meeting.[20]

After the meeting the British Prime Minister asked Churchill how long could Mr Collins be kept in London.

'It has been difficult to get him and it would be very difficult to keep him any length of time,' answered Churchill.

'Griffith stands by the Treaty and is willing to discuss it,' said Lloyd George. 'Collins was silent. I thought that ominous.'

The Prime Minister said that the British government would take action at once if the constitution were Republican. The British government would fight for allegiance to the king and they would have the whole British empire behind them.

Churchill did not dismiss war. 'Mr Collins said that in the event of a break, the Irish troops would probably be in uniform and able to conform to the laws of war. In my opinion they may resign.'

'Griffith is straight and means to be straight,' said Lloyd George.

'I doubt if Griffith will split with Collins,' answered Churchill.

Churchill then referred to a statement made by Collins that you cannot set bounds to the march of a nation and a statement made by De Valera's secretary – Boland – that 'if the constitution would be made Republican enough to be considered outside the Treaty there might instantly be a Coalition government.'

'It may be useful if you can get a split,' Lloyd George said.

Churchill agreed.

'We could ask Griffith if he could form a government. I am against going into the interior of Ireland with our troops in case of a massacre.'[21]

The British decided what sanctions should be applied if the Irish cabinet refused to give a guarantee to conform with the Treaty in the context of their constitution. Churchill proposed to cut off all revenue to the Irish Provisional Government, and to order the British navy to seize custom houses at three Irish ports.[22]

Lloyd George wrote to Arthur Griffith and the Irish delegation at their hotel in London, detailing a series of questions he wanted them to answer about the proposed constitution including the declaration to be signed by all members of the Irish Provisional Government after the election that they recognised the Treaty. If the four Republicans nominated to become ministers in a coalition government refused to do this they would disqualify themselves. Griffith discussed the position with O'Higgins, Duggan and Hugh Kennedy who were in London. Collins and Cosgrave had returned to Ireland. The Irish delegation were worried about the threatened sanctions and Griffith replied to Lloyd George's question on whether all the members of the Irish Government would be required to sign the declaration of acceptance of the Treaty – they would be so obligated.[23]

Back in Ireland plans were going ahead for the election. On 2 June correspondence was sent out by the Sinn Féin Executive, under the names of Austin Stack and Harry Boland (anti-Treaty) and P. Ó Caoimh (pro-Treaty) giving instructions in regard to the

Pact Election to secretaries of comhairle ceanntair of Sinn Féin. They told the secretaries of all cumainn to carry out joint canvassing and public meetings in favour of the Sinn Féin national panel of candidates.[24]

On 5 June Michael Collins and Éamon De Valera issued a joint statement:

> The terms of the agreement explicitly safeguard the right of all sections of the community ... We had hoped that the spirit of the Pact would have ensured that electoral contests would be reduced to a minimum ... We are confident that the spirit which suggested and underlies the agreement will find a response from all sections.[25]

Final nominations were accepted up to 6 June, 1922. When they closed there were twenty contested areas. The Pact agreement idea was complicated by the 47 Independent candidates. Labour had 18 candidates, there were 17 Independents representing business and professional interests and the Farmers' Party had 12.[26]

Although there was no contest in Roscommon Harry still campaigned. Speaking during the second week of June he first referred to the economic problems of his constituents:

> During the next six months there were big internal problems to be dealt with. The three most pressing of these were land settlement, housing and the unemployment problem. They (the anti-Treatyites) were out to help the Treaty side to build up the country to its very best.[27]

He believed the Pact was going to work. He believed if the coalition government lasted only six months it would get them over the danger of civil war:

> While the split was on, the people should not allow themselves to be divided. It was up to the men who led them into the mess to get them out of it. It was in the realisation that that duty lay upon the deputies that I did all I could to bring about agreement between the leaders. There had been many failures, but I had refused to believe that men who fought and worked together would fail to find a better remedy than pulling guns on one another.[28]

While praising Harry in some respects an editorial in *The Kilkenny People* of the following week, was also critical of his general policy. It described Harry as a very able, honest and courageous man and praised his presumption, that the Dáil would no longer be a talking shop or debating society but was going to tackle 'big internal problems'. The editor then pointed out that this policy justified the Farmers' Party, the Labour Party, and the commercial and professional interests in seeking representation in the new government. E. T. Keane, the writer of the editorial, then faulted Boland for contending that only candidates from the Sinn Féin coalition panel should be voted into the Dáil.[29]

A monster demonstration, under the auspices of the national Sinn Féin panel was held in the Round Room of the Mansion House at which Michael Collins, Éamon De Valera, Richard Mulcahy, Seán T. O'Kelly, Seán McGarry, Austin Stack, Harry and Mrs Tom Clarke came together on the same platform. Éamon de Valera said he was present as chairman of Sinn Féin and as the panel candidates were going forward under the auspices of Sinn Féin he would say very little but confine himself to the direction of the meeting. Michael Collins during a lengthy speech said that they had made the agreement in face of internal and external difficulties. It was only the enemies of Ireland who mistrusted the arrangements made, and 'where I find misgivings amongst the people it is easy, happily, to set their fears at rest by a little explanation'. Harry said he had never 'lost faith in unity and that the policy of Sinn Féin was to press ahead for the full national demand. In the best interests of the nation the national Sinn Féin Panel should be returned'.[30]

On 10 June Harry left Dublin with Éamon de Valera on an electioneering tour which brought him to the south-west, south and south-east of the country in a whirlwind tour. He was amongst the speakers selected to speak in North, Mid, South-West and South-East Cork constituency, the largest constituency in Ireland extending form Castletownbeare to Charleville – a distance of 130 miles. Although Michael Collins was one of the panel candidates in this huge constituency, he did not take part in this electioneering campaign. He was summoned to London on 12 June where it was officially announced that he and Arthur Griffith would meet with Winston Churchill the next day in the colonial office. Negotiations between the Irish and British governments on the constitution were then so advanced that the presence of Collins at these deliberations was considered desirable.

Harry and De Valera continued their journey into East Cork and addressed meetings in Midleton and Youghal. They passed over the border into Co. Waterford linking up with Cathal Brugha and they visited Lismore, Cappoquin, Dungarvan and Waterford. The Mall in Waterford was thronged and the speakers addressed the meeting from the windows of the town hall. The following day they spoke at Mooncoin, a quiet village but a Sinn Féin stronghold in South Kilkenny about 5 miles from Waterford City. They drove to Carrick-on-Suir and Clonmel where Harry told a big crowd: 'there were candidates coming along who were conspicuous by their absence when there was danger'. He referred to the desire of the people for peace and unity 'but now when there was unity they were doing their level best to upset it'.[31] Harry went with Éamon Dee, a Sinn Féin Republican candidate, to Cashel where they spoke and stayed overnight. On the 14 June Éamon de Valera, Harry and Austin Stack arrived into Kilkenny to address a large crowd at the Parade. In answer to a heckler who asked at what cost would his vote for an anti-Treaty Sinn Féiner be given, Harry retorted, 'the people or the man who would give up liberty to purchase a little safety, deserves neither'.[32] Harry then spoke in Dunlavin and Baltinglass in support of Robert Barton and the other Sinn Féin candidates in the Kildare-Wicklow constituency, while De Valera concentrated on Athy, Kildare and Naas. Harry ended his long electioneering tour in Carrickmacross and Monaghan.[33]

But the Pact Agreement suffered a serious set back on 14 June two days before polling day. Arriving back from London Michael Collins went straight to his native county and addressed a huge meeting in Cork City that night. He was accompanied by J. J. Walsh one of the Pro-Treaty deputies for that constituency. Speaking from Turner's Hotel, he said:

> You are facing an election here on Friday, and I am not hampered now by being on a platform where there are coalitionists and I can make a straight appeal to you, to the citizens of Cork, to vote for the candidates you think best of, whom the electors of Cork think will carry on best in the future the work that they want carried on. The country is facing a very serious situation, and if that situation is to be met as it should be, the country must have the representatives it wants and you understand fully what you have to do and I will depend on you to do it.[34]

J. J. Walsh spoke against the Pact in even stronger terms:

> In the impending election it is a matter for your own discretion. Simply cast those votes in whatever direction you think best for the Irish nation. In that spirit and with that intention alone I voted for the Treaty six months ago.[35]

Most newspapers printed the speeches the next day, 15 June, the day before the election. These words constituted a rupture of the Pact as according to the agreement each Coalition speaker was obliged to recommend the Sinn Féin coalition candidates and those alone to the electors. The voters must have been totally confused on voting day when they read in the papers Michael Collins had spoken again in Clonakilty and said he was in favour of the Pact:

> What I would ask you to do is to support the agreement that has been made in the spirit in which it was made, and that spirit was to establish a government that would secure proper order and stable conditions for the country.[36]

Speakers all over the country made appeals on that last day of electioneering for support for the coalition candidates. De Valera addressed a meeting from a platform erected at the steps of the town hall in Sligo. He spoke within the confines of the Pact agreement when he said that 'both parties in Dáil Éireann held their opinions honestly. Not being able to find a common basis they did the next best thing and agreed to differ'.[37] Tom O'Donnell, TD, who voted for the Treaty was on the same platform with the anti-Treaty leader.[38]

P. J. Little, an anti-Treaty supporter of Éamon de Valera, wrote a letter to one of the Dublin newspapers which refused to publish it. Little argued that 'the Provisional Government broke the Peace Pact directly contrary to the unanimous decision of the Second Dáil for a Peace Coalition'.[39]

The British government gave final approval to the amended constitution on 14 June. Griffith left the next day with the agreed text and hoped to put it before the new Irish parliament when it assembled in Dublin on 1 July. The Provisional Government held a meeting on 15 June. The attendance was small as many of the ministers were busy electioneering. The draft constitution as revised following the negotiations in London was read, together with a communication from Hugh Kennedy stating that the draft would probably be released that night for publication in the press.[40]

On the morning of 16 June, general election day, the daily newspapers printed the redrafted constitution. It differed greatly from the draft the constitution committee and the Provisional Government had first given to Arthur Griffith to be brought to

Lloyd George for approval. The position of the King in this approved constitution was stronger than even in the Articles of Agreement. The controversial oath of allegiance was inserted. There was no ambiguity about the compulsory taking of this oath, 'Such oath shall be taken and subscribed by every member of the Parliament/ Oireachtas before taking his seat therein before the representative of the crown, or some person authorised by him'. The governor-general represented the king.[41] Michael Collins said, after the negotiations, 'I'd rather go through everything from 1916 on than spend another week like this'.[42]

Many of the electorate did not have time to study the long and involved document before casting their votes and this was to the advantage of the pro-Treaty candidates. Frank Aiken said that 'the constitution was published on the morning of the election. Daily paper readers were small in number then'.[43] Éamon de Valera, interviewed on his return from the west on the morning of the election said, 'I have just got the paper. I have not read it'.[44]

The poll took place on 16 June and it went off peacefully. The pro-Treaty side did well and Michael Collins obtained the highest vote in the country. The anti-Treaty party fared badly and only gained nineteen seats in the twenty contested constituencies. Labour had a remarkable success. They nominated eighteen candidates and seventeen were elected. They obtained slightly more votes in the contested constituencies than the anti-Treaty side, but the Labour Party had not overtaken the anti-Treaty side because in the seven uncontested constituencies the anti-Treaty party tended to have stronger support than in the areas contested; Dan Breen's votes in Waterford-East Tipperary were not credited to the anti-Treaty total because he was described on the ballot paper as a joint nominee; these votes would have given the anti-Treaty side a slight edge over Labour if they had been included in the total anti-Treaty vote. Labour candidate, Pádraig Gaffney, a native of Killeshin, Co. Carlow, topped the poll in Carlow-Kilkenny ahead of W. T. Cosgrave. He was opposed to the oath of allegiance and refused to attend the assembly.[45] The Farmers' Organisation put forward twelve candidates and seven were elected.

In Dublin the anti-Treaty party suffered a severe reverse. Of the five deputies who supported the Republican outlook in the capital city, only one, Seán T. O'Kelly was elected. The Treaty Party retained its seven seats in Dublin. The strongest anti-Treaty representation from the contested constituencies was East Mayo-Sligo where they won three of the five seats.

Many of Harry's old friends lost their seats. Members of the Dáil who helped him in America were defeated – Liam Mellows failed to get elected in Galway and Lord Mayor Donal Óg O'Callaghan of Cork was defeated. Harry had campaigned for Éamon Dee in the Waterford-East Tipperary constituency but he was not re-elected. Veteran guerrilla fighter, Dan Breen, did not capture a seat either. In Dublin Mrs Kathleen Clarke, Countess Markievicz and Dr Ada English were defeated. Harry was very disappointed when Mrs Margaret Pearse, mother of Pádraig and Willie Pearse, failed to get elected in Co. Dublin.

But Mary MacSwiney, held her seat in Cork City and Patrick MacCartan on the opposite side now, but still a friend, was re-elected in Laois-Offaly. In Wexford Ald. Richard Corish and Denis O'Callaghan were elected for Labour and Michael Doyle (Farmer) and Seamus Doyle (anti-Treaty) were elected. Dr James Ryan and Seán Etchingham lost their seats.

The final result of the 1922 general election, taking into account the contested and uncontested constituencies was 58 pro-Treaty, 36 anti-Treaty, 17 Labour Party, Farmers' Party 7, Independents 6 and 4 Unionists representing Trinity College. Robert Barton felt that 'great numbers of the people were never Republican. They were sympathetic but not sincere Republicans. They were infused by the leaders'.[46]

An anti-Treaty supporter, Mr Henry from Co. Kildare, had some criticism of the voting register that was four years out of date. 'Young men and women who were good enough to fight were not good enough to vote. If Kevin Barry were alive today, Arthur Griffith would not allow him to vote'.[47]

Harry wrote to Joe McGarrity and said 'The election showed that the people favoured the Treaty and our party lost many seats'.[48] Éamon de Valera said in Dublin, 'the men and women who have been rejected by the electorate have gone down true to their principles, true to every pledge and promise they made'.[49] Harry expressed his deep disappointment to Éamon Dee when he wrote to him sending condolences on his defeat:

> You should be rather proud of the fact that you will not be a member of this coming assembly. My only regret is that we did not all go down together with our flag flying as you have done and the other members who

have suffered at this election.[50]

The second part of the Pact which promised a coalition government after the election had not been ruled out yet. Ninety-four
deputies on the pro-Treaty and anti-Treaty tickets had been elected
from the national coalition panel of Sinn Féin nominees. Would
the pro-Treaty party, headed by Griffith and Collins, go ahead
with the coalition idea or would they rule with their own 58 TDs
who would not be a majority in the next parliament if all elected
representatives attended? Harry waited and wondered.

THE WAR OF FRIENDS

The constitution was a huge disappointment to anti-Treaty members of the IRB. When interviewed about the constitution before leaving London for home Arthur Griffith said:

> The constitution is that of a free and democratic state, and under it Ireland for the first time for centuries secured the power and the opportunity to control and develop her own resources and to live her own national life.[1]

Francis Hackett, the Irish founder of the 'New Republic', reviewed the Irish constitution in the *Sunday Times:* 'The De Valera group will regard it as an English triumph. And on the face of it the Irish constitution is regarded as an English triumph'.[2]

Rory O'Connor told a *Daily Herald* correspondent, 'the thing is too rotten to talk about. The only good thing I can see in it is that it gives a holiday every four years. But it is only what I expected'.[3]

Dev waited until Wednesday, 21 June, to give his opinion on the new constitution:

> It is only a draft and I feel confident that Dáil Éireann will not pass it as it stands. As it stands it will exclude from the public service, and practically disfranchise every honest Republican ... Dáil Éireann will not dishonour itself by passing it.[4]

Harry considered that it was worse than the Treaty because he felt that 'Republicans are disfranchised under the constitution and representation is denied them in parliament by the oath of allegiance, etc.'[5] He realised now that achieving a Republic would be harder than ever before.[6]

One hundred and thirty thousand Irish people had cast their votes to elect 19 anti-Treaty deputies in the contested constituencies, aware that these representatives would not take the oath of allegiance. A further eleven thousand people had voted for Patrick Gaffney, the Labour TD who topped the poll in Carlow-Kilkenny, aware that he was not going to take this oath either. The British government made plans in the constitution to disfranchise these people. The British cabinet had forced the Irish delegation to accept the amended constitution, under a threat of occupying three ports. In order to exclude De Valera and three other Republican ministers from participating in a coalition interim government, the British government said they were prepared to go to war.

Harry wrote to Joe McGarrity on the 22 June and pointed out that Collins had won his majority for the Treaty on 'the specious plea that the Treaty clauses could be interpreted in a constitution, which would (in effect) ... eliminate the oath of allegiance, and the governor-general'. Harry said that he felt like 'two cents' for having even hoped that Collins would return to his allegiance to the Republic'. He described his inner thoughts at that moment:

> There are many in Ireland who believe that we must continue the fight at once, against England – others, there are who think that we must face the fact, i.e., that the people have repudiated our policy and consequently we should quit and give a free chance to the others to work out the Treaty. I am rent and torn between these two ideas and have not made up my mind as to which is best for Ireland, although I am inclined towards the war policy and will please God, be alongside any group who may take the bold and manly way.[7]

Harry said that he could not understand the minds of men like Mick and Griffith, who answered every crack of the whip from London and evidently preferred the terms imposed by Britain rather than stand with their old colleagues of the 'six glorious years'.[8]

Before the break on the Pact there had been talk that Seán T. O'Kelly would be welcomed by Mulcahy and Collins as Minister for Finance and De Valera as Minister for Education.[9] When he wrote to Joe McGarrity Harry said, 'I expected a call from Mick as to the men on our side who would be required to fill posts in the cabinet, in accordance with the agreement'.[10]

On 22 June two young men, Reginald Dunne and Joseph O'Sullivan (ex-soldiers of the British army), shot Sir Henry Wilson in London. Wilson, a native of Edgeworthstown, Co. Longford, was one of the most prominent English generals in the First World War. After the war he was appointed Chief of the Imperial General Staff. Joe Dolan, a member of the Free State army and a friend of Michael Collins said the reason for his assassination was 'the Belfast pogroms were on at the time and it was well known that Wilson played his part in them'.[11]

The death of Wilson was high on the agenda of a conference of ministers held at Downing Street shortly after the shooting. Amongst the documents found on one of those arrested was a printed scheme of organisation of the Irish Republican Army.[12] Another referred to re-organising the IRB in London and was signed 'Liam'. 'Now is the time to re-organise,' it said. 'If four of you go and see the Big Fellow [Collins] he would arrange an election'.[13] During the discussion the attention of the ministers was called to the situation in the Four Courts from which are believed 'to emanate the principal plots in southern Ireland, in northern Ireland and in the United Kingdom'.[14] It was recommended that a letter be sent to Michael Collins stating that information had been received connecting the assassins of Field Marshal Sir Henry Wilson with the IRA and that it was intolerable that Rory O'Connor should be permitted to remain with his followers in open rebellion in the heart of Dublin in possession of the Four Courts. The letter should contain a demand that the Irish Provisional Government, who were now supported by the declared will of the Irish people, should bring this state of affairs to an end. This letter was sent to Michael Collins by Lloyd George on the 22 June and the British Prime Minister offered assistance in the form of the necessary pieces of artillery which might be required to bring an end to the occupation of the Four Courts.[15]

On 23 June the Irish Provisional Government sent a reply, in the absence of Collins who had gone to Cork. They asked that the information to which Lloyd George had referred should be placed at their disposal.[16] They showed no urgency to attack the Four Courts.

'Personally, I am convinced Collins ordered it [Dunne and O'Sullivan to shoot Wilson],' said Joe Dolan.[17] Joe Sweeney, pro-Treaty deputy from Donegal, met Collins in Dublin the day after Wilson was shot. 'It was two men of ours who did it,' Collins said.[18] Oscar Traynor said that the shooting of Wilson was a complete surprise to the army executive in the Four Courts: 'It was believed to be an IRB action'.[19] De Valera suspected the IRB also.[20] But the British blamed the Four Courts' garrison for the assassination. (Reginald Dunne and Joe O'Sullivan were executed for the killing of Sir Henry Wilson.)

On 23 June Lloyd George discussed with other ministers a plan which General Macready had worked out for a surprise assault on the Four Courts by the British if the Irish Provisional Government did not make the assault themselves. It involved the use of a tank, and, if necessary of howitzers and aeroplanes.[21] At the conference of ministers on 24 June, Lloyd George passed round the reply he received from the Irish Provisional Government to his letter asking that Republican forces be dislodged from the Four Courts. The reply intimated 'that the Provisional Government had the matter in hand and that Mr Michael Collins would give his personal attention to it that day'. But the British government was not happy because they did not promise immediate action and implied a postponement of any action until after the meeting of parliament fixed for 1 July. The conference went on making their own plans for the Four Courts' attack which now included having a battleship off Kingstown to take prisoners from the Four Courts to a possible destination in Malta.[22] At their next meeting on Sunday, 25 June, the ministers agreed that notice should be given to the Irish Provisional Government that, if they did not deal with the occupation of the Four Courts within four days, the British government would do so. Finally the Secretary of State for the colonies, Winston Churchill, was authorised to make it quite clear in the House of Commons debate the following day that the British government could not proceed with the Treaty until the situation in the Four Courts was cleared up.[23]

A close American friend of Harry's, Mary McWhorter, who had an executive position in the AARIR, came to visit Ireland, hoping to find more peaceful conditions here because of the Pact. She arrived in Dublin on 20 June and met Harry the following day in the Gresham. She found that he was 'terribly disturbed' and he told her how hard Collins had worked to try and get him to go with the pro-Treaty side and that Harry had tried to get Mick to come back to his first principles. 'Night after night Mick walked out to Clontarf with me but I could not let him enter the house because my mother and sister did not want to see him because they thought he had betrayed his country'.[24]

That week, Michael Collins was grappling with the dilemma of what action he should take on the ultimatum delivered by Lloyd George in his letter and by Winston Churchill in his House of Commons speech. At first he was enraged. 'Let Churchill come over here and do his dirty work,' he snapped.[25] Collins knew that the executive of the anti-Treaty forces had quarrelled and there was a split at the top. Mellows, O'Connor and O'Malley were on one side and were still in the Four Courts. Liam Lynch and many other Munster officers were in a minority group and were staying in the Clarence Hotel. It would be an opportune time for the Provisional Government to attack the Four Courts. It might be over in a short time and the war might not spread to Munster, the most dangerous area of all. What Collins did not realise was that talks were going on between the two anti-Treaty factions and the split was virtually healed.

On Monday of the last week of June, Harry and Mary McWhorter were guests at a dinner at the home of Seán T. O'Kelly. They knew that earlier that day the Provisional Government had arrested Leo Henderson, who was prominent in the Four Courts' garrison. The Free State took him into custody for commandeering a number of cars, brought from Belfast, from a garage in Baggot Street. He wanted to enforce the boycott of goods from the six counties.[26] Word came during dinner that Rory O'Connor's Four Courts' garrison had seized the Deputy Chief-of-Staff of the Free State army, General 'Ginger' J. J. O'Connell, in retaliation. They were holding him in the Four Courts where he was playing bridge with Republican officers. Harry walked back to the hotel with Mary McWorther that evening and he said that he saw trouble brewing.

Arthur Griffith and the cabinet decided that this was the moment to strike. General O'Connell's kidnapping was reason enough for an attack on the Four Courts. After dark on Tuesday 27 June, Major-General Emmet Dalton went to General Macready's British army headquarters in Dublin with some motor-lorries and collected, by arrangement, some eighteen-pounder artillery field-guns and a reasonable supply of ammunition and towed them into town.[27]

Terence de Vere White said:

> One of his (Griffith's) first tasks after the June election was to order the army to bombard the Four Courts which Rory O'Connor and his companions had made into a fort. It was Griffith rather that Collins who took the initiative. Collins was prepared to go to almost any length before he fired on old comrades. 'We shall be considered the greatest poltroons in history if we don't take action,' said Griffith.[28]

There were rumours that the Four Courts was about to be attacked. Oscar Traynor, commanding officer of the Dublin Brigade of anti-Treaty forces went to the Four Courts and appealed to Mellows and O'Connor to come out of the building and take charge outside. He emphasised that there must not be another

Easter Week but they would not listen. Oscar told Liam Mellows that 'as far as I can see you are just vain glory seekers and you should come out.' Liam Mellows just put his arms around Oscar and said goodbye.[29]

At 3.40am on 28 June, Tom Ennis, a Free State officer, delivered a note to the Four Courts garrison demanding surrender within twenty minutes on behalf of the Provisional Government. No surrender was given and shortly after 4am the Free State army opened fire on the Four Courts with shells from the eighteen-pounders on the opposite side of the Liffey and with rifle and machine gun fire.

Traynor set up headquarters in the Plaza and sent out orders to all of the anti-Treaty Dublin Brigade commandants 'to stand to'. Harry reported to the Plaza and volunteered for service.[30] He had been waiting for the call from Mick to form the coalition Sinn Féin government but no word came. Instead the only message he had heard was the noise of the shells from the big guns as they exploded against the walls of the Four Courts.

Oscar Traynor conducted a brigade council meeting in the Plaza and the anti-Treaty forces seized Barry's Hotel for food and accommodation and for a while used it as HQ. Oscar sent men to occupy the Gresham and Hammam Hotels to force the Free Staters to negotiate and to relieve pressure on the Four Courts. Cathal Brugha, the former Minister for Defence, reported as a private. 'Well private,' said Traynor, 'you're promoted to commandant on the staff and I shall greatly value your wisdom and service'. He put Brugha in charge in Sackville Street.

Seán T. O'Kelly reported for duty to the Plaza. De Valera came to see Traynor and asked, 'what are your plans?'[31] Éamon de Valera later joined his old battalion in York Street as a private.[32]

Oscar decided to send couriers down the country to link up with the different divisions and to seek Republican reinforcements to come to the aid of the beleaguered Dublin Brigade. Harry was sent to Liam Lynch, Chief-of-Staff of the anti-Treaty forces, in Limerick with Oscar's plan for the defence of Dublin.[33] Lynch had slipped out of Dublin when the Four Courts was shelled to organise Republican forces in the south. The conflict was straightforward now – the forces who supported the Treaty became known as the Free State or regular army. Those who fought for a Republic were called Anti-Treaty, Republican or irregular forces.

ON THE DUBLIN MOUNTAINS

The firing from the Four Courts area was deafening as Harry made his way down Sackville Street in the direction of the quays. He met Corkman Moss Donegan and Seán Lehane who had come out of the Clarence Hotel and told them he had to get to Liam Lynch as soon as possible. They were going south too and they commandeered a car and drove out of Dublin. They were stopped again and again by Free State troops but they got through.[1]

They kept on travelling until it was dark. They needed food and a rest and Harry knew one place where he was assured of a welcome. They headed for Rockview House, Borris-in-Ossory, home of John Tynan. John and Cis welcomed him with open arms and they had a meal. John Joe and Tom, two of John's children, were sleeping upstairs and Harry wanted to see them so Cis brought him up to the bedroom and he tiptoed to the bedside and gave each of them a kiss on the forehead.[2] When he returned to the kitchen he told John that they had to move on.

Tom Smith of the Third Tipperary Brigade recalled that Harry called to the brigade headquarters in Clonmel looking for reinforcements to go to Dublin. He wanted to catch the night train from Thurles and he was driven to the station.[3]

Liam Lynch, Chief-of-Staff of the anti-Treaty forces, had special responsibility for the south and west and Ernie O'Malley, Assistant Chief-of-Staff, was O/C of the Dublin and northern areas.[4] On 1 July Lynch set out for Limerick with 'Sandow Donovan' who commanded a Cork column. Lynch immediately set up his headquarters in the New Military Barracks in Limerick. When he arrived, the Mayor of Limerick, Stephen O'Mara, arranged a meeting with Commandant-General Donnchadha Hannigan, O/C of the Free State forces who occupied another part of Limerick City, to try to avoid armed conflict. Liam Deasy, divisional O/C of the Republican forces, had already reached an agreement with Hannigan. Mick Leahy of Cork described the mood there:

> When we got down to Limerick, 'Sandow' was in charge of the columns. Negotiations were on and fighting was stopped there. That is what finished our fellows. 'Everything is going to be fixed up,' was the word and the waiting there demoralised the men.[5]

When Harry reached Limerick he asked Lynch to send on reinforcements to Oscar Traynor to defend Dublin. 'Lynch was more
concerned with peace than war', Harry reported back to Oscar
Traynor.[6] In fact Oscar sent out fourteen couriers in all but only got
a reply from Seamus Robinson and the O/C Belfast: 'Belfast sent
fifty half starved men without arms,' said Traynor.[7]

Harry reported to the South Dublin-North Wicklow area for
two reasons. He was expecting the reinforcements from Clonmel
barracks to come this way and his brother, Gerry Boland, was one
of the leaders in charge there. The column of 70 men from the
Third Tipperary Brigade left Clonmel Barracks and travelled
through Graignamanagh, Co. Kilkenny, New Ross and Enniscorthy on their way to North Wicklow. They travelled in a char-a-
banc, Crossley tenders and touring cars. Michael Sheehan was in
command. He had been quartermaster in the Third Tipperary
Brigade during the Black and Tan war.

Around the 1 July the Republican forces decided to establish
a base in Blessington to march on Dublin if the Dublin Brigade
could hold some of the buildings in the capital for long enough.
Finding that Bray would be too hard to defend they evacuated the
town and also left Cabinteely and Enniskerry. Before they left Bray
they tried, and failed, to burn the police barracks by soaking it
with petrol. They went round the shops and took away quantities
of overcoats, boots, blankets, cooking utensils and food stuffs but
left a receipt in each shop. They left Bray in 25 motor vehicles which
had been commandeered in garages and private dwellings and
drove to Blessington. The anti-Treatyites from Rathfarnham, and
the country areas of North Wicklow and East Kildare also went to
Blessington.[8] The Tipperary column under Michael Sheehan gathered there also.

The Four Courts garrison surrendered after a seventeen hours'
battle with Free State forces and 140 were taken prisoner. Seán
Lemass had been captured and he and a number of prisoners were
marched to the yard of a distillery in Stoneybatter. They were all
put in the enclosure but the door on the other side of the yard had
not been locked. A group of these prisoners including Lemass,
Ernie O'Malley, Joe Griffin and Paddy Rigney rushed out through
the door as soon as they saw the chance and they made their way
to Blessington.[9]

The anti-Treaty forces in Blessington had set up strong outposts in the neighbouring villages of Ballymore Eustace, which covered the Naas approach, and in Brittas which commanded the tram line and the main road from Dublin. Smaller outposts were spread round in a circle at places such as Poulaphouca and Kilbride to give early warning of a flank attack.[10] Commandant Gerry Boland was in control of Crooksling.

Ernie O'Malley took over the defence preparations of Blessington. The small town was almost entirely one long street and it lay under a ridge of mountains that cut Wicklow into two parts, east and west, with Blessington on the western side. The first thing O'Malley did was to appoint a defence team with Harry as Quartermaster and Seán Lemass as Director of Operations.[11] They established their headquarters in the strongly fortified Ulster Bank and they also occupied the premises of the Bank of Ireland across the road. Everybody entering or leaving the village had to produce a permit. A hospital was fitted up in a dairy and they recruited a full hospital staff including a doctor and nurses, some of whom were Cumann na mBan members.[12] The roads around Blessington were mined to prevent the approach of armoured cars. Barricades were placed near the village.[13]

At midnight on the day Lemass and O'Malley arrived, O'Malley led an anti-Treaty force in a convoy of cars towards Dublin. They brought mines and explosives with them and their advance guard was instructed to capture some of the canal bridges from Free State sentries to open up a road into Dublin. The main body was to take the College of Science where most of the ministers of the Provisional Government had taken shelter. A messenger from the Republican forces in the city centre halted them at Crooksling. Traynor, the O/C of the Dublin Brigade, sent word that he had disbanded his men from the occupation of the hotels they had taken over in Sackville Street because these buildings were now on fire. Only a rearguard of forty men under Cathal Brugha remained to put up a token fight until he got the remainder of his forces away from the centre of the city. He did not think it wise for O'Malley to enter the city with his forces at that stage.[14] Though not fully happy with these instructions or tactics, O'Malley turned around and brought his forces back to Blessington. The Tipperary men were not happy either because they had travelled to Blessington to relieve Dublin. Tom Derrig, a Republican leader from Mayo, came out from Dublin and he brought more news of the fighting and confirmed the news that the scout had brought from Oscar Traynor.[15]

Ernie O'Malley decided to move south to North Wexford with the column of Tipperary men who were anxious to return to their own county where hostilities had already broken out. Before leaving Blessington he left instructions that the town should be used as a base to attack posts in the neighbourhood and to worry the pro-Treaty forces in the Curragh. He planned to capture posts in North Wexford and then to link up with Blessington again and establish an anti-Treaty stronghold in the Wicklow-Wexford area.[16] Harry assumed command in Blessington itself because Seán Lemass went south with Ernie O'Malley.

Jack Myles of Fethard, Co. Tipperary was with the Tipperary column and before they moved out he was one of twenty-one men under the command of Martin 'Sparky' Breen who attacked Baltinglass barracks on the first Sunday afternoon in July.[17] The residents of the town were attending the monthly meeting of the Sacred Heart confraternity in the local church. The anti-Treaty group began a fierce sustained attack with rifles and the outnumbered garrison replied with a strong burst of fire. The assault lasted an hour before the occupants surrendered. Both sides chatted together after the surrender and the Republicans released their prisoners.[18] The anti-Treaty group stayed in the captured barracks that night and before they departed they left a skeleton Republican garrison made up of Dublin men. The following day 'Sparky' led his group to Castledermot in South Kildare where they billeted in several houses in the town. They commandeered anything they needed from the shops and issued receipts to re-imburse all concerned 'after the war was won'. They stayed the night and they left on Tuesday afternoon before a much bigger contingent of Free State troops arrived – they were coming from Carlow to take part in an encirclement movement on Blessington.[19] Some of the group from Tipperary joined Ernie O'Malley and the rest of Michael Sheehan's column in Carlow but more of them found their way back to Blessington.[20]

Tipperary man Mick Burke, having taken part in the fighting with the anti-Treaty forces in the Gresham Hotel, made his way out from Dublin because he heard that the Tipperary column was in Blessington and he wanted to join them.[21] He was known to his fellow volunteers as the man who had nine lives.[22] When he got to

Blessington he heard that the Tipperary column had gone to Baltinglass so he got a car and drove there to catch up with them. They were not in Baltinglass either and then anti-Treaty occupiers of the barracks gave him a guide, Laurence Sweeney, to bring him to Castledermot where they thought Breen's group was still billeted. As Burke drove into the town he did not see the Lancia armoured car facing him until he was forty yards away from it. He stuck the car into reverse gear and began to move backwards but a burst of fire from a Lewis machine gun killed Laurence Sweeney. Burke was slightly wounded but he rolled out of the car opposite a cottage gate. He ran into the cottage, past an old lady at the door and got through a window leading to a field. He got into a drain and crossed some fields. He finished up in Blessington safe and sound. In the meantime the pro-Treaty troops continued their advance from Castledermot and captured the village of Ballytore about eight miles further up towards Dublin where they found a group of anti-Treaty soldiers. The Republican forces suffered one casualty in the gun battle at Ballytore when Sylvester Sheppard of Monasterevan was killed in action.

Harry was busy in the Blessington area. Con O'Donovan, Vice O/C of the Third Battalion, wrote to Gerry Boland, his commanding officer, to inform him that it had been decided to attack Naas barracks that night. He told him that Harry had just come in to see them and explained the plans they had for taking the barracks. Captain Dowd, had drawn up the plan and he would be in charge of the operation but he wanted Captain Watkins to assist. Dowd suggested that Gerry Boland should snipe at the Tallaght and Baldonnel posts from 1am to 2am continually. O'Donovan said that Harry 'must parade in Blessington at 10pm tonight'.[23] The attack did not take place afterwards as another group of Republicans ambushed an armoured car driven by Free State soldiers on the Naas Road and this put the Naas garrison on the alert.

Éamon de Valera was following newspaper accounts of what was happening in the Wicklow area and he drew the attention of Oscar Traynor to statements that the Free State troops were slowly but surely encircling the anti-Treaty troops in Blessington. De Valera asked Traynor to go out and extricate them.[24] Oscar wanted to have the two battalions out there – one under Gerry Boland and the other under Andy McDonnell – dispersed in small formations. Traynor told the two commandants what the Free State troops were planning. Arrangements were being made to split up the two battalions to get them out of the area when a message arrived to say that some of the anti-Treaty troops were surrounded in Cobb's Lodge in Glenasmole but were holding out against Free State troops. Oscar decided that he would take a group to rescue the Republican forces in Cobb's Lodge. Traynor gave command of the advance party to Harry with orders to keep in communication with the main party – only a mile or less to his rear. With Harry were Captain Tom Watkins and two other Volunteers, O'Hanlon and Devine. Commandant Gerry Boland was in charge of the main party and Oscar Traynor took charge of the rearguard. Glenasmole was about eight or ten miles away through difficult terrain across the mountains. The country was bare and there was an absence of trees. There were long stretches of heather and soggy bogland that impeded and delayed progress. After some hours of heavy trudging Harry reached Cobb's Lodge and found that the building was deserted. He sent back word that there was no battle in progress. Oscar Traynor gathered together all the men who had marched to Glenasmole. They stopped for over an hour at Ballinascorney House and were given tea and food by the owners. Traynor advised the officers to get their men back to their home areas to await fresh orders from GHQ. Then he made his own way back to Dublin.[25]

When Oscar Traynor returned to Dublin he wrote a report to Liam Lynch: 'Commandant Gerry Boland was working like a hero'. He claimed that 'he regarded the continuance of activities in Dublin as the most essential thing for the present'. He also asserted that 'they (Free State troops) may concentrate on the south next if we do not keep things going in the city'.[26]

Éamon de Valera was right – the anti-Treaty forces in the Blessington area were being encircled. In a clever and well planned move the Free State military army was converging on Blessington from three directions. From the south and the east the round-up was conducted by a contingent of the Curragh Brigade under Commandant Bishop. The party that had come from Carlow through Castledermot and Ballytore supported them in the rear. From the north Commandant Heaslip advanced from the Dublin area. From the west a smaller force was moving east under Commandant McNulty. He had the difficult task of pushing his way over high mountains mostly with practically no roads on which troops could move. They tramped over bluish gaunt rocks with furze up to their waists and soft sodden ground underneath.

Commandant Bishop coming from the east first came in contact with the anti-Treaty forces at Ballymore-Eustace. The anti-Treaty forces retreated after four hours' fighting and Commandant Dineen of the Free State army was wounded in the foot. Commandant Bishop established his headquarters in the town and then began to advance on Blessington until he was about a mile and a half from the town. The detachment under Commandant Heaslip moved cautiously through Tallaght and other villages that skirt the base of the Dublin hills. In a skirmish near Brittas, Private Patrick Smith of the Free State army received a wound from which he subsequently died. As these forces advanced on the road between Saggart and Crooksling, one of their transport drivers, Private Patrick Doyle, was shot dead by a Republican sniper from a nearby wood. The advance continued and they did not meet much more opposition from the anti-Treaty troops who had retired towards their main base in Blessington.

A party of pro-Treaty soldiers under Colonel Hugo McNeill[27] moving between Kilteel and Hempstown met a Republican post at a farmhouse near Crosschapel, two miles from Blessington. The Free State soldiers attacked with rifle fire and the occupants fired many grenades in their direction. After a half an hour's fighting, the Republicans, some of whom were wounded, evacuated the position. The Free State troops took over the farmhouse and they had just done so when their scouts reported that three motor cars were approaching. The pro-Treaty occupiers guessed that they could be anti-Treaty reinforcements on their way and remained in hidden positions. The anti-Treaty party included Commandants Boland, McDonnell and Captain Tom Watkins, nearly all the top officers of the anti-Treatyites in the area. Unaware of the circumstances, they drove up confident that they were approaching friends and they were much taken aback when they got the order 'Hands Up!' from troops whom they first thought were their own. They were captured and taken away quickly in the direction of Tallaght.[28] Oscar Traynor said that 'they (Free State troops) had taken the sentry prisoner and then manned the barricade with one of their men garbed to look like our man'.[29] Gerry Boland summed up his capture, 'I was glad. After all it was Civil War. None of us wanted that'.[30]

The encircling movement of the National troops around Blessington was almost complete. Not a mouse would escape through the cordon. Harry was inside the trap and in charge. An *Irish Times* reporter returning to Dublin from the besieged area noted that he encountered a formidable array of Free State reinforcements going towards Blessington which included a heavy field piece and a turret car called 'The Kerry Blue'.[31]

Commandant McNulty, coming from the western direction found the forces under his command insufficient and he had to slow down to await reinforcements. Commandants Bishop and Heaslip were in place for the final assault on Blessington. In fact Commandant Bishop had sent a party to make a reconnaissance trip into Blessington and some shots had been exchanged.[32] This put Harry and the garrison on their guard.

At daybreak Harry and Mick Burke decided to go up into the hills to the west to size up the situation. When they got up far enough they saw the column of Free State troops coming in from the Wicklow direction. Mick Burke said that Harry decided that the way out was in that direction and back to Dublin.[33] Harry and Mick Burke went down to their men and quickly organised a hasty withdrawal. They asked for volunteers to form a rearguard action to allow the main garrison to escape and gave them a plentiful supply of ammunition and told them to fire away and give the impression that there were more than fifteen in the Blessington garrison. They hurried their other men towards the hills. Luck was with them. A sudden mist came down on the mountain and though McNulty was close by, the fog screened them from his view. A high line of hills under which they passed on their way into the mountains hid them from being observed by Commandant Bishop on the east and south and from the gaze of Commandant Heaslip in the north. When the Free State troops entered Blessington, after more than an hour's gun battle with the Republican rearguard, they were amazed to find only fifteen men in the town whom they took as prisoners.[34]

'We beat it across the hills,' remarked Mick Burke, 'and some of the Free State columns were only a few hundred yards away from us'.[35] The *Irish Times* reported that 'the elusive commander of the Irregulars in Blessington has escaped through the only opening in the whole circle of his enemies'.[36] Harry and his band made their way quickly over the mountains and reached Rathfarnham that night. They went to St Enda's, the former home of Pádraig and Willie Pearse, now occupied by their mother and they dumped their stuff. 'Harry and I then went to Phil Shanahan,' said Mick Burke, 'he looked after the men and the stuff was brought into the city'. They put all the Tipperary men in a train to Tipperary.[37]

Harry wrote to Joe McGarrity telling him that he had just had a narrow escape. He began by saying, 'I may not be in a position to write again for some time and it may very well be that I shall fall in this awful conflict'. He went on to express his opinion on 'this British manufactured war on the Republic':

> I have been in the fray since the start ... I do not know what may happen in Munster if the Free State troops invade the area. Of one thing I am certain we cannot be defeated even if Collins and his British guns succeed in garrisoning every town in Ireland ... Mick has outdone Greenwood ... Can you understand the mentality of men who are prepared to carry Ireland into the Empire over the bodies of Republicans?[38]

Harry – it has Come to This

When Harry reached Rathfarnham he was elated but that feeling did not last long. He was told that Cathal Brugha had died in the Mater Hospital. Brugha, who had been in charge of the occupation of the Hammam Hotel, had been fighting a rearguard action until his comrades had escaped. Oscar Traynor had sent word to Cathal Brugha that it was time to surrender but the word 'surrender' was never in Brugha's vocabulary. When the hotel was burning around him, Brugha called the last seventeen defenders and the three nurses together and ordered them to lay down their arms before the blazing wall toppled down on them. One of the nurses, Linda Kearns and Dr J. P. Brennan fearing that Brugha would not surrender himself stayed with him, but he stole back after they had gone out the door. Those who had left the building stood in a lane behind the hotel. The lane was crowded with pro-Treaty soldiers. Then Cathal appeared at the doorway, a revolver in each hand. The pro-Treaty troops had their rifles levelled in self-defence. Brugha darted forward. It was difficult to see down the lane because of a barricade of handcarts and a cloud of smoke. One shot was first heard and Cathal fell amid a volley of shots.[1]

Dr Seán Geraghty, Dr Joseph Brennan and two Red Cross personnel took him to the side of the lane near a wooden telegraph post and gave him every help they could. An ambulance arrived and they took the badly wounded leader to the Mater Hospital where, in spite of surgical treatment, he died two days later.[2]

When Harry wrote to Joe McGarrity on 13 July, he expressed his great admiration for Cathal who had organised the coming together of the First Dáil and who was Minister for Defence during the Black and Tan War. 'Cathal Brugha is dead! No man is here to replace him. He was easily the greatest man of his day'.[3]

Gerry Boland was a prisoner in Mountjoy; Ned, the youngest was involved with the anti-Treaty forces, Kathleen, reported for duty to the Plaza when the Four Courts was shelled. Harry himself was now back on the run – 'Poor mother' he exclaimed.[4]

Harry became morose and downhearted in July. In his letters he spoke a lot about death and in his personal contact with people he talked as if his future was very unsure. In a letter to an Ameri-

235

can friend he showed that a sense of bitterness had entered his life where there was never any trace of it before:

> Lloyd George has bought half of those who made the fight for the past six years ... and who now make war upon the Republic at the bidding of the British prime minister, with British guns, armoured cars, artillery, etc. – the Black and Tans have given way to the Green and Tans ...[5]

But Civil War was not something Harry wanted and he said that it was forced on him:

> The fight has been forced upon us – we must bear it. I am in it with a heavy heart, but yet not without hope. The world will honour Ireland for her devotion to freedom ... the world shall know that there is one land which preferred death to dishonour. Ireland is not, never was and never will be a part of the British empire, we shall keep faith with the Dead and shall not betray our trust.[6]

It pained him that the IRB was so involved in Civil War politics:

> The Supreme Council IRB are being rewarded for their treachery by being placed as military governors of his majesty's prisons. O'Hegarty is governor of Mountjoy and Ó Muirthile is in command at Kilmainham.[7]

During July, the Labour Party repeatedly demanded that the Dáil should be summoned but again and again it was prorogued. Neither the ministry of the Second Dáil nor the ministry of the Irish Provisional Government gave any recognition to the parliament elected on 16 June. Professor O'Rahilly of Cork who supported the Treaty and was a member of the Irish constitution committee set up by Collins said that in his opinion 'Michael Collins received no mandate from parliament, not even from the parliament recently elected to which he professed to be responsible'.[8] Cathal O'Shannon, poll-topper for Labour in Louth-Meath, while making it clear that he was not to be taken as lending support to the Republican Party's policy, declared 'that without the sanction of the Dáil and without giving any satisfactory explanation of their change of policy, they [Provisional Government] precipitated an attack on the headquarters of the forces with whose leaders they had been in negotiation ...'[9]

Ernie O'Malley called Harry and others to a meeting and he appointed a staff to deal with matters in the area under his command. Harry was appointed Quartermaster, Tom Derrig became Adjutant, Seán Lemass was Director of Communications and Austin Stack was in charge of accounts and records.[10]

The anti-Treaty Dublin Brigade was weak because of frequent raids and numerous arrests and there was a feeling that the fight was hopeless. Public opinion was against the anti-Treaty forces in the metropolis more than anywhere else. Catholic clergy, with few exceptions throughout the country, pounded the pulpits and called the anti-Treaty IRA all types of names – looters, bank robbers, murderers. It was very difficult to recruit any new members and almost impossible to get a room anywhere to hold a meeting. Ernie O'Malley held his staff meetings at eight o'clock in the morning in different safe houses in the city.[11]

On 12 July the Provisional Government created a war council of three. Michael Collins was appointed the General Commanding-in-Chief, Richard Mulcahy was General Chief-of-Staff and Minister for Defence and Eoin O'Duffy became General in Command south-western division.[12] William T. Cosgrave, Minister for Local Government was appointed to act as temporary Chairman of the Provisional Government.[13] Harry made a comment on these appointments in his diary, 'Mick, Dick and Eoin "the big three". What a change!'

Harry, as quartermaster, wanted to hold a meeting in Dublin but he knew it would have to be brought together under some other guise. Mary McWhorter was still visiting Dublin and Harry asked her to approach the manageress of the Clarence Hotel saying she was returning to America and wanted to give a farewell dinner to about 25 of her friends. Kathleen Clarke and Harry's sister, Kathleen, were amongst the women inveigled to attend the fabricated dinner party. As soon as the meal was over, the women went into the drawing-room and took turns playing the piano and left the men to their own devices in the dining-room. After about twenty minutes Harry knocked on the drawing-room door and told the women that they had finished their business, and all the guests left quickly in case of a sudden raid.[14]

Harry was not happy because he felt that no further progress could be made in Dublin and he wanted to join the fight in Tipperary.[15] He told Mary McWhorter in Dublin that 'I am pinned up here like a rat in a trap when I'd a million times rather be out in the hills fighting with Dev'.[16]

Ernie O'Malley said 'that it was impossible to make him [Harry] take proper precautions because he could not adjust himself to the new conditions'.[17] Harry tended to move around Dublin as he did in the War of Independence but many of his former comrades were on the opposite side now. They knew his regular haunts and many of the general public were ready to inform on him. He was staying at home in Marino Crescent some nights and this was a big risk although he had the usual escape route through the skylight upstairs and along the roofs. But this was no longer safe as some of his pursuers had been given shelter in the Boland home in the earlier days of the Tan War and knew about the skylight.

He returned home on 22 July to join Mary McWhorter for dinner. They were enjoying themselves when a messenger arrived to report that the Free State troops had raided Mick Foley's print shop. In the course of the raid they had taken away a bundle of papers which included an order for two typewriters which Harry had bought in his capacity as quartermaster on Ernie O'Malley's staff. It was obvious he was being trailed and he said to Mary 'that the quicker he got away to the hills where Dev was the happier he would be'.[18] That very day Éamon de Valera had left Carrick-on-Suir for Clonmel because Waterford City had been taken by the Free State army under General John T. Prout who had moved 700 troops from Kilkenny. Dev was now in the heart of Mick Burke's territory in Tipperary where Harry wanted to be.[19]

'Surely, Harry, you are not in any real danger,' said Mary, 'Mick Collins can't be so ignorant or cold to the canons of friendship to allow harm to come to you.'

'God bless you, Mrs McWhorter,' answered Harry. 'You don't know Mick. Having set his hand to the plough, there is no turning back for him. My life to him now does not mean the snap of a finger. Then, too, I am not considered a safe man to be allowed to live. I know too much'.[20]

Later Harry called to Mick Foley's print shop, believing that lightning does not strike twice in the same place, and a slip of paper was handed to him. 'Counsels me to take every precaution,' wrote Harry.[21]

Luckily Harry did not go home that night as his home was raided again and this time Seán O'Donovan, Kathleen's fiance, was arrested and ended up in Mountjoy Jail.[22]

Harry returned when he had heard of the raid. He was worried about his mother and Kathleen and he found his mother was weeping silently. 'Harry, I had a terrible dream last night,' she sobbed. 'I don't like telling you but I saw you lying lifeless on a couch. It frightened me.'[23]

'Arah, go on,' said Harry in his funny drawl, 'Sure you must be dying to get rid of me – all the trouble I'm causing ye.'

He made his mother laugh.

'Harry,' she said. 'Promise me you'll be careful.'

Kathleen and Mary McWhorter were there and Harry whispered to Kathleen as he said goodbye at the door: 'If anything happens to me, look after mother. She deserves better.'

Harry knew the Free State soldiers were at his heels. Wherever he went, a raid followed. It was only a matter of time and he did not want to go home again because he felt it wasn't fair on his family.

When Kathleen Clarke arrived home that evening she found Harry was settled in and doing some secretarial work – sending out notices under his own name and that of Seán T. O'Kelly to members of the Republican Party to attend a meeting of Cumann na Poblachta on the following Thursday, 27 July, to be held in the printing offices of the Republican newspaper, *Republic of Ireland*. Harry stayed a few days in Mrs Clarke's house. On 25 July he wrote a letter to Joe McGarrity in Philadelphia: 'Can you imagine me on the run from Mick Collins? ... Well, I am, together with many others'. Then he went on to give a heart-breaking description of Ireland:

> Raids and arrests are again the order of the day. Mrs Pearse has had her house raided in the dead of night. My house was raided on Sunday morning, Mrs de Valera's house was raided ... Seán T. O'Kelly's house was also raided and so it goes. We are back again to the terror, the only change is the uniform. The Supreme Council have been rewarded for their treachery by serving posts as gaol governors.[24]

On the 27 July, while still staying in Mrs Clarke's house he wrote to Seán T. O'Kelly. He had a letter from Joe McGarrity in which Joe asked for a representative of the anti-Treaty side to be sent to a convention of the re-organised Clan-na-Gael that was fixed for early in the second week of August. Harry emphasised to O'Kelly that:

> as the fight is likely to be long drawn out, we shall require money and

material. Joe promises the full support of clan. You could bring back with you all available money and arrange with the clan to supply Thompsons, revolvers, .303, .405 etc. You could also organise a campaign in the USA. Your name and record will stand to you over there. I cannot imagine another man for the job. Dev read this letter last night en route and added a note saying that 'someone must go'.[25]

The next day Kathleen Clarke went to the Cumann na Poblachta headquarters in Suffolk Street and delivered Harry's letter to Seán. As she chatted to O'Kelly and other workers Free State troops burst in the door. Political documents were discovered, including Harry's letter. Kathleen Clarke hurried back home to warn Harry and she told him to destroy all the papers he had. As she was telling him about the arrest of Seán T., she saw a party of Free State soldiers coming up the street to her house.

'Get out quick, Harry,' she shouted, 'They're coming.'

Harry got away safely.[26] He breathed a sigh of relief but he knew how close the chase was. It was worse than the Tan days. There was no doubt in his mind that there was a concerted campaign from the highest authorities in Beggar's Bush down to the bottom, to catch him – he was only minutes ahead of the posse each time.

That day Michael Collins wrote to Harry and he showed concern for his former great friend, he knew that if Harry was ever cornered he would fight like a tiger:

Harry – it has come to this! Of all things it has come to this.

It is in my power to arrest you and destroy you. This I cannot do. If you will think over the influence which has dominated you it should change your mind.

You are walking under false colours. If no words of mine will change your attitude then you are beyond all hope – my hope.[27]

But no one in the world could change Harry now. He wrote to Mrs Wyse Power the next day protesting against the closing down of the Sinn Féin headquarters in Harcourt Street:

Altho' dictatorship is now the rule, I hope you will not attempt to imitate 'Mick', 'Dick' and 'Owney' (O'Duffy) by arrogating to yourself the functions of the Ard Fheis as they have attempted to usurp the functions of the new National Government.[28]

I'M GOING TO CATHAL BRUGHA

Harry drove to Upper Mount Street on Sunday to meet some of his anti-Treaty friends. He met Joe Griffin and Austin Stack and invited them to go with him for a breath of fresh air. Joe accepted and they drove through Fairview in the direction of Skerries.[1]

On his way out Harry visited the home of his brother Gerry who had been captured in the fighting in Blessington and was now in Mountjoy. He had a chat with Gerry's wife and he played with his nephews. Kevin Boland was only five years old but he can still remember Harry taking off his coat and sitting down to drink a cup of tea.[2]

Harry and Joe Griffin drove towards Skerries and went through Swords. They booked into the Grand Hotel in Skerries. As the hotel stood in a square in the centre of this seaside town it could easily be surrounded by troops who would have no difficulty in blocking all avenues of escape. It was not an ideal location for a wanted Republican officer to spend the night.

Harry had stayed in Skerries before while on the run. He may have gone there to see Captain Martin, a native of Skerries, whom he knew frequently sailed boats across to Liverpool. He may have wanted Captain Martin to arrange passage for him to Liverpool so he could get to America where he could appeal for more men, money, and weapons from the re-organised Clan-na-Gael.[3] The McGarrity clan were sympathetic to the Republican cause.

Joe and Harry relaxed that night and had a few drinks in the bar. Joe was the first to feel tired and he went up to bed and Harry followed him soon after. They shared the same room.[4] Some time after 1am while they slept soundly, lorries of Free State troops invaded the square in Skerries and quickly surrounded the Grand Hotel. The manageress was forced to open up and six of the soldiers compelled her to show them the room where Harry slept.[5]

The soldiers entered his bedroom and went to Harry first and woke him up. He got up and partly dressed himself. He had no gun. But then Harry tackled one of the soldiers and tried to seize his gun. The scuffle went on until they were both in the corridor. A shot was fired over Harry's head to warn him to desist. He continued the struggle and practically had the gun in his hand when another shot was fired and Harry collapsed on the floor with a bad abdominal wound.[6] Joe who had not taken part in the struggle was arrested. Before he was taken out to another room he pleaded with the troops to get a priest and doctor.[7]

Those who had carried out the raid were all from the Fingal Brigade of the Free State army and were stationed in Balbriggan Coastguard Station – all except one who was sent to identify Harry Boland when arrested. Harry was wounded between 1am and 2am on 31 July. A priest and doctor were summoned. The doctor dressed the wound and requested an ambulance. The raiding party phoned for an ambulance[8] but Harry was not moved from the Grand Hotel until 6.30am – over four hours later.[9] Though carrying a seriously injured man the ambulance crew passed the Mater Hospital and did not stop to have him urgently admitted. Instead they brought him to Portobello barracks where they kept him for at least two more hours although he was badly in need of surgical treatment. He was not transferred to St Vincent's Hospital until 10am that morning.[10]

This delay was indefensible. Harry Boland had three life threatening injuries. His diaphragm was pierced and his spleen and liver were lacerated. There was extensive internal bleeding which caused severe pain.[11] Even with today's improved methods of surgery and anaesthesia, it would be touch and go whether he would survive. But to hold him eight hours before bringing him to a hospital where surgical treatment was available, was bordering on criminal negligence by the Free State authorities. This long delay merited a thorough public investigation that was never carried out.

Surgeon Kennedy, of St Vincent's Hospital decided on an immediate operation but Harry asked him to give him a little time until he had the opportunity of speaking to his sister, Kathleen. Fr Thornton, the chaplain at the hospital, went to Marino Crescent and brought Kathleen to the hospital. Harry was conscious when she arrived and motioned to her with his hand to come closer to him. Kathleen went to his bed and knew from the way he looked that he was dying.

'You'll get over this, Harry,' she said although she saw death in his face.

'Ah! no Kit. I don't think so.'

Kathleen asked him who shot him.

'The only thing I'll say is that it was a friend of my own who was in Lewes Prison with me. I'll never tell the name and don't try to find out. I forgive him and want no reprisals. I want to be buried in the grave in Glasnevin with Cathal Brugha.'

He asked to see Gerry, his brother. Kathleen went to Mountjoy to get parole for him. The deputy governor told her she would have to take the request to Portobello barracks. She went there and asked for the adjutant general who could not see her. He sent the assistant adjutant general, Kevin O'Higgins to meet her. She told him what she wanted. He refused permission and his attitude was hostile and cold. She came back and told Harry that Gerry would not be allowed to see him. Harry reminded Kathleen that the Russian jewels were still hidden in the family home in Marino Crescent and he told her to hold them until De Valera got back into power. If ever the Republic were declared by De Valera she was to hand the jewels over to him.[12] (The Boland family respected his wishes and when De Valera had succeeded in getting his 1937 Constitution passed into law and had recovered the ports, they considered that Harry's wishes were fulfilled. They handed the Russian jewels into the safe keeping of the Irish government who eventually handed them back to the Russian government and redeemed the loan.)[13]

When Harry had settled these affairs with Kathleen, Surgeon Kennedy went ahead with the operation. Harry did not regain consciousness until the next morning. He then had a long talk with his mother and as he felt he was going to die, he gave her some advice on how she would carry on.

Several friends had gathered beside Harry's bedside. Fr Hyland, Muriel MacSwiney, widow of Terence MacSwiney and Kathleen Clarke, wife of Tom Clarke, first president of the Irish Republic, kept a vigil with Harry's family as he became weaker.[14]

Patrick McCartan, although he had taken the opposite side to Harry on the Treaty issue, came to see his friend and described his visit in a letter to Joe McGarrity:

> He recognised me though a bit delirious and wanted to get out of bed. Poor Harry. One felt on leaving him to curse the whole lot more than one feels inclined to do so at other times ... Poor big-hearted, good-natured Harry to be shot by his own friends.[15]

Michael Collins was distressed to hear that Harry was gravely ill.

He wrote to his Director of Intelligence and asked him to send some good officer to St Vincent's Hospital to make a report on the exact medical condition of Harry. 'It is necessary to find out whether he has been operated on and what the doctors think of his condition.' He ordered that no guard be placed over him.[16]

Mary McWhorter described Harry's last hour before he died:

> Harry went peacefully to his Maker just at ten minutes after nine in the evening of 1 August. It was a beautiful evening ... still broad daylight. There was a picture of the Sacred Heart hanging on the wall at the foot of the bed and Harry kept his eyes on it constantly until the very last. It was a lovely peaceful going and somehow sorrow had no place there.[17]

Fionán Lynch was sleeping in his room in Mountjoy Street, when Collins burst in, weeping uncontrollably at the news.[18] 'The Big Fella' wrote to Kitty Kiernan on 2 August:

> Last night I passed St Vincent's Hospital and saw a crowd outside. My mind went to him lying dead and I thought of the times together, and whatever good there is in any wish of mine he certainly had it. Although the gap of 8 or 9 months was not forgotten – of course no one can forget it – I only thought of him with the friendship of the days of 1918 and 1919.[19]

Kitty was very sad and she wrote to Michael Collins:

> Poor Harry, may he rest in peace. I murmured little aspirations all day yesterday to our Lord, to have pity on the dying. I had an idea he might die, strong and all as he was ... I have lost a good friend in Harry – and no matter what, I'll always believe in his genuineness, that I was the one and only.[20]

Down in the hills where De Valera was – between Clonmel and Fermoy – and where Harry wanted to go but delayed too long, Kathleen O'Connell heard about Harry's death from a sister of Kevin Barry:

> She told me that Harry was dead and would be buried in the morning. Poor old Harry ... It was a fearful shock. I wept. God rest his generous soul. I dread telling the Chief about it. Couldn't sleep that night.[21]

Kathleen wondered how she could break the news to Éamon de Valera, but when she met him she knew that he had heard about it:

He was broken-hearted and said he felt it terrible. He looked crushed and broken. He lost his most faithful friend. On that long journey between Fermoy and Clonmel he never spoke a word. Kathy Barry was with us too. Oh! the loneliness and the thought that Harry was gone forever ... Cathal gone and now Harry – when will be the end.[22]

Denis Riordan, the leader of the Republican forces in the Borris-in-Ossory area of Co. Leix on the Co. Tipperary border, brought word of Harry's death to John Tynan. Tom Tynan, his six and a half year old son, never forgot that evening when Denis Riordan called to his father in their home in Rockview House. He remembers Denis Riordan speaking to his father.

'John, Harry Boland is dead,' Riordan said slowly. 'The Free State army shot him in a hotel.'

John Tynan went into the front room of the house and he lay down on the sofa. He remembered old times. Then he cried like a child. 'Lord have Mercy on your soul, Harry Boland,' he said as he sobbed. 'You were one of nature's gentlemen. Anywhere and everywhere you went love and happiness went with you.'[23]

On 5 August Patrick McCartan wrote to Joe McGarrity:

Harry was buried yesterday ... I sent a wreath from 'Joe McGarrity, Phila'. I knew you would like to be represented in some way.[24]

As Harry's funeral passed through O'Connell Street on its way to Glasnevin from the Carmelite church, Whitefriar Street, a Lancia car full of pro-Treaty soldiers met the funeral. The vehicle stopped, and the troops having laid down their arms, removed their caps and stood up reverently until the hearse had passed.[25]

Éamon de Valera wrote a long letter to Joe McGarrity on 10 September in which he discussed Harry's biggest political achievement – the Collins–De Valera Pact and how it nearly achieved peace before the disastrous Civil War. If only Britain had stayed out of the reckoning what a difference it would have made:

The Pact meant, in effect, acceptance of the people's decision as the final count, that is, defeat by the Republicans, so I told Harry when I signed it, unless Mick were to stand up to Lloyd George and bring in a constitution which would leave open a path for the achievement of the Republic ... had the coalition come into existence, I'd have nominated Harry as one of the ministers from our side – and then he would have had his chance ... Loyal, generous, big-souled, bold, forceful Harry – Harry of the keen mind and broad sympathies. Incapable of the petty or the mean ... Harry was fit to be anything. Since I have heard of his death I have lived with him more intimately even than when he was alive. His stories, his snatches of song, his moods – how can one get the idea of what he was who did not know him?[26]

Just three weeks later, Harry's friend, Michael Collins was killed in an ambush in Beál na mBlath, Co. Cork. The two of them had served Ireland in the way each of them thought best but had died, on opposite sides, from bullets fired by their own countrymen.

There is a better title in Irish for the type of Civil War we had in Ireland – 'Cogadh na gCarad' – 'The War between Friends'.

Notes

Born into Patriotism

1 Memoir of Mrs Seán O'Donovan (*nee* Kathleen Boland).
2 Gerry Boland in an interview with Michael McInerney, *The Irish Times*, 9 October, 1968.
3 Ó Beoláin, Caoimhghín, *James Boland 1857–1895*.
4 *Ibid.*
5 Interview with Tom Tynan, Navan Road, Dublin, 30 September 1997.
6 Ó Beoláin, Caoimhghín, *James Boland 1857–1895*.
7 *Ibid.*
8 *Ibid.*
9 Census 1901, Boland family, 28 Wexford Street, Dublin.
10 Ó Beoláin, Caoimhghín, *James Boland 1857–1895*.
11 Interview with Kevin Boland, Rathcoole, 8 September 1997.
12 Ó Beoláin, Caoimhghín, *James Boland 1857–1895*.
13 Memoir of Mrs Seán O'Donovan (nee Kathleen Boland).
14 *Ibid.*
15 Ó Beoláin, Caoimhghín, *James Boland 1857–1895*.
16 *Ibid.*
17 Gerry Boland in an interview with Michael McInerney, *The Irish Times*, 9 October 1968.
18 *Ibid.*
19 Interview with Tom Tynan, Navan Road, Dublin, 30 September 1997.
20 Interview with Br Hermes, Castletown De La Salle College, 24 September 1997.
21 Interview with Edmund Tynan, Donoughmore, Johnstown, Co. Kilkenny, 25 September 1997.
22 Interview with Tom Tynan, Navan Road, Dublin, 30 September 1997.

In the GAA

1 Ó Beoláin, Caoimhghín, *James Boland 1857–1895*.
2 Gerry Boland in an interview with Michael McInerney, *The Irish Times*, 9 October 1968.
3 Interview with Mrs Eileen Barrington, Dún Laoghaire, 12 November 1997.
4 Interview with Kevin Boland, Rathcoole, 8 September 1997.
5 Gerry Boland in an interview with Michael McInerney, *The Irish Times*, 9 October 1968.
6 Interview with Mrs Eileen Barrington, Dún Laoghaire, 12 November 1997.
7 Gerry Boland in an interview with Michael McInerney, *The Irish Times*, 9 October 1968.
8 *The Freeman's Journal*, 9 April 1906.
9 *Ibid.*, 17 December 1906.
10 Interview with Mrs Eileen Barrington, Dún Laoghaire, 12 November 1997.
11 De Búrca, Marcus, *The GAA – A History*, Cumann Lúthchleas Gael, Dublin 1980, p. 87.
12 *The Freeman's Journal*, 23 February 1909.
13 *Ibid.*, 4 January 1909.
14 *Ibid.*, 22 March 1909.
15 *Ibid.*, 26 April 1909.
16 *The Kilkenny Journal*, 3 July 1909.
17 *The Freeman's Journal*, 6 May 1909.
18 Interview with Annraoi Ó Beoláin, Sutton, Co. Dublin, 4 September 1997.
19 Interview with Kevin Boland, Rathcoole, 8 September 1997.
20 *The Freeman's Journal*, 23 October 1911.
21 O'Neill, Phil (Sliabh Ruadh), *History of the GAA (1910–1930)*, Kilkenny Journal 1931, p. 89.
22 *Freeman's Journal*, 24 March 1913.

HURLING AND VOLUNTEERS
1   Interview, Mrs Fionnuala Crowley, Cork, 24 November 1997.
2   Interview, Mrs Eileen Barrington, Dún Laoghaire, 12 November 1997.
3   Gerry Boland, *Irish Times,* Michael McInerney, 9 October 1968, Franciscan Library Killiney.
4   Interview with Kevin Boland, 8 September 1997.
5   O'Brien, Séamus, *Dublin's Fighting Story,* 'The Great Dublin Strike and Lockout', 1913, Tralee 1947, p. 12.
6   Statement of Mrs Seán O'Donovan (nee Kathleen Boland).
7   Conversation with Annraoi Ó Beoláin, Sutton, 4 November 1997.
8   Bowman, John, *Saturday Eight-Thirty,* 'Erskine Childers', 29 November 1997.
9   Macardle, Dorothy, *The Irish Republic,* Irish Press, Dublin 1951, p. 118.
10 *Ibid.,* p. 122.
11 *Irish Independent,* 5 October 1914.
12 Boland, Harry, 'Draft of Manifesto to the People of Ireland', 10 October 1918.
13 Interview, Mrs Eileen Barrington, Dún Laoghaire, 12 November 1997.
14 Interview with Kevin Boland, Dublin, 8 September 1997.
15 *Ibid.*
16 *Ibid.*

FROM FAIRVIEW TO THE GPO
1   Memoir of Mrs Seán O'Donovan (nee Kathleen Boland).
2   *Ibid.*
3   Heuston, OP, John M., *Headquarters Battalion, Easter Week, 1916,* p. 20.
4   Lynch, Diarmuid, *The IRB and the 1916 Insurrection,* Mercier Press, Cork 1957, p. 158.
5   Leonard, Hugh, *1916 Insurrection,* RTE, 1966.
6   Lynch, Diarmuid, *The IRB and the 1916 Insurrection,* Mercier Press, Cork 1957.
7   Interview with Kevin Boland, Dublin, 8 September 1997.
8   *The Irish Independent,* 26 April–5 May 1916.
9   Ó Ceallaigh, Seán T., arna chur in eagar ag Proinsias Ó Conluain, *Seán T.,* Foilseacháin Náisiúnta Teoranta, Baile Átha Cliath 1963, leath. 172, 173.
10 Memoir of Mrs Seán O'Donovan (nee Kathleen Boland).
11 Caulfield, Max, *The Easter Rebellion,* Four Square Book, London 1965, p. 183.
12 *Ibid.*
13 Lynch, Diarmuid, *The IRB and the 1916 Insurrection,* Mercier Press, Cork 1957, p. 165.
14 Memoir of Mrs Seán O'Donovan (nee Kathleen Boland).
15 MacThomáis, Éamon, *Down Dublin Streets,* Irish Book Bureau, Dublin 1965, p. 23.
16 *Times History of the War,* London, August 1916, p. 433.

LIVED TO SEE AN IRISH REPUBLIC
1   Lynch, Diarmuid, *The IRB and the 1916 Insurrection,* Mercier Press, Cork 1957, p. 166.
2   Peter Carpenter Interview, 1965.
3   Lynch, Diarmuid, *The IRB and the 1916 Insurrection,* Mercier Press, Cork 1957, p. 166.
4   Frank Thornton, memoir.
5   Caulfield, Max, *The Easter Rebellion,* Four Square Book, London, 1965, p. 276.
6   *Ibid.*
7   Ryan, Desmond, *The Rising,* Golden Eagle Books, Dublin 1966, p. 152.
8   Lynch, Diarmuid, *The IRB and the 1916 Insurrection,* Mercier Press, Cork 1957, p. 177.
9   Ryan, Desmond, *The Rising,* Golden Eagle Books, Dublin 1966, p. 152.
10 *Evening Herald,* 15 May 1916.
11 Lynch, Diarmuid, *The IRB and the 1916 Insurrection,* Mercier Press, Cork 1957, p. 178.
12 Interview with Kevin Boland, Dublin, 8 September 1997.
13 Caulfield, Max, *The Easter Rebellion,* Four Square Book, London, 1965, p. 345.
14 *Evening Herald,* 'Thirteen of Us', Private William Richardson, 15 May 1916.

A Prisoner after 1916

1 Memoir of Mrs Seán O'Donovan (nee Kathleen Boland).
2 *Ibid.*
3 *The Freeman's Journal,* Saturday, 13 May 1916.
4 PRO, Kew, London, HO 144\1453\31\980.
5 *Ibid.*
6 Memoir of Frank Thornton.
7 Memoir of Mrs Seán O'Donovan (nee Kathleen Boland).
8 Memoir of Frank Thornton.
9 *Ibid.*
10 Beáslaí, Piaras, *Michael Collins,* Talbot Press, Dublin 1937, p. 47.
11 Jones, Thomas, *Whitehall Diary,* Volume III: *Ireland 1918–25,* Edited by Keith Middlemas, Oxford University Press, Oxford 1971, p. 81.
12 *The Roscommon Herald,* 30 November 1918.
13 Thornton Memoir.
14 PRO, Kew, London, File HO 144\1453\311980.
15 Brennan, Robert, *Allegiance,* Browne and Nolan Ltd., Dublin 1950, p. 101.
16 *Ibid.*
17 Béaslaí, Piaras, *Michael Collins and the Making of a New Ireland,* Harrap, London 1926, p. 148.
18 PRO, Kew, London, File HO\144\1453\311980.
19 Memoir of Mrs Seán O'Donovan (nee Kathleen Boland).
20 Ó Beoláin, Caoimhghín, *Jim Boland, 1857–1895.*
21 PRO, Kew, London, File 144\1453\311980.
22 *Ibid.*
23 *Ibid.*
24 *Ibid.*
25 Béaslaí, Piaras, *Michael Collins and the Making of a New Ireland,* Harrap, London 1926, p. 152.
26 Longford, O'Neill, *Éamon de Valera,* Gill and Macmillan Ltd., Dublin 1970, p. 57.
27 *Ibid.,* p. 58.
28 PRO, Kew, London, File 144\1453\311980.
29 *Ibid.*
30 *Ibid.*
31 Brennan, Robert, *Allegiance,* Browne and Nolan Ltd., Dublin 1950, p. 132.
32 PRO, Kew, London, File 144\1453\311980.
33 Mrs Seán O'Donovan (nee Kathleen Boland) Memoir.
34 Harry Boland letter, National Library of Ireland, Kildare Street, Dublin.
35 PRO, Kew, London, File 144\1453\311980.
36 Longford, O'Neill, *Éamon de Valera,* Gill and Macmillan, Dublin 1970, p. 56.
37 PRO, Kew, London, File 144\1453\311980.
38 *Ibid.*
39 Memoir of Mrs Seán O'Donovan (nee Kathleen Boland).

The German Plot

1 Béaslaí, Piaras, *Michael Collins and the Making of a New Ireland,* Harrap, London 1926, p. 161.
2 Brennan, Robert, *Allegiance,* Browne and Nolan Limited, Dublin 1950, pp. 152, 153.
3 Ó Broin, Leon, *Revolutionary Underground – The Story of the IRB, 1858–1924,* Gill and Macmillan, Dublin 1976, p. 178.
4 Hogan, David, *The Four Glorious Years,* Irish Press, Dublin 1953, p. 20.
5 *The Freeman's Journal,* 26 and 27 October 1917.
6 O'Neill, Phil, *History of the GAA, 1910–30,* Kilkenny Journal 1931, p. 148.
7 Memoir of Senator Seán O'Donovan.

8   Interview with Kevin Boland, Dublin, 8 September 1997.
9   *The Freeman's Journal,* 12 November 1917.
10   De Búrca, Marcus, *The GAA, A History,* Dublin 1980, p. 137.
11   Coogan, Tim Pat, *Michael Collins,* Hutchinson, London 1990, p. 90.
12   Béaslaí, Piaras, *Michael Collins and the Making of a New Ireland,* Harrap, London 1926,
       p. 189
13   UCD Archives, O'Malley Notebooks, File No: P\7b\98, Broy.

BOLAND FILLS THE GAP
1   Greaves, C. Desmond, *Liam Mellows and the Irish Revolution,* Lawrence and Wishart,
       London 1971, p. 145.
2   Béaslaí, Piaras, *Michael Collins and the making of a new Ireland,* London 1926, p. 196.
3   Interview with Kevin Boland, Rathcoole, 25 February 1998.
4   Memoir of Mrs Seán O'Donovan (nee Kathleen Boland).
5   Interview with Eileen Barrington, Dúnlaoghaire, 12 November 1997.
6   Interview with Fionnuala Crowley, Cork, 24 November 1997.
7   De Búrca, Marcus, *The GAA – A History,* Cumann Lúthchleas Gael, Dublin 1980, p. 141.
8   Hogan, David, *The Four Glorious Years,* Irish Press Ltd, Dublin 1953, p. 36.
9   *Ibid.,* p. 36.
10   *Ibid.,* p. 38.
11   *The Freeman's Journal,* 31 October 1918.
12   *Ibid.*
13   Béaslaí, Piaras, *Michael Collins and the making of a new Ireland,* Harrap, London 1926, pp.
       236, 237.
14   *Ibid.,* p. 239.
15   *The Freeman's Journal,* 30 October 1918.

BOLAND WINS SOUTH ROSCOMMON
1   *The Freeman's Journal,* 2 November 1918.
2   Béaslaí, Piaras, *Michael Collins and the making of a new Ireland,* Harrap, London 1926, p.
       240.
3   *Ibid.,* p. 240.
4   Brennan, Robert, *Allegiance,* Browne and Nolan Ltd., Dublin 1950, p. 183.
5   *Ibid.,* p. 172.
6   Valiulis, Maryann, *General Richard Mulcahy,* Irish Academic Press, Dublin 1992, p. 32.
7   Boland family archives.
8   Brennan, Robert, *Allegiance,* Browne and Nolan Ltd, Dublin 1950, p. 239.
9   *Ibid.,* p. 168.
10   Béaslaí, Piaras, *Michael Collins and the making of a new Ireland,* Harrap, London 1926, p.
       246.
11   *The Roscommon Herald,* 30 November 1918.
12   *Ibid.,* 14 December 1918.
13   Hogan, David, *The Four Glorious Years,* Irish Press Ltd., Dublin 1953, p. 52.
14   *Ibid.,* p. 50.
15   Mitchel, Arthur, *Revolutionary Government in Ireland,* Gill and Macmillan, Dublin 1995,
       p. 15.
16   *The Freeman's Journal,* 22 January 1919.

THE PROFESSIONAL DECAMPED
1   Peter de Loughry statement, De Loughry Family Papers, Kilkenny.
2   Béaslaí, Piaras, *Michael Collins and the making of a new Ireland,* Harrap, London 1926, p.
       263.
3   Memoir of Mrs Seán O'Donovan (nee Kathleen Boland).
4   Ó Beoláin, Caoimhghín, *James Boland 1857–1895,* p. 8.

5   Memoir of Mrs Seán O'Donovan (nee Kathleen Boland).
6   Béaslaí, Piaras, *Michael Collins and the making of a new Ireland*, Harrap, London 1926, p. 264.
7   *The Kilkenny People*, 25 January 1919.
8   De Loughry, Anna T., 'Remembering Lincoln Prison Escape', *Old Kilkenny Review*, 1982, p. 468.
9   Interview with Pádraigín Ní Dhubhluachra, Kilkenny, February 1998.
10 De Loughry, Anna T., 'Remembering Lincoln Prison Escape', *Old Kilkenny Review*, 1982, p. 468.
11 Béaslaí, Piaras, *Michael Collins and the making of a new Ireland*, Harrap, London 1926, p. 265.
12 Memoir of Mrs Seán O'Donovan (nee Kathleen Boland).
13 Coogan, Tim Pat, *De Valera*, Hutchinson, London 1993, p. 125.
14 Longford, O'Neill, *Éamon de Valera*, Gill and Macmillan Ltd., Dublin 1970, p. 85.
15 *Ibid.*, p. 85.
16 Béaslaí, Piaras, *Michael Collins and the making of a new Ireland*, Harrap, London 1926, p. 267.
17 Longford, O'Neill, *Éamon de Valera*, Gill and Macmillan Ltd., Dublin 1970, p. 86.
18 Coogan, Tim Pat, *De Valera*, Hutchinson, London 1993, p. 126.
19 *The Freeman's Journal*, 5 February 1919.
20 Longford, O'Neill, *Éamon de Valera*, Gill and Macmillan Ltd., Dublin 1970, p. 89.
21 *The Kilkenny People*, 15 March 1919.
22 Longford, O'Neill, *Éamon de Valera*, Gill and Macmillan Ltd., Dublin 1970, p. 89.
23 Béaslaí, Piaras, *Michael Collins and the making of a new Ireland*, Harrap, London 1926, p. 269.

SPECIAL ENVOY TO USA
1   Carroll, Denis, *They have fooled you again, Micheál Ó Flanagáin*, The Columba Press, Dublin 1993, p. 103.
2   Boland family archives.
3   MacEoin, Uinseann, *Survivors*, Argenta Publications, Dublin 1987, p. 86.
4   *Minutes of Proceedings of the First Dáil*, Stationery Office, Dublin, p. 36.
5   *Ibid.*, p.46.
6   *The Freeman's Journal*, 10 April 1919.
7   *Ibid.*
8   *Ibid.*
9   Hogan, David, *The Four Glorious Years*, Irish Press Ltd., Dublin 1954, p. 121.
10 Béaslaí, Piaras, *Michael Collins and the making of a new Ireland*, Harrap, London 1926, p. 304.
11 *Ibid.*, pp. 305 and 306.
12 *The Freeman's Journal*, 21 April 1919.
13 De Búrca, Marcus, *The GAA – A History*, Cumann Lúthchleas Gael, Dublin 1980, p. 145.
14 *The Freeman's Journal*, 21 April 1919.
15 *Ibid.*
16 De Valera Papers, Franciscan Library, Killiney, File 1473.
17 *Ibid.*, File 1302.

DISUNITY IN AMERICA
1   Béaslaí, Piaras, *Michael Collins and the making of a new Ireland*, Harrap, London 1926, p. 307.
2   Coogan, Tim Pat, *Michael Collins*, Hutchinson, London 1990, p. 114.
3   Memoir of Mrs Seán O'Donovan (nee Kathleen Boland).
4   *Ibid.*

5 Béaslaí, Piaras, *Michael Collins and the making of a new Ireland*, Harrap, London 1926, p. 308.
6 Memoir of Mrs Seán O'Donovan (nee Kathleen Boland).
7 Coogan, Tim Pat, *Michael Collins*, Hutchinson, London 1990, p. 85.
8 Lynch, Diarmuid, *The IRB and the 1916 Insurrection*, Mercier Press Cork 1957, Chapter X1, 'Diarmuid Lynch as National Secretary, Friends of Irish Freedom' by Florence O'Donoghue, p. 192.
9 *Ibid.*, p. 209.
10 Macardle, Dorothy, *The Irish Republic*, Irish Press Ltd., Dublin 1937, p. 128.
11 Cronin, Seán, *The McGarrity Papers*, Anvil Books, Tralee 1972, p. 63.
12 Greaves, C. Desmond, *Liam Mellows and the Irish Revolution*, Lawrence and Wishart, London 1971, p. 117.
13 Cronin, Seán, *The McGarrity Papers*, Anvil Books, Tralee 1972, p. 69.
14 Lynch, Diarmuid, *The IRB and the 1916 Insurrection*, Mercier Press, Cork 1957, Chapter X1, 'Diarmuid Lynch as National Secretary, Friends of Irish Freedom' by Florence O'Donoghue, p. 207.
15 *Ibid.*
16 McCartan, Dr Patrick, *With De Valera in America*, Dublin 1932, p. 94.
17 Cronin, Seán, *The McGarrity Papers*, A Clan-na-Gael Book, 1993, Appendix VIII, p. 9.
18 Lynch, Diarmuid, *The IRB and the 1916 Insurrection*, Mercier Press, Cork 1957, Chapter X11, 'Diarmuid Lynch as National Secretary, Friends of Irish Freedom' by Florence O'Donoghue, p. 209.
19 Cronin, Seán, *The McGarrity Papers*, A Clan-na-Gael Book, 1993, Appendix VIII, p. 9.
20 Interview with Kevin Boland, Rathcoole, on 8 September 1997.
21 Cronin, Seán, *The McGarrity Papers*, A Clan-na-Gael Book, Appendix VIII, p. 8.
22 McCartan, Dr Patrick, *With De Valera in America*, Fitzpatrick Ltd, Dublin 1932, p. 136.
23 Harry Boland to De Valera, May 1919, Franciscan Library, Killiney, De Valera Papers, File 96.
24 *Ibid.*, 4 June 1919.
25 Cronin Seán, *The McGarrity Papers*, A Clan-na-Gael Book, 1993, Appendix VIII, p. 7.
26 Harry Boland to De Valera, 4 June 1919, Franciscan Library, Killiney, De Valera Papers, File 96.
27 *Ibid.*
28 *Ibid.*
29 McCartan, Dr Patrick, *With De Valera in America*, Fitzpatrick Ltd, Dublin 1932, p. 136.
30 De Valera to Harry Boland, 11 June 1919, Franciscan Library, Killiney, De Valera Papers, File 1214.

I FEEL AT HOME AT THIS WORK
1 Handwritten note by Harry Boland on letter from De Valera to Harry Boland, *circa* June 1919, De Valera Papers, Franciscan Library, Killiney, File 1214.
2 *Ibid.*
3 *New York Times*, 21 June 1919, Johns Hopkins University, Baltimore, Maryland, USA.
4 McCartan, Dr Patrick, *De Valera in America*, Fitzpatrick Ltd, Dublin 1932, pp. 137, 138, 139.
5 Minutes of Dáil Éireann, 17 June 1919, p. 114.
6 *Ibid.*, 17 June 1919, p. 112.
7 *Ibid.*, 19 June 1919, p. 135.
8 McCartan, Dr Patrick, *De Valera in America*, Fitzpatrick Ltd, Dublin 1932, pp. 139, 140.
9 *New York Times*, 22 June 1919, Johns Hopkins University, Baltimore, Maryland, USA.
10 *Ibid.*, 23 June 1919.
11 *Ibid.*
12 *Ibid.*, 24 June 1919.
13 McCartan, Dr Patrick, *De Valera in America*, Fitzpatrick Ltd, Dublin 1932, p. 21.

14 *New York Times,* 25 June 1919.
15 Kathleen O'Connell's statement given before the Referee and Advisory Committee, 28 June 1945, De Valera Papers, Franciscan Library, Killiney, File 1473.
16 Harry Boland to his mother, 8 July 1919, De Valera Papers, Franciscan Library, Killiney, File 1302.
17 *The New York Times,* 22 June 1919.
18 Harry Boland to his mother, 8 July 1919, De Valera Papers, The Franciscan Library, Killiney, File 1302.
19 Diarmuid Ó hÉigeartaigh to Harry Boland, 12 July 1919, De Valera Papers, Franciscan Library, Killiney, File 96.
20 McCartan, Dr Patrick, *De Valera in America,* Fitzpatrick Ltd, Dublin 1932, p. 23.
21 Harry Boland to Arthur Griffith, 29 July 1919, Franciscan Library, Killiney, File 1226.
22 Arthur Griffith to Harry Boland, 1 August 1919, Franciscan Library, Killiney, File 1226.
23 Longford, O'Neill, *Éamon de Valera,* Gill and Macmillan, Dublin 1970, p.100.
24 McCartan, Dr Patrick, *De Valera in America,* Fitzpatrick Ltd, Dublin 1932, p. 23.

ON TOUR IN AMERICA
1 Harry Boland Diary, De Valera Papers, Franciscan Library, Killiney, File 2172\1.
2 *Ibid.*
3 Ó Broin, Leon and Ó hÉigeartaigh, Cian, *In Great Haste,* Gill and Macmillan, Dublin 1996, p. 8.
4 *Indianapolis News,* 11 October 1919, Indianapolis State Library, Indianapolis.
5 *Ibid.,* 13 October 1919.
6 *Ibid.*
7 Harry Boland Diary, De Valera Papers, Franciscan Library, Killiney, File 2172\1.
8 *Ibid.*
9 *Ibid.*
10 *Ibid.*
11 Harry Boland to E. de Valera, 4 November 1919, De Valera Papers, Franciscan Library, Killiney, File 1214.
12 Harry Boland Diary, De Valera Papers, Franciscan Library, Killiney, File 2172\1.
13 *Ibid.*
14 *Ibid.*
15 *Gaelic American,* 8 November 1919, Belch Institute for Ethnic Studies Library, Philadelphia, USA.
16 Harry Boland Diary, De Valera Papers, Franciscan Library, Killiney, File 2172\1.
17 *The New York Times,* 14 November 1919, Indiana State Library, Indianapolis, Indiana.
18 Maher, Jim, *The Flying Column – West Kilkenny,* Geography Publications, Dublin 1987, p. 4.
19 Harry Boland Diary, De Valera Papers, Franciscan Library, Killiney, File 2172\1.
20 McCartan, Dr Patrick, *With De Valera in America,* Fitzpatrick Ltd, Dublin 1932, p. 144.
21 *Gaelic American,* 7 June 1919, Belch Institute for Ethnic Studies Library, Philadelphia, USA.
22 *Ibid.,* 27 December 1919.
23 McCartan, Dr Patrick, *With De Valera in America,* Fitzpatrick Ltd, Dublin 1932, p. 147.
24 Macardle, Dorothy, *The Irish Republic,* Irish Press Ltd, Dublin 1951, p. 320.
25 McCartan, Dr Patrick, *With De Valera in America,* Fitzpatrick Ltd, Dublin 1932, p. 147.
26 Harry Boland Diary, De Valera Papers, Franciscan Library, Killiney, File 2172\1.
27 *Ibid.*
28 *Ibid.*
29 *Ibid.*

1   Harry Boland Diary, De Valera Papers, Franciscan Library, Killiney, File 2172\1.
2   *Gaelic American,* 17 January 1920, Belch Institute for Ethnic Studies Library, Philadelphia, USA.
3   Harry Boland Diary, De Valera Papers, Franciscan Library, Killiney, File 2172\1.
4   *Ibid.*
5   *Ibid.*
6   McCartan, Dr Patrick, *With De Valera in America,* Fitzpatrick Ltd, Dublin 1932, p. 150.
7   *Gaelic American,* 21 February 1920, Belch Institute for Ethnic Studies Library, Philadelphia, USA.
8   *Ibid.*
9   Cronin, Seán, *The McGarrity Papers,* A Clan-na-Gael Book, 1993, Appendix VIII, p. 11.
10 *Ibid.*
11 Harry Boland Diary, De Valera Papers, Franciscan Library, Killiney, File 2172\1.
12 Harry Boland to Thomas J. Lynch, 25 February 1920, De Valera Papers, Franciscan Library, Killiney, File 1226.
13 Cronin, Seán, *The McGarrity Papers,* A Clan-na-Gael Book, 1993, Appendix VIII, p. 12.
14 Harry Boland Diary, De Valera Papers, Franciscan Library, Killiney, File 2172\1.
15 *Ibid.*
16 *Ibid.*
17 McCartan, Dr Patrick, *With De Valera in America,* Fitzpatrick Ltd, Dublin, 1932, pp. 160, 161.
18 *Ibid.,* pp. 164, 166.
19 Harry Boland Diary, De Valera Papers, Franciscan Library, Killiney, File 2172\1.
20 McCartan, Dr Patrick, *With De Valera in America,* Fitzpatrick Ltd, Dublin 1932, p. 151.
21 Harry Boland Diary, De Valera Papers, Franciscan Library, Killiney, File 2172\1.
22 *Ibid.*
23 Lavelle, Patricia, *James O'Mara,* Clonmore and Reynolds Ltd, London 1961, p. 155.
24 Harry Boland Diary, De Valera Papers, Franciscan Library, Killiney, File 2172\1.
25 Lavelle, Patricia, *James O'Mara,* Clonmore and Reynolds Ltd, London 1961, p. 151.
26 Harry Boland Diary, De Valera Papers, Franciscan Library, Killiney, File 2172\1.
27 Lavelle, Patricia, *James O'Mara,* Clonmore and Reynolds Ltd, London 1961, p. 156.
28 *Ibid.*
29 Harry Boland Diary, De Valera Papers, Franciscan Library, Killiney, File 2172\1.
30 McCartan, Dr Patrick, *With De Valera in America,* Fitzpatrick Ltd, Dublin pp. 167, 168, 169.
31 *Ibid.*
32 Interview with Kevin Boland, 8 September 1997.
33 *Ibid.*
34 *Gaelic American,* 26 June 1920, Belch Institute for Ethnic Studies Library, Philadelphia, USA.
35 McCartan, Dr Patrick, *With De Valera in America,* Fitzpatrick Ltd, Dublin, pp. 167, 168, 169.
36 Harry Boland Diary, De Valera Papers, Franciscan Library, Killiney, File 2172\1.
37 Coogan, Tim Pat, *De Valera,* Hutchinson, London 1993, p. 171.
38 McCartan, Dr Patrick, *With De Valera in America,* Fitzpatrick Ltd, Dublin, p. 166.
39 Harry Boland Diary, De Valera Papers, Franciscan Library Killiney, File 2172\1.
40 *Kentucky Irish American,* 21 June 1920, University of Notre Dame, Indiana, USA.
41 Harry Boland Diary, De Valera Papers, Franciscan Library, Killiney, File 2172\1.
42 Kathleen O'Connell to Liam Mellows, 31 March 1920, De Valera Papers, Franciscan Library, Killiney, File 1473.
43 Liam Ó Maelíosa, Norfolk, to Kathleen O'Connell, Washington, 1 April 1920, De Valera Papers, Franciscan Library, Killiney, File 1473.
44 McCartan, Dr Patrick, *With De Valera in America,* Fitzpatrick Ltd, Dublin, p. 182.

45 Harry Boland Diary, De Valera Papers, Franciscan Library, Killiney, File 2172\1.
46 Lavelle, Patricia, *James O'Mara*, Clonmore and Reynolds Ltd, London 1961, pp. 167, 168.
47 Micheál Ó Coileáin to Harry Boland, 19 April 1920, De Valera Papers, Franciscan Library, Killiney, File 1694.
48 McCartan, Dr Patrick, *With De Valera in America*, Fitzpatrick, Dublin 1932, pp. 201, 202.
49 Harry Boland Diary, De Valera Papers, Franciscan Library, Killiney, File 2172\1.
50 *Ibid.*
51 *Ibid.*
52 Boland Family Archive, Fionnuala Crowley, Waterfall, Cork.
53 Harry Boland Diary, De Valera Papers, Franciscan Library, Killiney, File 2172\1.
54 T. P. O'Neill, Lecture on First Dáil, Kilkenny, March 1989, Tape with John Cahill, Great Oak, Callan.
55 Harry Boland Diary, De Valera Papers, Franciscan Library, Killiney, File 2172\1.
56 *Ibid.*

BOLAND REPORTS HOME

1   Harry Boland Diary, De Valera Papers, Franciscan Library, Killiney, File 2172/1.
2   *Ibid.*
3   *Ibid.*
4   Brennan, Robert, *Allegiance*, Browne and Nolan Ltd, Dublin 1950, p. 265.
5   Kitty Kiernan to Harry Boland, 31 May, 1920, Boland family Archive, Annraoi Ó Beoláin, Sutton.
6   Ua Ceallaigh (Sceilg), Seán, *Cathal Brugha*, M. H. Macanghoill agus a mhac Teo, Baile Átha Cliath 1942, p. 142.
7   Harry Boland Diary, De Valera Papers, Franciscan Library, Killiney, File 2172/1.
8   *Ibid.*
9   *Ibid.*
10 *Ibid.*
11 Dáil Éireann 1/2, Ministry and Cabinet Minutes, 5 June 1920, National Archives, Bishop Street, Dublin.
12 *Gaelic American*, 5 June 1920, Belch Institute for Ethnic Studies Library, Philadelphia.
13 Ó Broin, Leon, Ó hÉigeartaigh, Cian, *In Great Haste*, Gill and Macmillan Ltd, Dublin 1996, p. 8.
14 Harry Boland Diary, De Valera Papers, Franciscan Library, Killiney, File 2172/1.
15 *Ibid.*
16 Ó Broin, Leon, Ó hÉigeartaigh, Cian, *In Great Haste*, Gill and Macmillan Ltd, Dublin 1996, p. 10.

BOLAND PACKED A PUNCH

1   Harry Boland Diary, De Valera Papers, Franciscan Library, Killiney, File 2172/1.
2   *Ibid.*
3   McCartan, Dr Patrick, *With De Valera in America*, Fitzpatrick Ltd, Dublin 1932, p. 196.
4   Harry Boland Diary, De Valera's Papers, Franciscan Library, Killiney, File 2172/1.
5   Longford, O'Neill, *Éamon de Valera*, Gill and Macmillan Ltd, Dublin 1970, p. 111.
6   O'Donoghue, Florence, 'Diarmuid Lynch as national secretary, Friends of Irish Freedom', Chapter XI, *The IRB and the 1916 Rising*, Lynch, Diarmuid, Mercier Press, Cork 1957, p. 210.
7   *Gaelic American*, 20 July 1920, Belch Institute for Ethnic Studies Library, Philadelphia.
8   Harry Boland Diary, De Valera Papers, Franciscan Library, Killiney, File 2172/1.
9   Cronin, Seán, *The McGarrity Papers*, A Clan-na-Gael Book, 1993, Appendix VIII, p. 12.
10 *Gaelic American*, 20 July 1920, Belch Institute for Ethnic Studies Library, Philadelphia.
11 Harry Boland Diary, De Valera Papers, Franciscan Library, Killiney, File 2172/1.
12 Boland Family Archive, Annraoi Ó Beoláin, Sutton, Co. Dublin.
13 Harry Boland to Kitty Kiernan, Boland Family Archive, Annraoi Ó Beoláin, Sutton,

Co. Dublin.

14 Cronin, Seán, *The McGarrity Papers*, Anvil Books, Tralee 1972, p. 83.
15 *Ibid.*, p. 84.
16 Cronin, Seán, *The McGarrity Papers*, A Clan-na-Gael Book, 1993, Appendix VIII, p. 12.
17 *Ibid.*, p. 13.
18 Cronin, Seán, *The McGarrity Papers*, Anvil Books, Tralee 1972, p. 84.
19 Harry Boland to Kitty Kiernan, 18 September 1920, Boland Family Archive, Annraoi Ó Beoláin, Sutton, Co. Dublin.
20 *Kentucky Irish American*, 30 October 1920, The University of Notre Dame, Indiana.
21 McCartan, Dr Patrick, *With De Valera in America*, Fitzpatrick, Dublin 1932, p. 213.
22 Cronin Seán, *The McGarrity Papers*, A Clan-na-Gael Book, 1993, Appendix VIII, p. 13.
23 Coogan, Tim Pat, *De Valera*, Hutchinson, London 1993, p. 190.
24 Cronin, Seán, *The McGarrity Papers*, A Clan-na-Gael Book, 1993, Appendix VIII, p. 14.
25 Harry Boland to Kitty Kiernan, 18 September 1920, Boland Family Archive, Annraoi Ó Beoláin, Sutton, Co. Dublin.
26 Greaves, C. Desmond, *Liam Mellows and the Irish Revolution*, Lawrence and Wishart, London 1971, p. 218.
27 Cronin, Seán, *The McGarrity Papers*, Anvil Books, Tralee 1972, p. 87.
28 Harry Boland to Kitty Kiernan, 24 September 1920, Boland Family Archive, Annraoi Ó Beoláin, Sutton, Co. Dublin.
29 McCartan, Dr Patrick, *With De Valera in America*, Fitzpatrick, Dublin 1932, p. 214.
30 Harry Boland to Éamon de Valera, 14 October 1920, De Valera Papers, Franciscan Library, Killiney, File No. 1214.
31 *Gaelic American*, 30 October 1920, Belch Institute for Ethnic Studies Library, Philadelphia.
32 Cronin, Seán, *The McGarrity Papers*, Anvil Books, Tralee 1972, p. 99.
33 *Gaelic American*, 30 October 1920, Belch Institute for Ethnic Studies Library, Philadelphia.
34 *Ibid.*, 13 November 1920.
35 McCartan, Dr Patrick, *With De Valera in America*, Fitzpatrick, Dublin 1932, p. 186.
36 Cronin, Seán, *The McGarrity Papers*, Anvil Books, Tralee 1972, p. 95.
37 *The Kilkenny People*, 2 September 1922, Letter from John Devoy.
38 *Ibid.*
39 Cronin, Seán, *The McGarrity Papers*, A Clan-na-Gael Book, 1993, Appendix VIII, p. 14.
40 Harry Boland to Éamon de Valera, 17 August 1920, De Valera Papers, Franciscan Library, Killiney, File 1214.
41 Lavelle, Patricia, *James O'Mara*, Clonmore and Reynolds Ltd, Dublin 1962, p. 184.
42 *The Gaelic American*, 5 December 1920.
43 Lynch, Diarmuid, *The IRB and the 1916 Insurrection*, Chapter X1, O'Donoghue, Florence, 'Diarmuid Lynch as national secretary, Friends of Irish Freedom', Mercier Press, Cork 1957, p. 214.
44 McCartan, Dr Patrick, *With De Valera in America*, Fitzpatrick, Dublin 1932, p. 216.
45 *Gaelic American*, 5 December 1920.
46 *Kentucky Irish American*, 3 July 1920.
47 *Ibid.*, 16 October 1920.
48 McCartan, Dr Patrick, *With De Valera in America*, Fitzpatrick, Dublin 1932, p. 221.
49 Éamon de Valera to H. J. Boland, 27 October 1920, Fionnuala Crowley, Waterfall, Cork.
50 L. Martens to the Government of the Republic of Ireland, 29 October 1920, *ibid.*
51 McCartan, Dr Patrick, *With De Valera in America*, Fitzpatrick, Dublin 1932, p. 221.
52 *Ibid.*, p. 221.
53 Macardle, Dorothy, *The Irish Republic*, Irish Press, Dublin 1951, p. 410.
54 Coogan, Tim Pat, *De Valera*, Hutchinson, London 1993, p. 194.
55 Éamon de Valera to Harry Boland, December 1920, De Valera Papers, Franciscan

Library, Killiney, File 1302.
56 Coogan, Tim Pat, *De Valera*, Hutchinson, London 1993, p. 195.

A Joyous Day
1   Lavelle, Patricia, *James O'Mara*, Clonmore and Reynolds, Dublin 1961, p. 220.
2   Mary MacSwiney to Harry Boland, 26 January 1921, De Valera Papers, Killiney, File 1444.
3   Kitty Kiernan to Harry Boland, 15 April 1921, Boland Family Archive, Annraoi Ó Beoláin, Sutton, Co. Dublin.
4   Éamon de Valera to Harry Boland, December 1920, De Valera Papers, Killiney, File 1302.
5   McCartan, Dr Patrick, *With De Valera in America*, Fitzpatrick, Dublin 1932, p. 232.
6   *Ibid.*
7   Éamon de Valera to Harry Boland, 1 January 1921, De Valera Papers, Killiney, File 1215.
8   De Valera to Harry Boland, December 1920, De Valera Papers, Franciscan Library, Killiney, File 1302.
9   Lavelle, Patricia, *James O'Mara*, Clonmore and Reynolds Ltd, Dublin 1961, p. 200.
10 Interview with Kevin Boland, Rathcoole, 8 September 1997; *Kilkenny People*, 11 September 1998.
11 Harry Boland to Éamon de Valera, 13 January 1921, De Valera Papers, Franciscan Library, Killiney, File 1215.
12 Lavelle, Patricia, *James O'Mara*, Clonmore and Reynolds Ltd, Dublin 1961, p. 224.
13 Harry Boland to Éamon de Valera, 13 January 1921, De Valera Papers, Franciscan Library, Killiney, File 1215.
14 Éamon de Valera to Harry Boland, January, 1921, De Valera Papers, Franciscan Library, Killiney, File 1215.
15 Harry Boland to Éamon de Valera, 11 February 1921, De Valera Papers, Franciscan Library, Killiney, File 1215.
16 Cronin, Seán, *The McGarrity Papers*, Anvil Books, Tralee 1972, p. 98.
17 Kathleen O'Connell's statement, 28 June 1945, De Valera Papers, Franciscan Library, Killiney, File 1473.
18 Cronin, Seán, *The McGarrity Papers*, A Clan-na-Gael Book, 1993, Appendix VIII, p. 15.
19 *Ibid.*, p. 2.
20 *Ibid.*, p. 16.
21 Cronin, Seán, *The McGarrity Papers*, Anvil Books, Tralee 1972, p. 99.
22 Memoir of Mrs Seán O'Donovan (nee Kathleen Boland).
23 Enclosure No. 3, State Department, National Archives, Washington DC.
24 Éamon de Valera to Harry Boland, 23 May 1921, De Valera Papers, Franciscan Library, Killiney, File 1215.
25 Cronin, Seán, *The McGarrity Papers*, Anvil Books, Tralee 1972, p. 99.
26 Minutes of Dáil Éireann, 11 March 1921, p. 267.
27 Memo from Harry Boland to Éamon de Valera, 28 April 1921, De Valera Papers, Franciscan Library, Killiney, File 1215.
28 Lavelle, Patricia, *James O'Mara*, Clonmore and Reynolds Ltd, Dublin 1961, p. 244.
29 Memo from Éamon de Valera to Harry Boland, 29 April 1921, De Valera Papers, Franciscan Library, Killiney, File 1215.
30 Memo from Harry Boland to Éamon de Valera, 28 April 1921, De Valera Papers, Franciscan Library, Killiney, File 1215.
31 Lavelle, Patricia, *James O'Mara*, Clonmore and Reynolds Ltd, Dublin 1961, p. 249.
32 Memo from De Valera to Harry Boland, 13 May 1921, De Valera Papers, Franciscan Library, Killiney, File 1215.
33 Dáil Éireann 1/2, Ministry and Cabinet Meetings, 25 May 1921.
34 Lavelle, Patricia, *James O'Mara*, Clonmore and Reynolds Ltd, Dublin 1961, p. 262.

35 *Gaelic American,* 30 April 1921, Belch Institute for Ethnic Studies Library, Philadelphia.

36 *Ibid.*

37 Kitty Kiernan to Harry Boland, 15 April 1921, Boland Family Archive, Annraoi Ó Beoláin, Sutton, Co. Dublin.

38 Walker, Brian M, *Parliamentary Election Results in Ireland 1918–92,* Royal Irish Academy, 1992.

39 Harry Boland to James O'Mara, 4 April 1921, De Valera Papers, Franciscan Library, Killiney, File 1226.

40 Jones, Thomas, *Whitehall Diary,* Volume 111, *Ireland 1918–1925,* Edited by Keith Middlemas, Cabinet Meeting, 12 May 1921, Oxford University Press, Oxford 1971, p. 68.

41 *Ibid.,* p. 69.

42 *Ibid.,* p. 72.

43 *Ibid.,* pp. 74, 75.

44 *Ibid.,* pp. 78, 79.

45 Macardle, Dorothy, *The Irish Republic,* Irish Press Ltd, Dublin 1951, p. 474.

46 American Consul, London to State Department, Washington DC, National Archives, Washington, File No. 800–Treaty (20).

47 Harry Boland to Éamon de Valera, 20 July 1921, De Valera Papers, Franciscan Library, Killiney, File 1215.

48 *Gaelic American,* 20 August 1921, Belch Institute for Ethnic Studies Library, Philadelphia.

GAIRLOCH AND KITTY KIERNAN

1 Minutes of Dáil Éireann, 16 August 1921, p. 10.

2 *Ibid.,* 17 August 1921, p. 18.

3 *Ibid.,* p. 20.

4 Minutes of Dáil Éireann, Private Session, 25 August 1921, pp. 62, 63, 64.

5 *Ibid.,* 26 August 1921, p. 84

6 Official correspondence relating to the Peace Negotiations, De Valera Papers, Franciscan Library, Killiney, File 1374.

7 Macardle Dorothy, *The Irish Republic,* Irish Press, Dublin 1951, p. 499.

8 Ministry and Cabinet Minutes, Dáil Éireann 1/3, Special Meeting, 27 July 1921.

9 Harry Boland Diary, 25 August 1921, De Valera Papers, Franciscan Library, Killiney.

10 Taylor, Rex, *Michael Collins,* Four Square Book, London 1961, p. 113.

11 Robert Barton to Dr Mannix, De Valera Papers, Franciscan Library, Killiney, File 1296.

12 Ó Broin, Leon, Ó hÉigeartaigh, Cian, *In Great Haste,* Michael Collins to Kitty Kiernan, 2 August 1921, Gill and Macmillan, Dublin 1996, p. 13.

13 *Ibid.,* 21 August 1921, p. 14.

14 Harry Boland Diary, 28 August 1921, De Valera Papers, Franciscan Library, Killiney.

15 Minutes of Dáil Éireann, 26 August 1921, pp. 80, 82.

16 *Ibid.,* p. 81.

17 *Ibid.,* p. 80.

18 Ó Broin, Leon, Ó hÉigeartaigh, Cian, *In Great Haste,* Michael Collins to Kitty Kiernan, 31 August 1921, Gill and Macmillan, Dublin, 1996, p. 15.

19 Harry Boland to Kitty Kiernan, 1 September 1921, Boland Family Archive, Annraoi Ó Beoláin, Sutton, Co. Dublin.

20 Harry Boland Diary, De Valera Papers, Franciscan Library, Killiney.

21 *Ibid.*

22 Ó Broin, Leon, Ó hÉigeartaigh, Cian, *In Great Haste,* Michael Collins to Kitty Kiernan, 8 September 1921, Gill and Macmillan, Dublin, 1996, p. 18.

23 Official Correspondence Relating to the Peace Negotiations, De Valera Papers, Franciscan Library, Killiney, File 1374, Lloyd George.

24 Bishop Fogarty to Michael Collins, 1 September 1921, De Valera Papers, Franciscan Library, Killiney, File 151.

25 Diary of Éamon de Valera, De Valera Papers, Franciscan Library, Killiney.
26 Ministry and Cabinet Minutes, Dáil Éireann 1/3, 9 September 1921, National Archives, Bishop Street, Dublin.
27 *Ibid.*, 10 September 1921.
28 Diary of Kathleen O'Connell, De Valera Papers, Franciscan Library, Killiney.
29 Interview with John Roberts, Kilkenny All-Ireland hurler, summer 1987.
30 Brennan, Robert, *Allegiance*, Browne and Nolan Ltd, Dublin 1950, pp. 318, 319.
31 *Ibid.*, pp. 318, 319.
32 *Ibid.*, p. 319.
33 Minutes of Dáil Éireann, Private Session, 14 September 1921.
34 *Ibid.*, 3 October 1921.
35 Murphy, Brian P., *John Chartres Mystery Man of the Treaty*, Irish Academic Press, Dublin 1995, p. 49.
36 Ó Broin, Leon, Ó hÉigeartaigh, Cian, *In Great Haste,* Gill and Macmillan, Dublin 1996, Harry Boland to Kitty Kiernan, 20 September 1921, p. 18.
37 Éamon de Valera to Harry Boland, 20 September 1921, De Valera Papers, Franciscan Library, Killiney, File 1302.
38 R. Ó Breandáin to Harry Boland, 23 September 1921, De Valera Papers, Franciscan Library, Killiney, File 1302.
39 Harry Boland to Kitty Kiernan, 24 September 1921, Boland Family Archive, Annraoi Ó Beoláin, Sutton, Co. Dublin.
40 *Ibid.*
41 *Ibid.*, 30 September 1921, Boland Family Archive, Annraoi Ó Beoláin, Sutton, Co. Dublin.
42 *Ibid.*
43 *Ibid.*
44 *Ibid.*
45 Ó Broin, Leon, Ó hÉigeartaigh, Cian, *In Great Haste,* Gill and Macmillan, Dublin 1996, Harry Boland to Kitty Kiernan, 1 October 1921.
46 *Ibid.*
47 *Ibid.*, 2 October 1921.

HOME TO VOTE ANTI-TREATY

1   *Irish Independent*, 3 October 1921, National Archives, Washington DC.
2   *Cork Examiner*, 3 October 1921, National Archives, Washington DC.
3   Minutes of Dáil Éireann, 7 January 1922, p. 307.
4   *Irish Independent*, 18 October 1922.
5   *Ibid.*, 31 January 1923.
6   *Ibid.*, 18 October 1922.
7   Minutes of Dáil Éireann, 14 September 1921, pp. 94–96.
8   Robert Barton to Dr Mannix, De Valera Papers, Franciscan Library, Killiney, File 1296.
9   *Irish Independent*, 18 October 1922.
10 Macardle, Dorothy, *The Irish Republic,* Irish Press Ltd, Dublin 1951, p. 529.
11 *Ibid.*
12 *Irish Independent*, 18 October 1922.
13 American Consul, Mason Mitchel to Secretary of State, Washington, 3 October 1921, Enclosure 1397, National Archives, Washington, 12–9–64.
14 Byron, H. UHL, Assistant Commissioner to Commissioner General of Immigration, Washington DC, Enclosure 1397, National Archives, Washington DC.
15 Ó Broin, Leon, Ó hÉigeartaigh, Cian, *In Great Haste,* Gill and Macmillan, Dublin 1996; Harry Boland to Kitty Kiernan, 11 October 1921, p. 26.
16 Harry Boland to Kitty Kiernan, 17 October 1921, Boland Family Archive, Annraoi Ó Beoláin, Sutton, Co. Dublin.
17 *Ibid.*, 19 October 1921.

18 *Ibid.*
19 *Ibid.*, 26 October 1921.
20 Ó Broin, Leon, Ó hÉigeartaigh, Cian, *In Great Haste,* Gill and Macmillan, Dublin 1996, Kitty Kiernan to Michael Collins, Letter 23A, p. 32.
21 *Ibid.*, Kitty Kiernan to Michael Collins, probably 14 October 1921.
22 *Ibid.*, Kitty Kiernan to Michael Collins, probably October 1921.
23 Article by Harry J. Boland, 'Irish Diplomatic Rep. in the U.S.A.', October 1921, De Valera Papers, Franciscan Library, Killiney, File 1302.
24 Letter from Harry Boland to Kathleen O'Connell, (to be passed to the Chief), 18 October 1921, De Valera Papers, Franciscan Library, Killiney, File 1215.
25 Harry Boland to Kitty Kiernan, 26 October 1921, Boland Family Archive, Annraoi Ó Beoláin, Sutton, Co. Dublin.
26 *Gaelic American,* 8 April 1922, Belch Institute for Ethnic Studies Library, Philadelphia.
27 National Archives, Washington DC, File 84/do/B11/7.
28 Letter from Harry Boland to Kitty Kiernan, 30 October 1921, Fionnuala Crowley Archive, Waterfall, Cork.
29 Ó Broin, Leon, Ó hÉigeartaigh, Cian, *In Great Haste,* Gill and Macmillan, Dublin, 1996, Kitty Kiernan to Michael Collins, 10 November 1921, p. 61.
30 *Ibid.*, 15 November 1921, p. 65.
31 *Ibid.*
32 Harry Boland to Éamon de Valera, 30 November 1921, De Valera Papers, Franciscan Library, Killiney, File 1215.
33 Daniel Sheehy to Harry Boland, December 1921, De Valera Papers, Franciscan Library, Killiney, File 1226.
34 Mitchell, Arthur, *Revolutionary Government in Ireland 1919–22,* Gill and Macmillan Ltd, Dublin 1995, p. 313.
35 *Gaelic American,* 10 September 1921.
36 *The New York Times,* 1 December 1921.
37 *The New York Tribune,* 3 December 1921.
38 *Ibid.*, 5 December 1921.
39 *Ibid.*
40 *The New York Times,* 6 December 1921.
41 *Ibid.*, 7 December 1921.
42 *Ibid.*
43 *Ibid.*
44 *The New York World,* 7 December, 1921.
45 *The New York Herald,* 8 December 1921, Library of Congress, Washington DC.
46 *The New York Tribune,* 8 December 1921, Library of Congress, Washington DC.
47 *The New York Times,* 9 December 1921.
48 Minutes of Dáil Éireann, 7 January 1921, p. 335.
49 *Ibid.*, pp. 301, 302.
50 *The New York Times,* 9 December 1921.
51 *Ibid.*
52 Diary of Harry Boland, 9 December 1921, De Valera Papers, Franciscan Library, Killiney, File 2172.
53 *The New York Herald,* 11 December 1921, Library of Congress, Washington DC.
54 Cronin, Seán, *The McGarrity Papers,* Anvil Books, Tralee 1972, pp. 114, 115.
55 *Ibid.*
56 *The New York Herald,* 7 December 1921.
57 *Ibid.*
58 *The New York Times,* 7 December 1921.
59 *The New York Tribune,* 11 December 1921, Library of Congress, Washington DC.
60 *The New York Times,* 10 December 1921.
61 *Kentucky Irish American,* 10 December 1921, University of Notre Dame, Indiana.

62 *The New York Tribune*, 8 December, 1921.
63 Minutes of Dáil Éireann, 7 January 1922, p. 303.
64 Harry Boland to Kitty Kiernan, 12 December 1921, Boland Family Archive, Annraoi Ó Beoláin, Sutton, Co. Dublin.
65 Minutes of Dáil Éireann, 19 December 1921, p. 20.
66 Diary of Harry Boland, De Valera Papers, Franciscan Library, Killiney, File 2172.
67 De Valera Papers, Franciscan Library, Killiney, File 1302.
68 *Ibid.*
69 De Valera Papers, Franciscan Library, Killiney, File 1226.
70 Harry Boland Diary, De Valera Papers, Franciscan Library, Killiney, File 2172.
71 *Ibid.*

LIKE FATHER – LIKE SON
1 Memoir of Seán O'Donovan, Clontarf Road, Dublin; Eileen Barrington, Dunlaoghaire, daughter.
2 Minutes of Dáil Éireann, 19 December 1921, p. 20.
3 Proinsias Ó Druacháin do Cheann Chomhairle na Dála, Minutes of Dáil Éireann, 5 January 1922, p. 269.
4 Kathleen O'Connell Diary No. 3, De Valera Papers, Franciscan Library, Killiney.
5 Béaslaí, Piaras, *Michael Collins*, The Talbot Press, Dublin and Cork 1937, p. 342.
6 Minutes of Dáil Éireann, Private Session, 6 January 1922, p. 275.
7 *Ibid.*, p. 282.
8 Ludwig Martens to Harry Boland, 29 October 1920, in possession of Fionnuala Crowley, Waterfall, Cork.
9 Béaslaí, Piaras, *Michael Collins*, The Talbot Press, Dublin and Cork 1937, p. 342.
10 Memoir of Mrs Seán O'Donovan (nee Kathleen Boland).
11 Ó Broin, Leon, Ó hÉigeartaigh, Cian, Michael Collins to Kitty Kiernan, 6 January 1922, *In Great Haste*, Gill and Macmillan, Dublin 1996, p. 102.
12 Minutes of Dáil Éireann, 6 January 1922, p. 273.
13 *Ibid.*, 10 January 1922, p. 409.
14 *Ibid.*, 6 January 1922, p. 277.
15 *Ibid.*, p. 279.
16 *Ibid.*, p. 281.
17 *Ibid.*
18 Memoir of Mrs Seán O'Donovan (nee Kathleen Boland).
19 Special Correspondent, *Irish Times*, 9 January 1921.
20 Minutes of Dáil Éireann, 7 January 1922, p. 301.
21 *Ibid.*, p. 304.
22 *Ibid.*
23 *Ibid.*, p. 330.
24 *Ibid.*, p. 344.
25 *Ibid.*, p. 346.
26 *Ibid.*, p. 347.

THE SHIP HAS A NEW CAPTAIN
1 Diaries of Éamon de Valera, 7 January 1922, De Valera Papers, Franciscan Library, Killiney.
2 *Ibid.*
3 Minutes of Dáil Éireann, 9 January 1922, pp. 349, 350.
4 Clarke, Kathleen, *My Fight for Ireland's Freedom*, edited by Helen Litton, The O'Brien Press, Dublin 1991, pp. 193, 194.
5 Minutes of Dáil Éireann, 9 January 1922, p. 374.
6 *Ibid.*, p. 378.
7 *Ibid.*, p. 381.

8   *Ibid.*, 10 January 1921, pp. 392, 393.
9   *Ibid.*, p. 410.
10 *Ibid.*, p. 411.
11 *Ibid.*, p. 414.
12 Diaries of Kathleen O'Connell, De Valera Papers, Franciscan Library, Killiney.
13 Minutes of Dáil Éireann, 3 January 1922, p. 190.
14 Harry Boland to Kitty Kiernan, 10 January 1922, Fionnuala Crowley, Waterfall, Cork.
15 Harry Boland to Kitty Kiernan, 16 January 1922, Boland Family Archive, Annraoi Ó Beoláin, Sutton, Co. Dublin.
16 *Ibid.*
17 *The Irish Times*, 18 January 1922.
18 Memoir of Mrs Seán O'Donovan (nee Kathleen Boland).
19 *The Irish Times*, 10 January 1922.
20 Macardle, Dorothy, *The Irish Republic*, Irish Press Ltd, Dublin 1951, p. 651.
21 *The Irish Times*, 13 January 1922.
22 Minutes of Provisional Government, 16 January 1922, G 1/1 16 January – 24 March 1922, National Archives, Dublin.
23 Éamon de Valera to Harry Boland, 8 January 1922, De Valera Papers, Franciscan Library, Killiney, File 1302.
24 Diaries of Harry Boland, 16 January 1922, De Valera Papers, Franciscan Library, Killiney, File 1302.
25 Dáil cabinet meeting, 11 January 1922, Dáil Ministry and Cabinet Minutes, National Archives, Dublin.
26 Harry Boland to Kitty Kiernan, 16 January 1922, Fionnuala Crowley, Waterfall, Cork.
27 Diaries of Harry Boland, 23 January 1922, De Valera Papers, Franciscan Library, Killiney, File 1302.
28 Diaries of Éamon de Valera, De Valera Papers, 29 January 1922, Franciscan Library, Killiney.
29 The *Nationalist and Leinster Times*, 25 February 1922.
30 *The Irish Times*, 31 January 1922.
31 De Valera Papers, Franciscan Library, Killiney, File 253.
32 Foreign Office Memorandum No. 1, 1922, De Valera Papers, Franciscan Library, Killiney.
33 Gavan Duffy to Harry Boland, 28 January 1922, De Valera Papers, Franciscan Library, Killiney, File 253.

BOLAND LOSES OUT
1   Harry Boland to Gavan Duffy, 30 January 1922, De Valera Papers, Franciscan Library, Killiney, File 253.
2   Gavan Duffy to Harry Boland, 2 February 1922, De Valera Papers, Franciscan Library, Killiney.
3   Harry Boland to Gavan Duffy, 9 February 1922, De Valera Papers, Franciscan Library, Killiney.
4   Gavan Duffy to Harry Boland, 16 February 1922, De Valera Papers, Franciscan Library, Killiney.
5   Dáil cabinet meeting on 3 February 1922, Dáil Minstry and Cabinet Minutes, National Archives, Dublin.
6   Minutes of Dáil Éireann, 1 March 1922, p. 135.
7   Harry Boland to Stephen O'Mara, 16 February 1922, De Valera Papers, Franciscan Library, Killiney, File 1450.
8   Kate Boland to Éamon de Valera, 16 June 1923, De Valera Papers, Franciscan Library, Killiney, File 1302.
9   UCD Archives, File P/4/299, Hugh Kennedy Papers.
10 *The Nationalist*, Clonmel, 22 February 1922.

11 *The Irish Times*, 23 February 1922.
12 *Ibid.*, 22 February 1922.
13 *Ibid.*
14 Kathleen O'Connell's Diaries, 22 February 1922, De Valera Papers, Franciscan Library, Killiney.
15 Akenson, D. H. and Fallin, J. F., 'The Drafting of the Irish Constitution', *Éire–Ireland*, St Paul, Minnesota, 1970.
16 *The Tipperary Star*, 18 February 1922.
17 Stephen O'Mara to Harry Boland, 15 February 1922, De Valera Papers, Franciscan Library, Killiney, File 1450.
18 *The Irish Times*, 27 February 1922.
19 *The Tipperary Star*, 11 March 1922.
20 John Moore to Harry Boland, De Valera Papers, Franciscan Library, Killiney, File 253.
21 Hanna Sheehy Skeffington to Harry Boland, February 1922, De Valera Papers, Franciscan Library, Killiney.
22 Liam Mellows, Statement by Alfred White, De Valera Papers, Killiney, File 1457.
23 Cronin, Seán, *The McGarrity Papers*, Anvil Books, Tralee 1972, Harry Boland to Luke Dillon, 22 January 1922, p. 113.
24 Oscar Traynor, De Valera Papers, Franciscan Library, Killiney, File 1527/2.
25 Mulcahy Papers, UCD Archives, File P7/C/10.

DRIFTING TOWARDS CIVIL WAR
1 Papers of Florence O'Donoghue, MS 31242, Manuscript Room, National Library of Ireland.
2 Minutes of Dáil Éireann, 10 January 1922, p. 424.
3 MacCárthaigh, Cormac, Micheál Ó Coileáin – 'Cé dhein a Bhás a Phleanáil?' *Agus*, Bealtaine 1968.
4 Ua hUallacháin, Gearóid, *A Scéal Féin*, le cead on Athair Maoilíosa Ó hUallacháin, Baile Átha Cliath.
5 Letter to Richard Mulcahy, Minister of Defence, 11 January 1922.
6 Dáil Éireann 1/4, Ministry and Cabinet minutes, Dáil Cabinet, 12 January 1922, National Archives.
7 O'Donoghue, Florence, *No Other Law*, Irish Press, Dublin 1954, p. 210.
8 *Ibid.*
9 *Ibid.*, pp. 210, 211.
10 Harry Boland Diary, 26 March 1922, De Valera Papers, Franciscan Library, Killiney.
11 UCD Archives, Mulcahy Papers, File P7/B/191.
12 *Ibid.*
13 *Ibid.*
14 *Ibid.*
15 Harry Boland Diary, De Valera Papers, Franciscan Library, Killiney, 9 March 1922.
16 Letter from Liam Lynch to *Irish Independent*, 27 April 1922.
17 *Ibid.*
18 *Ibid.*
19 UCD Archives, Mulcahy Papers, File P7/B/191.
20 Hopkinson, Michael, *Green against Green*, Gill and Macmillan, Dublin 1988, p. 66.
21 O'Donoghue, Florence, *No Other Law*, Irish Press, Dublin 1954, p. 220.
22 Griffith's instructions to the Minister for Defence, 23 March 1922, UCD Archives, Mulcahy Papers, File M31, 249.
23 Dáil Éireann 1/4, Ministry and Cabinet Minutes, Meeting of Ministry, 15 March 1922, National Archives, Dublin.
24 UCD Archives, Mulcahy Papers, File M31, 249.
25 O'Donoghue, Florence, *No Other Law*, Irish Press, Dublin 1953, p. 221.
26 De Valera Papers, Franciscan Library, Killiney, Oscar Traynor, File 1527/2.

27 Gerry Boland in an interview with Michael McInerney, *Irish Times*, 9 October 1968.
28 Interview with Ned Aylward, Callan 1966.
29 O'Donoghue, Florence, *No Other Law*, Irish Press, Dublin 1953, p. 233.
30 *Ibid.*
31 Béaslaí, Piaras, *Michael Collins*, The Talbot Press, Dublin, 1937, p. 343.
32 Domhnall Ó Ceallacháin to Harry Boland, 8 March 1922, De Valera Papers, Franciscan Library, Killiney, File 253.
33 Harry Boland to Domhnall Ó Ceallacháin, 10 March 1922, De Valera Papers, Franciscan Library, Killiney.
34 Liam Pedlar to Harry Boland, 13 April 1922, De Valera Papers, Franciscan Library, Killiney.
35 Lavelle, Patricia, *James O'Mara*, Clonmore and Reynolds, Dublin 1961, p. 293.
36 Cronin, Seán, *The McGarrity Papers*, Anvil Books, Tralee 1972, p. 114.
37 Harry Boland to Joe McGarrity, 12 April 1922, De Valera Papers, Franciscan Library, Killiney, File 1302.
38 Harry Boland to Liam Lynch, 30 May 1922, De Valera Papers, Franciscan Library, Killiney, File 1302.
39 *Ibid.*
40 Interview with Kevin Boland, 8 September 1922.
41 Harry Boland to Kitty Kiernan, 10 April 1922, Boland Family Archive, Annraoi Ó Beoláin, Sutton, Co. Dublin.
42 Kitty Kiernan to Michael Collins, 4 August 1922, Fionnuala Crowley, Waterfall, Cork; Ó Broin, Leon, Ó hÉigeartaigh, Cian, *In Great Haste*, Gill and Macmillan, Dublin 1996, Kitty Kiernan to Michael Collins, 4 August 1922, p. 220.
43 *The Irish Times*, 12 April 1922.
44 *Ibid.*, 10 April 1922.
45 *Ibid.*, 7 April 1922.
46 Harry Boland to Commander Liam Lynch, 20 April 1922, De Valera Papers, Franciscan Library, Killiney, File 1302.
47 Liam Lynch to Harry Boland T.D., 24 April 1922, De Valera Papers, Franciscan Library, Killiney.
48 Batt O'Connor to Harry Boland, 7 April 1922, De Valera Papers, Franciscan Library, Killiney.
49 *The Irish Times*, 4 April 1922.
50 *The Nationalist and Leinster Times*, 22 April 1922.
51 *Ibid.*, 17 April 1922.
52 *Ibid.*, 25 April 1922.
53 *The Kilkenny People*, 1 April 1922.
54 Cronin, Seán, *The McGarrity Papers*, Anvil Books, Tralee 1972, p. 117.

There'll be No Civil War
1 Interview with Mick Ruth, Kilkenny 1966.
2 Memoir of Michael MacSweeney, Kilkenny.
3 Interview with Mick Ruth, Kilkenny 1966.
4 Memoir of Michael MacSweeney, Kilkenny.
5 *Ibid.*
6 *Ibid.*
7 Younger, Calton, *Ireland's Civil War*, Fontana Books, Glasgow, 1968, p. 287.
8 Interview with Martin Murphy, Grange, Mooncoin, 1966.
9 Interview with Ned Halley, Ballycloven, Callan 1966.
10 Interview with Mick Ruth, Kilkenny 1966.
11 Dáil Debates, 3 May 1922, p. 358.
12 Richard Mulcahy to Micheál Ó Coileáin, 25 March 1922, UCD Archives, File P/7b/192.

13 Minutes of Dáil Éireann, 3 May 1922, p. 366.
14 *Ibid.*
15 *Ibid.*, p. 367.
16 *Ibid.*
17 Diary of Harry Boland, De Valera Papers, Franciscan Library, Killiney.
18 UCD Archives, O'Malley Notebooks, P/17b/100, Seán Moyler.
19 Diary of Harry Boland, De Valera Papers, Franciscan Library, Killiney.
20 Harry Boland to Joe McGarrity, 13 July 1922, National Library of Ireland, Manuscript Room, Joseph McGarrity Papers, 1922.
21 Minutes of Dáil Éireann, 11 May 1922, p. 402.
22 Brennan, Robert, *Allegiance,* Browne and Nolan, Dublin 1950, p. 337.
23 UCD Archives, O'Malley Notebooks, P/7b/90, Frank Aiken.
24 Minutes of Dáil Éireann, 17 May 1922, p. 415.
25 *Ibid.*, p. 418.
26 *Ibid.*, p. 421.
27 *Ibid.*, p. 429.
28 *Ibid.*, p. 439.
29 UCD Archives, O'Malley Notebooks, P/17b/100, Seán Moyler.
30 Minutes of Dáil Éireann, 19 May 1922, p. 462.
31 *Ibid.*, p. 465.
32 *Ibid.*
33 Franciscan Library, Killiney, *The Capuchin Annual,* 1966, article on Arthur Griffith by Seán T. Ó Ceallaigh, pp. 147, 148,149.
34 *The Irish Independent,* 22 May 1922.
35 Minutes of Dáil Éireann, 20 May 1922, p. 480.
36 *The Irish Independent,* 22 May 1922.
37 *The Free Press,* Wexford, 27 May 1922.
38 *The Nationalist,* Carlow, 26 May 1922.
39 *The Waterford News,* 26 May 1922.
40 National Library of Ireland, Manuscript Room, Harry Boland to Joe McGarrity, File 17424.
41 Harry Boland to Joe McGarrity, 30 May 1922, National Library of Ireland, Manuscript Room, File 17424.

BOLAND'S PEACE PACT ON THE ROCKS
1   Liam Pedlar to Harry Boland, 24 May 1922, De Valera Papers, Franciscan Library, Killiney, File 1302.
2   James K. McGuire to Harry Boland, 24 May 1922, De Valera Papers, Franciscan Library, Killiney.
3   Dáil Debates, 20 May 1922, p. 479.
4   Minutes of Dáil Éireann, 7 January 1922, pp. 345, 346.
5   *The Free Press,* Wexford, 8 April 1922.
6   *Ibid.,* 17 May 1922.
7   *Ibid.,* 3 June 1922.
8   *Ibid.,* 27 May 1922.
9   *Ibid.*
10 British Cabinet Minutes, CAB 43/7, British Cabinet Sub-committee on Ireland, 24 May 1922, Kew, PRO, London.
11 *Ibid.*
12 *Ibid.,* CAB 43, 26 May 1922, PRO, Kew, London.
13 *The Free Press,* Wexford, 27 May 1922.
14 *Ibid.*
15 Minutes of Provisional Government, 25 May 1922, National Archives, Dublin.
16 *Ibid.*

17 British Cabinet Minutes, CAB 43, 27 May 1922, PRO, Kew, London.

18 *Ibid.*, CAB 23/30, 30 May 1922.

19 *Ibid.*, CAB 47/7, Interview between Tom Jones and Arthur Griffith and Michael Collins, 31 May 1922.

20 *Ibid.*, CAB 47/7. Interview between Lloyd George, Arthur Griffith and Michael Collins on 1 June 1922.

21 British Cabinet Minutes. CAB 47/7, 1 June 1922, PRO, Kew, London.

22 UCD Archives, Hugh Kennedy Papers, File P4/352 (1).

23 *Ibid.*, File P4/353 (1–4).

24 *The Freeman's Journal*, 3 June 1922.

25 *The Free Press*, Wexford, 10 June 1922.

26 *Ibid.*

27 *Ibid.*

28 *Ibid.*

29 *The Kilkenny People*, 10 June 1922.

30 *The Irish Independent*, 13 June 1922.

31 *Ibid.*, 14 June 1922.

32 *Ibid.*, 15 June 1922.

33 Harry Boland Diary, De Valera Papers, Franciscan Library, Killiney.

34 *The Irish Independent*, 15 June 1922.

35 *Ibid.*

36 *Ibid.*, 16 June 1922.

37 *Ibid.*

38 *Ibid.*

39 De Valera Papers, Franciscan Library, Killiney, File 1403.

40 Minutes of the Provisional Government, 15 June 1922, The National Archives, Dublin.

41 Akenson D. H. and Fallin, J. F., 'The Irish Civil War and the Drafting of the Irish Constitution', *Éire–Ireland*, St Paul, Minnesota, 1970.

42 *The Irish Independent*, 15 June 1922.

43 UCD Archives, O'Malley Papers, File P/7b/90, Frank Aiken.

44 *The Waterford News*, 16 June 1922.

45 Burns, Alec, 'Pádraig MacGamhna', *Carloviana 1965*

46 Robert Barton to Dr Mannix, De Valera Papers, Franciscan Library, Killiney, File 1296.

47 *The Nationalist and Leinster Times*, 29 April 1922.

48 Harry Boland to Joseph McGarrity, 13 July 1922, National Library of Ireland, Manuscript Room, File 17424.

49 *The Free Press*, Wexford, 24 June 1922.

50 Harry Boland to Éamon Dee, De Valera Papers, Franciscan Library, Killiney, File 253.

THE WAR OF FRIENDS

1 *The Free Press*, Wexford, 24 June 1922.

2 *Ibid.*

3 *The Waterford News*, 16 June 1922.

4 *The Free Press*, Wexford, 24 June 1922.

5 Harry Boland to a friend, 21 June 1922, De Valera Papers, Franciscan Library, Killiney, File 253/3.

6 *Ibid.*

7 Harry Boland to Joe McGarrity, 22 June 1922, De Valera Papers, Franciscan Library, Killiney, File 253.

8 *Ibid.*

9 Dictated by Éamon de Valera to Marie O'Kelly, 17 January 1964, De Valera Papers, Franciscan Library, Killiney, File 1527/2.

10 Harry Boland to Joe McGarrity, 12 July 1922, National Library of Ireland Manuscript Room, File 17424.

11 *The People,* 6 August 1961, Joe Dolan, De Valera Papers, Franciscan Library, Killiney, File 132.

12 British Cabinet Minutes, CAB 21/255, 22 June 1922, PRO, Kew, London.

13 *Ibid.*

14 *Ibid.*

15 *Ibid.*

16 Macardle, Dorothy, *The Irish Republic,* Irish Press Ltd, Dublin 1951, p. 738.

17 *The People,* 6 August 1961, Joe Dolan, De Valera Papers, Franciscan Library, Killiney, File 132.

18 UCD Archives, O'Malley Notebooks, File P/7b/97, Joe Sweeney, Donegal.

19 Oscar Traynor, De Valera Papers, Franciscan Library, Killiney, File 1527/2.

20 *Ibid.*

21 Conferences of Ministers, 23 June 1922, CAB 21/255, PRO, Kew, London.

22 *Ibid.,* 24 June 1922.

23 *Ibid.,* 25 June 1922.

24 Memoir of Mrs Mary F. McWhorter, De Valera Papers, Franciscan Library Killiney, File 253.

25 Coogan, Tim Pat, *Michael Collins,* Hutchinson, London 1990, p. 330.

26 Macardle, Dorothy, *The Irish Republic,* Irish Press, Dublin 1951, p. 742.

27 *Ibid.,* p. 744

28 De Vere White, Terence, 'Arthur Griffith', Thomas Davis Lecture, De Valera Papers, Franciscan Library, Killiney, File 1379.

29 UCD Archives, O'Malley Notebooks, File P/17b/96, Oscar Traynor.

30 Harry Boland Diary, De Valera Papers, Franciscan Library, Killiney.

31 UCD Archives, O'Malley Notebooks, File P/17b/96, Oscar Traynor.

32 Kathleen O'Connell Diary, De Valera Papers, Franciscan Library, Killiney.

33 UCD Archives, O'Malley Notebooks, File P/17b/96, Oscar Traynor.

On the Dublin Mountains

1 UCD Archives, O'Malley Notebooks, File P/7b/108, Moss Donegan, Cork.

2 Interview with Thomas Tynan, Navan Road, Dublin, 30 September 1997.

3 UCD Archives, O'Malley Notebooks, File P/7b/103, Tom Smith.

4 Neeson, Eoin, *The Civil War 1922–23,* Mercier Press, Cork 1966, p. 140.

5 UCD Archives, O'Malley Notebooks, File P/7b/108, Mick Leahy, Cork.

6 UCD Archives, O'Malley Notebooks, File P/7b/96, Oscar Traynor.

7 *Ibid.*

8 *The Irish Times,* 10 July 1922.

9 Seán Lemass in an interview with Michael Mills, *Irish Press,* 22 January 1969.

10 *The Irish Times,* 10 July 1922.

11 O'Malley, Ernie, *The Singing Flame,* Anvil Books, Dublin 1978, p. 129.

12 *The Irish Times,* 10 July 1922.

13 O'Malley, Ernie, *The Singing Flame,* Anvil Books, Dublin 1978, p. 129.

14 *Ibid.*

15 *Ibid.*

16 *Ibid.,* p. 131.

17 Interview with Jack Myles, Fethard, 1967.

18 *The Nationalist and Leinster Times,* 8 July 1922.

19 *Ibid.*

20 Jack Myles.

21 UCD Archives, O'Malley Notebooks, File P/17 b/ 103, Mick Burke.

22 Maher, Jim, Interview with Jack Gardiner, *The Flying Column – West Kilkenny,* Geography Publications, Dublin 1987, p. 37.

23 UCD Archives, Mulcahy Papers, File P7/B/106.

24 De Valera Papers, Franciscan Library, Killiney, Oscar Traynor File 1572/2.

25 *Ibid.*
26 UCD Archives, Mulcahy Papers, Documents captured in Blessington.
27 Interview with Kevin Boland, 8 September 1997.
28 *The Irish Times*, 10 July 1922.
29 De Valera Papers, Franciscan Library, Killiney, File 1572/2, Oscar Traynor.
30 Gerry Boland in an interview with Michael McInerney, *Irish Times*, 9 October 1968.
31 *The Irish Times*, 10 July 1922.
32 *Ibid.*
33 UCD Archives, O'Malley Notebooks, File P/17b/103, Mick Burke.
34 *The Irish Times*, 10 July 1922.
35 UCD Archives, O'Malley Notebooks, File P/17b/103. Mick Burke.
36 *The Irish Times*, 10 July 1922.
37 UCD Archives, O'Malley Notebooks, File P/17b/103, Mick Burke.
38 Harry Boland to Joseph McGarrity, 13 July 1922, National Library of Ireland, Manuscript Room, McGarrity Papers, File 17424.

HARRY – IT HAS COME TO THIS

1 De Valera Papers, Franciscan Library, Killiney, File 1305, Seán Brady; Macardle, Dorothy, *The Irish Republic*, Irish Press Ltd., Dublin 1951, p. 153.
2 Letter from Seán Geraghty to Ruairi Brugha, 7 February 1966, De Valera Papers, Franciscan Library, Killiney, File 1315/2.
3 Harry Boland to Joe McGarrity, 13 July 1922, National Library of Ireland, Manuscript Room, File 17424.
4 Diary of Harry Boland, De Valera Papers, Franciscan Library, Killiney.
5 Harry Boland to an American friend, 13 July 1922, De Valera Papers, Franciscan Library, Killiney, File 253.
6 *Ibid.*
7 Harry Boland to Joe McGarrity, McGarrity Papers, National Library of Ireland, Manuscript Room, 13 July 1922, File 17424.
8 Macardle, Dorothy, *The Irish Republic*, Irish Press Dublin, 1951, p. 773.
9 *Ibid.*, p. 774.
10 O'Malley, Ernie, *The Singing Fame*, Anvil Books, Dublin, 1978, p. 149.
11 *Ibid.*
12 Minutes of Provisional Government, 12 July 1922 (evening), National Archives, Dublin.
13 *Ibid.* (morning).
14 Memoir of Mrs Mary McWhorter, De Valera Papers, Franciscan Library, Killiney, File 253.
15 UCD Archives, O'Malley Notebooks, File P/17b/103, Mick Burke.
16 Memoir of Mrs Mary McWhorter, De Valera Papers, Franciscan Library, Killiney, File 253.
17 O'Malley, Ernie, *The Singing Flame*, Anvil Books, Dublin 1978, p. 149.
18 Memoir of Mrs Mary McWhorter, De Valera Papers, Franciscan Library, Killiney, File 253.
19 Diary of Éamon de Valera, De Valera Papers, Franciscan Library, Killiney.
20 Memoir of Mrs Mary McWhorter, De Valera Papers, Franciscan Library, Killiney, File 253.
21 Diary of Harry Boland, De Valera Papers, Franciscan Library, Killiney.
22 Memoir of Mrs Mary McWhorter.
23 *Ibid.*
24 Cronin, Seán, *The McGarrity Papers*, Anvil Books, Tralee 1972, p. 121.
25 Harry Boland to Seán T. O'Kelly, UCD Archives, Mulcahy Papers, File P/7B/155.
26 Clarke, Kathleen, *My Fight for Ireland's Freedom*, The O'Brien Press, Dublin 1991, p. 199.
27 Taylor, Rex, *Michael Collins*, Four Square Book, Hutchinson and Co., Great Britain, p.

194.

28 Coogan, Tim Pat, *Michael Collins*, Hutchinson, London 1990, p. 388.

I'M GOING TO CATHAL BRUGHA

1   Joe Griffin's account to Éamon de Valera, 18 April 1963, De Valera Papers, Franciscan
    Library, Killiney, File 1302.
2   Interview with Kevin Boland, Rathcoole, 2 March 1998.
3   *Ibid.*
4   Joe Griffin's account to Éamon de Valera, 18 April 1963, De Valera Papers, Franciscan
    Library, Killiney, File 1302.
5   Memoir of Mrs Mary McWhorter, De Valera Papers, Franciscan Library, Killiney, File
    253.
6   *The Freeman's Journal*, 1 August 1922.
7   Joe Griffin's account to Éamon de Valera, 18 April 1963, De Valera Papers, Franciscan
    Library, Killiney, File 1302.
8   UCD Archives, Mulcahy Papers, File MP/P7/B/107.
9   *Irish Independent*, 1 August 1922.
10 Memoir of Mrs Mary McWhorter, De Valera Papers, Franciscan Library, Killiney, File
    253.
11 Medical Evidence at inquest on Harry Boland, *Irish Independent*, 4 August 1922.
12 Memoir of Mrs Seán O'Donovan (nee Kathleen Boland).
13 *Ibid.*
14 *The Freeman's Journal*, 2 August 1922.
15 Cronin, Seán, *The McGarrity Papers*, Anvil Books, Tralee 1972, p. 122.
16 Coogan, Tim Pat, *Michael Collins*, Hutchinson, London 1990, p. 388.
17 Memoir of Mrs Mary McWhorter, De Valera Papers, Franciscan Library, Killiney, File
    253.
18 Coogan, Tim Pat, *Michael Collins*, Hutchinson, London, 1990, p. 388.
19 Ó Broin, Leon, Ó hÉigeartaigh, Cian, *In Great Haste*, Gill and Macmillan, Dublin 1996,
    Michael Collins to Kitty Kiernan, 2 August 1922, p. 219.
20 *Ibid.*, Kitty Kiernan to Michael Collins, 2 August 1922, pp. 219, 220.
21 Kathleen O'Connell, Diary No 3, De Valera Papers, Franciscan Library, Killiney.
22 *Ibid.*
23 Interview with Tom Tynan, Dublin, 30 September 1997.
24 Cronin, Seán, *The McGarrity Papers*, Anvil Books, Tralee 1972, p. 122.
25 *The Evening Mail*, 3 August 1922; Doherty, Gabriel and Keogh, Dermot, *Michael Collins
    and the Making of the Irish State*, Mercier Press, Cork 1998, p. 191.
26 Cronin, Seán, *The McGarrity Papers*, Anvil Books, Tralee 1972, p. 127.

BIBLIOGRAPHY

PRIMARY SOURCES

De Loughry Family Papers, Kilkenny.

Lalor, Jimmy, Kilkenny, Papers and documents relating to military pension claims.

Letters of Harry Boland, Boland Family Archive, Annraoi Ó Beoláin, Sutton, Co. Dublin.

Letters of Harry Boland, Boland Family Archive, Fionnuala Crowley, Waterfall, Cork.

McSweeney, Michael (Jnr), Kilkenny, Memoir.

Ó Beoláin, Caoimhghín, *James Boland 1857–1895*.

O'Donovan, Seán, Mrs (nee Kathleen Boland), Memoir.

O'Donovan, Seán, Senator, Memoir, Eileen Barrington, Dún Laoghaire.

O'Neill, T. P., Lecture on First Dáil, Kilkenny, 1989.

Ruth, Mick, Kilkenny, Memoir.

Ua h-Uallacháin, Gearóid, *A Scéal Féin*.

ARCHIVES CONSULTED

Franciscan Library, Killiney, Co. Dublin.

De Valera Papers.

Kathleen O'Connell Papers.

Harry Boland Diaries

Diaries of Éamon de Valera.

Diaries of Kathleen O'Connell.

Seán MacEoin Papers.

University College, Dublin.

Ernie O'Malley Papers.

Ernie O'Malley Notebooks.

Hugh Kennedy Papers.

Richard Mulcahy Papers.

National Library of Ireland.

Harry Boland Letters.

Papers of Florence O'Donoghue.

Papers of Joseph McGarrity.

National Archives, Bishop Street, Dublin.

Census 1901.

Census 1911.

Dáil Éireann Ministry and Cabinet Minutes.

Minutes of Irish Provisional Government, 1922.

Military Archives, Cathal Brugha Barracks, Dublin.

Documents captured in Civil War.

Dublin University (Trinity College).

Erskine Childers Papers.

Irish Stationery Office, Dublin.

Dáil Debates: First Dáil 1919–1921 (Private Sessions); Second Dáil 1921–1922.

Treaty Debates (Public Sessions) 1921–1922 and subsequent meetings of the
  Dáil until June 1922.
National Archives, Washington DC.
State Department Files.
Public Record Office, Kew, London.
British Cabinet Minutes and Papers.
File on Irish Prisoners in English Jails, 1916–1917.
Minutes of British Cabinet Subcommittee on Ireland, 1922.
Minutes of Conferences of Ministers, June 1922.

PAMPHLETS AND ARTICLES
Akenson, D. H. and Fallin, J. F., 'The Irish Civil War and the Drafting of the
  Free State Constitution', *Eire-Ireland*, Irish American Cultural Institute, St
  Paul, Minnesota 1970.
Boland, Harry, 'Draft of Manifesto to the People of Ireland', 10 October 1918.
Burns, Alec, 'Pádraig MacGamhna', *Carloviana* 1965,
De Loughry, Anna T., 'Remembering Lincoln Prison Escape', *Old Kilkenny
  Review*, 1982.
MacCárthaigh, Cormac, 'Micheál Ó Coileáin – Cé a dhein a bhás a phleanáil?'
  Agus, Bealtaine 1968.
Ó Ceallaigh, Seán T., 'Arthur Griffith', *The Capuchin Annual*, 1966.
Old Timer, 'Harry Boland', *Dublin GAA Yearbook* of 1966.

ORAL TESTIMONY
I interviewed Kevin Boland, Annraoi Ó Beoláin, Eileen Barrington, Fionnuala
  Crowley, Ruairí Brugha, Éamon Ó Cuiv, TD, Senator Maurice Manning, Tom
  Tynan, Padraigín Ní Dhubhluachra, Bro. Hermes, Seán Fleming, TD, Tom
  Ryall, and the late Ned Aylward, Jack Gardiner, Jack Myles, Mick Ruth,
  Michael McSweeney, Ned Halley, Martin Murphy, John Roberts and
  Edmund Tynan.

NEWSPAPERS AND PERIODICALS
Gilbert Library, Dublin: *The Freeman's Journal, Irish Independent, Evening Herald,
  The Irish Press, The Evening Mail.*
National Library of Ireland: *The Cork Examiner, The Roscommon Herald.*
Franciscan Library, Killiney, De Valera Papers
The People, Sunday Graphic and Sunday News
Irish Times (Waterford Public Library): *The Kilkenny People* (Kilkenny Public Lib-
  rary); *The Kilkenny Journal* (Rothe House, Kilkenny); *The Nationalist and
  Leinster Times* (Carlow Public Library); *The Clonmel Nationalist* (Thurles Pub-
  lic Library); *The Tipperary Star* (Thurles Public Library); *The Free Press, Wex-
  ford* (Wexford Public Library); *The Carlow Nationalist* (Carlow Public Lib-
  rary); *The Waterford News* (Waterford Public Library).
USA: Library of Congress, Washington DC.
The New York Tribune; The New York World; The New York Herald.
Other USA Centres: *New York Times* (Indiana State Library, Indianapolis, Indiana; Johns Hopkins University, Baltimore, Maryland); *Indianapolis News*

(Indianapolis State Library, Indianapolis, Indiana, USA); *The Gaelic American* (Belch Institute for Ethnic Studies Library, Philadelphia, USA); *The Kentucky Irish American* (University of Notre Dame, Indiana, USA)

RADIO DOCUMENTARIES
Bowman, John, *Saturday Eight-Thirty,* 'Erskine Childers', 29 November, 1997.
De Vere White, Terence, 'Arthur Griffith', Thomas Davis Lecture.

TELEVISION DOCUMENTARY
Leonard, Hugh, *Insurrection 1916,* RTE, 1966.

SELECT BIBLIOGRAPHY
Béaslaí, Piaras, *Michael Collins and the making of a new Ireland,* George Harrap, London, 1926.
Béaslaí, Piaras, *Michael Collins,* Talbot Press, Dublin 1937.
Bourke, Marcus, *The O'Rahilly,* Anvil Books, Tralee 1967.
Brennan, John, *Dublin's Fighting Story,* 'Seán Mac Diarmada', The Kerryman, Tralee 1947.
Brennan, Robert, *Allegiance,* Browne and Nolan, Dublin 1950.
Bromage, Mary C., *De Valera and the March of a Nation,* Hutchinson, London 1956.
Carroll, Denis, *They have fooled you again, Micheál Ó Flanagáin,* The Columba Press, Dublin 1993.
Caulfield, Max, *The Easter Rebellion,* A Four Square Book, London 1965.
Clarke, Kathleen, ed. Helen Litton, *My Fight for Ireland's Freedom,* The O'Brien Press, Dublin 1991.
Coogan, Tim Pat, *Michael Collins,* Hutchinson, London 1990.
Coogan, Tim, Pat, *De Valera,* Hutchinson, London,1993.
Cronin, Seán, *The McGarrity Papers,* A Clan-na-Gael Book, 1993, Appendix VIII.
Cronin, Seán, *The McGarrity Papers,* Anvil Books, Tralee 1972.
Cumann na n-Uaigheann Náisiúnta, *The Last Post,* Áth Cliath 1985.
De Búrca, Marcus, *One Hundred Years of Faughs Hurling,* Faughs HC, Dublin 1985.
De Búrca, Marcus, *The GAA – A History,* Cumann Lúthchleas Gael, Dublin 1980.
De Búrca, Seamus, *Soldier's Song,* P. J. Bourke, Dublin 1955.
De Rossa, Peter, *Rebels,* Bantam Press, London, 1990.
Doherty, Gabriel and Keogh, Dermot, *Michael Collins and the Making of the Irish State,* Mercier Press, Cork and Dublin 1998.
Dwyer, T. Ryle, *Michael Collins – The man who won the war,* Mercier Press, Cork and Dublin 1990.
Forester, Margery, *Michael Collins – The Lost Leader,* Gill and Macmillan, Dublin 1989.
Greaves, C. Desmond, *Liam Mellows and the Irish Revolution,* Lawrence and Wishart, London 1971.
Griffith, Kenneth and O'Grady, Timothy, *Curious Journey: An Oral History of Ireland's Unfinished Revolution,* Mercier Press, Cork and Dublin 1998.

Heuston, John M., OP, *Headquarters Battalion Easter Week 1916*, Author, 1966.

Hogan, David, *The Four Glorious Years*, Irish Press, Dublin 1954.

Hopkinson, Michael, *Green against Green*, Gill and Macmillan, Dublin 1988.

Jones, Thomas, *Whitehall Diary*, Volume 111, *Ireland 1918–25*, Edited by Keith Middlemas, Oxford University Press, Oxford 1971.

Lavelle, Patricia, *James O'Mara*, Clonmore and Reynolds, Dublin 1961.

Longford, Lord and O'Neill, T. P., *Éamon de Valera*, Gill and Macmillan, Dublin 1970.

Lynch, Diarmuid, *The IRB and the 1916 Insurrection*, Mercier Press, Cork 1957.

Mac Thomáis, Éamon, *Down Dublin Streets*, Irish Book Bureau, Dublin 1965.

Macardle, Dorothy, *The Irish Republic*, Irish Press, Dublin 1951.

MacEoin, Uinseann, *Survivors*, Argenta Publications, Dublin 1987.

MacManus, M. J., *Éamon de Valera*, Talbot Press, Dublin 1962.

Maher, Jim, *The Flying Column – West Kilkenny*, Geography Publications, Dublin 1987.

McCartan, Patrick, Dr, *With de Valera in America*, Fitzpatrick Ltd. Dublin 1932.

Mitchell, Arthur, *Revolutionary Government in Ireland*, Gill and Macmillan, Dublin 1995.

Murphy, Brian P., *John Chartres – Mystery Man of the Treaty*, Irish Academic Press, Dublin 1995.

Murphy, Brian P., *Patrick Pearse and the Lost Republican Ideal*, James Duffy, Dublin 1991.

Neeson, Eoin, *The Civil War 1922–23*, Mercier Press, Dublin 1966.

O'Brien, Seamus, *Dublin's Fighting Story*, The Kerryman, Tralee 1947.

Ó Broin, Leon, Ó hÉigeartaigh, Cian, *In Great Haste*, Gill and Macmillan, Dublin 1996.

Ó Broin, Leon, *Revolutionary Underground – The Story of the IRB, 1858–1924*, Gill and Macmillan, Dublin 1976.

Ó Ceallaigh, Seán T., arna chur in eagar ag Proinsias Ó Conluain, *Seán T.*, Foilseacháin Náisiúnta Teo., Baile Átha Cliath 1963.

O'Connor, Frank, *The Big Fellow*, Poolbeg, Dublin 1979.

O'Donoghue, Florence, *No Other Law*, Irish Press, Dublin 1954.

O'Farrell, Padraic, *Who's Who in the War of Independence – Civil War*, Lilliput Press, Dublin 1997.

Ó Labhra, Colm, *Trodairí na Treas Briogáide*, Clo Uí Mheara, Aonach Urmhumhan 1955.

O'Malley, Ernie, *The Singing Flame*, Anvil Books, Dublin 1978.

O'Neill, Philip, *History of the GAA 1910–1930*, Kilkenny Journal, Kilkenny 1931.

Pakenham, Frank, *Peace by Ordeal*, Mentor Books, London 1967.

Ryall, Tom, Kilkenny, *The GAA Story, 1884–1984*, Kilkenny 1984.

Ryan, Desmond, *The Rising*, Golden Eagle Books, Dublin 1966.

Ryan, Media, *Michael Collins and the women in his life*, Mercier Press, Cork and Dublin 1996.

Sinnott, Richard, *Irish Voters Decide*, Manchester University Press, Manchester 1995.

Taylor, Rex, *Michael Collins*, Four Square Book, London 1961.

The men who made it, *Dublin's Fighting Story*, Kerryman, Tralee 1947.

Times History of the War, London, August 1916.

Ua Ceallaigh, (Sceilg), Seán, *Cathal Brugha*, M. H. Macanghoill agus a mhac Teoranta, Baile Átha Cliath 1942.

Valiulis, Maryann, Gialanella, *General Richard Mulcahy*, Irish Academic Press, Dublin 1992.

Walker, Brian, M., *Parliamentary Election Results in Ireland 1918–1992*, Royal Irish Academy, Dublin 1992.

Younger, Calton, *Ireland's Civil War*, Fontana Press, Glasgow 1968.

INDEX

Nowlan, Ald. James, 83, 152
Nunan, Seán, 100–1, 107, 113–4, 116, 123–4, 127, 170–1
Nuorteva, Mr (Russian delegation to USA), 110, 115–6, 132
O'Brien, Art, 136, 144, 181
O'Brien, Pat, MP, 11–2, 14
O'Byrne, J. J., 207
O'Callaghan, Denis, 207, 218
O'Callaghan, Katherine, 143
Ó Ceallacháin, Domhnall, Lord Mayor, Cork, 193, 218
O'Connell, Kathleen, 95, 114, 137, 150, 178, 186, 244
O'Connell, 'Ginger' J. J., 224
O'Connell, Cardinal, Boston, 134
O'Connell, Daniel, 69
O'Connor, Batt, 118, 196
O'Connor, Joseph, MP, 44
O'Connor, Rory, 52, 80, 192, 220, 222–224
O'Donnell, Tom, 178, 216
O'Donoghue, Florence, 191–193
O'Donoghue, Paddy, 73–77
O'Donovan, Con, 41–2, 230
O'Donovan, Senator Seán, 54, 171, 238
O'Duffy, Eoin, 192, 237, 240
O'Dwyer, Seamus, 200–1
O'Flanagan, Father Michael, 41, 53, 59, 60, 63, 68, 79
O'Grady, Capt James, MP, 62
O'Hanlon, Irish Party, 60
O'Hanlon, Volunteer, 231
O'Hegarty, Diarmuid, 51, 97, 138, 236
O'Hegarty, P. S., 129
O'Hegarty, Seán, 199
O'Higgins, Kevin, 154, 203, 208–9, 212, 243
O'Keeffe, Patrick, 203, 212
O'Kelly, Seamus, 67
O'Kelly, Seán T., 28, 64, 71–2, 181–184, 203–4, 214, 217, 221, 224–5, 239, 240
O'Leary, John, 16
O'Mahoney, John, 73
O'Mahony, Fr Charles, 76
O'Mahony, Seán, 180
Ó Maille, Padraic, 63, 154, 200
O'Malley, Ernie, 223, 226–229, 236–238
Ó Maoileain, Tomas, 80
O'Mara, James, 69, 103–105, 107, 109–117, 122, 125, 135–137, 139–141, 143

O'Mara, Patricia, 110, 116
O'Mara, Stephen, 141, 145, 159, 163–4, 166, 169, 185, 187, 190–1, 226
Ó Muirthile, Seán, 52, 119, 236
O'Neill, Dick, 92
O'Rahilly, Prof., 236
O'Rahilly, The, 31, 35
O'Reilly, Joe, 117, 138
O'Rourke, Daniel (Dan), 143, 206
O'Shannon, Cathal, 236
O'Shea, Fr Edmund, 83
O'Sullivan, Gearóid, 119, 138, 199
O'Sullivan, Joseph, 221–2
Old Church Street, Dublin, 131
Pact Election, 206–7, 209, 213, 217, 221, 223
Parkhurst Prison, England, 49
Parnell, Charles Stewart, 10
Parnellite Split, 182
Parnellites, 11
Partition Election, May, 1921, 143
Paulstown, Co. Kilkenny, 198
Peace Committee of Ten, 199, 200
Peace Conference, 66, 77, 81, 93, 96, 150, 157
Peafield House, Mountrath, 9–13
Pearse, Mrs Margaret, 143, 218, 239
Pearse, Pádraig, 20, 22, 25–6, 31, 34, 36–7, 64, 218
Pearse, Willie, 218, 234
Pedlar, Liam, 170–1, 194, 206
Pentonville Prison, England, 50
Phelan, Bishop, Australia, 159, 160
Philadelphia Public Ledger, 127
Philadelphia, Pennsylvania, 83, 85, 88–9, 92–3, 99, 102, 124, 167, 239
Pilkington, General Liam, 196
Pittsburg, Pennsylvania, 99, 134, 141
Plaza, Dublin, 225, 235
Plunkett, Count, 49, 53, 57, 72, 80, 93, 110
Plunkett, Joseph Mary, 25, 34, 37, 53
Portland Prison, England, 49
Portland, Oregon, USA, 103
Portobello Barracks, Dublin, 242, 243
Pro–Treaty Forces (Free State Army or Regular Army), 189, 190, 198–9, 207, 225–227, 229–234, 238–240, 245
Prout, Comdt J. T., Free State Army, 198, 238
Pulleyn, J. J., 135

MICHAEL COLLINS
AND THE MAKING OF THE IRISH STATE

EDITED BY GABRIEL DOHERTY AND DERMOT KEOGH

Michael Collins was one of the most important leaders of his or any other age in Irish history. His contribution to the founding of the Irish state was immense even by the standards of a talented generation which included politicians of the calibre of Éamon de Valera, Arthur Griffith, Willam T. Cosgrave, Richard Mulcahy, Kevin O'Higgins, Patrick McGilligan, Harry Boland, Seán Lemass, Frank Aiken and Seán MacEntee.

Collins has generally been portrayed in writing and film as a revoloutionary man of action, a guerrilla leader, a military tactician and a figure of great personal charm, courage and ingenuity. He was in fact a man of many parts.These essays illustrate the multifaceted and complex character that was Michael Collins.

This book is a professional evaluation of Michael Collins and his contribution to the making of the Irish state. With contributions from many of the leading historians working in the field, and written in an accessible style, the essays make full use of archival material and provide new findings and insights into the life and times of Michael Collins.

The contributors examine Collins as Minister for Finance, his role in intelligence, his policy towards the north, his career as Commander-in-Chief, the origins of the Civil War, his relationship with De Valera and how academics view his place in Irish history.

The collection also includes two personal memoirs by Fr Gearóid O'Sullivan and Margot Gearty on Collins and the Kiernans of Granard, County Longford. Both shed new light on Kitty and on her remarkable sisters.

MICHAEL COLLINS
THE MAN WHO WON THE WAR

T. RYLE DWYER

In formally proposing the adoption of the Anglo-Irish Treaty on 19 December 1921 Arthur Griffith referred to Michael Collins as 'the man who won the War', much to the annoyance of the Defence Minister Cathal Brugha, who questioned whether Collins 'had ever fired a shot at any enemy of Ireland'.

Who was this Michael Collins, and what was his real role in the War of Independence? How was it that two sincere, selfless individuals like Griffith and Brugha, could differ so strongly about him?

This is the story of a charismatic rebel who undermined British morale and inspired Irish people with exploits, both real and imaginary. He co-ordinated the sweeping Sinn Féin election victory of 1918, organised the IRA, set up the first modern intelligence network, masterminded a series of prison escapes and supervised the fundraising to finance the movement.

Collins probably never killed anybody himself, but he did order the deaths of people standing in his way, and even advocated kidnapping an American President. He was the prototype of the urban terrorist and the real architect of the Black and Tan War.

CURIOUS JOURNEY
AN ORAL HISTORY OF IRELAND'S
UNFINISHED REVOLUTION

KENNETH GRIFFITH & TIMOTHY O'GRADY

The first twenty-five years of this century saw a profound trans-
formation in Irish life. There was a growing political awakening
among th people which spread throughout the country. The ending of British rule after many centuries in most of the island cul-
minated in civil war. *Curious Journey* is the story of those years
told by people who participated in the 1916 uprising and the subsequent civil war. The authors interviewed nine veterans – Tom
Barry, Máire Comerford, Seán Harling, Seán Kavanagh, David
Neligan, John L. O'Sullivan, Joseph Sweeney, Brighid Lyons Thornton and Martin Walton – and they tell their dramatic stories with
vividness, humour and sometimes shocking clarity.

THE PATH TO FREEDOM

MICHAEL COLLINS

Many books have been written about the life and death of Michael
Collins. *The Path to Freedom* is the only book he wrote himself.

These articles and speeches, first published in 1922, throw
light not only on the War of Independence, the Civil War and the
foundation of the Free State but on crucial contemporary issues.

> The actions taken indicated an over-keen desire for peace, and although
> terms of truce were virtually agreed upon, they were abandoned be-
> cause the British leaders thought their actions indicated weakness, and
> they consequently decided to insist upon the surrender of our arms. The
> result was the continuance of the struggle.

Michael Collins on efforts to bring about a truce earlier in 1920.

HARD TIME
ARMAGH GAOL 1971–86

RAYMOND MURRAY

Raymond Murray was Catholic chaplain of Armagh Women's Gaol from 1971 to 1986. The number of women political prisoners increased from two in 1971 to more than one hundred in the 1972–76 period. Thirty-two of these women were imprisoned without trial. Most of the political prisoners in gaol were girls in their teenage years and one internee was in her sixties. In the 1972–76 period the prisoners had 'special category' or 'political' status.

Raymond Murray's reports became more hard-hitting as injustices increased and oppression grew. Some prisoners in Armagh Gaol alleged beatings by male officers, strip-searches, denial of access to toilets, denial of laundry, denial of visits from concerned persons, the use of 23-hour lock-up and other degrading practices.

DEMOCRACY DENIED

DESMOND WILSON

The name of Des Wilson has always meant two things: integrity and controversy. The diocesan priest whose mission to Bally-murphy, one of West Belfast's poorest ghettos, caused him to try an alternative theology and reject the irrelevant instructions of his bishops, has now turned an informed eye upon the 'Northern situation'.

The author's challenging, anti-establishment analysis of the history of the six counties in the past hundred years demands a close reading and evaluation at the highest level. He argues that all British governments have deliberately manipulated both Protestants and Catholics for their own economic purposes and that the Dublin government and the Church have co-operated in the matter. This contention, argued with compelling logic, cries out for a rebuttal.